Con...

Introduction

PART ONE—*The Autobiography*

Note   **15**

PART TWO—*Selected Writings*

I   The Way to Wealth   **181**

Plan for Future Conduct, 182; Advice to a Young Girl, 183; The Art of Conversation, 184; Advice to a Young Tradesman, 184; "The Way to Wealth," 187.

II   Essays to Do Good   **196**

Standing Queries for the Junto, 197; "A Short Account of the Library," 199; Fire-Fighting, 201; The American Philosophical Society, 204; The Pennsylvania Academy, 207.

III   The New Prometheus, I: Franklin the Scientist   **215**

The Young Naturalist, 217; The Meteorologist, 222; Experimenter in Electricity, 226; Franklin's Kite, 232; The Lightning Rod, 233; Humane Slaughtering, 234; The Franklin Stove, 237; The First American Catheter, 242; The Glass Harmonica, 243; Youthful Inventor, 248; Bifocals, 250; The Long Arm, 251.

IV   The New Prometheus, II: Franklin and the Revolution   **253**

The Stamp Act, 253; After Repeal, 258; The Weapon of Satire, 259; A Counsel of Moderation, 264; America in

Arms, 266; The French Alliance, 270; Busy Days, 272; "Let Us Now Forgive and Forget," 274; "Sketch of the Services of B. Franklin to the United States of America," 276.

V   The Family Man   **279**

Deborah Read, 280; Franky Franklin's Death, 281; Katy Ray, 282; Franklin's London Family, 284; Polly Stevenson, 291; The Shipley Girls, 293; Deborah's Last, Lonely Years, 298; "A Thorough Courtier," 305; The Ladies of France, 307; A Treaty of the Heart, 308; Rejected Suitor, 311; Home Again, 313.

VI   Something of His Religion   **315**

A Practical Theology, 316; "A Dissertation on Liberty and Necessity, Pleasure and Pain," 318; A Reconsideration of Freethinking, 325; Articles of Belief and Acts of Religion, 326; A Summary of Belief, 333; "Here is My Creed," 333.

Notes on the Sources   **337**

The Sources   **341**

Additional Reading   **342**

Afterword: Imagining Benjamin Franklin   **344**

BENJAMIN FRANKLIN, statesman, philosopher, and man of letters, was born in Boston in 1706 of Protestant parents. He entered Boston Grammar School when he was eight and later attended George Browell's school. When he was twelve, his father apprenticed him to his half brother James as a printer. James was later the publisher of the *New England Courant*, where Franklin's first articles, *The Dogood Papers*, were published before he was seventeen. He went to Philadelphia in 1723 and pursued his trade of printer. He was befriended by William Keith, Governor of Pennsylvania, who offered to help the young man get started in business. Franklin left for England, where he hoped to arrange for the purchase of printing equipment. Arriving in London in 1724, he was soon deserted by Keith and again turned to printing for a livelihood. His privately printed *Dissertation on Liberty and Necessity, Pleasure and Pain* (1725) introduced him to leading Deists and other intellectuals in London. A year later, he returned to Philadelphia, and by 1730, he had been appointed public printer for Pennsylvania. In 1731, he established the first circulation library in the United States and, in 1743–44, the American Philosophical Society. In 1748, he retired from the trade of printer but continued to advise and back his partner and to draw profit from the business. His most spectacular success as a publisher, *Poor Richard's Almanack*, went through numerous editions and was translated in many languages. Over the next thirty-five years, he devoted himself largely to politics and diplomacy, but still wrote and engaged in scientific ventures. He resigned as Minister to France in 1785, returned to America, and was elected President of the Commonwealth of Pennsylvania. Still concerned with the rights of the individual, he published papers encouraging the abolition of slavery. He died in Philadelphia in 1790.

CARLA MULFORD has been teaching early American literature and culture and Native American studies at the Pennsylvania State University, University Park, since 1986. While taking her Ph.D. at the University of Delaware, she taught at Temple University, and then at Villanova University, prior to taking the post at Penn State. The Founding President of the Society of Early Americanists, she has published books related to Franklin's associates and contemporaries John Leacock, Annis Stockon, William Hill Brown, and Hannah Webster Foster. She has also compiled (with Amy E. Winans and Angela Vietto) two collections: a biographical dictionary, *American Women Prose Writers to 1820*, and an anthology of readings, *Early American Writings*. She has over the past decade published several essays on Benjamin Franklin, and she will soon complete a book-length study of Franklin called *Benjamin Franklin and the Ends of Empire*.

THE AUTOBIOGRAPHY AND OTHER WRITINGS

Benjamin Franklin

Selected and Edited
and with an
Introduction by L. Jesse Lemisch

With a New Afterword
by Carla Mulford

SIGNET CLASSICS

SIGNET CLASSICS
Published by New American Library, a division of
Penguin Group (USA) Inc., 375 Hudson Street,
New York, New York 10014, USA
Penguin Group (Canada), 90 Eglinton Avenue East, Suite 700, Toronto,
Ontario M4P 2Y3, Canada (a division of Pearson Penguin Canada Inc.)
Penguin Books Ltd., 80 Strand, London WC2R 0RL, England
Penguin Ireland, 25 St. Stephen's Green, Dublin 2,
Ireland (a division of Penguin Books Ltd.)
Penguin Group (Australia), 250 Camberwell Road, Camberwell, Victoria 3124,
Australia (a division of Pearson Australia Group Pty. Ltd.)
Penguin Books India Pvt. Ltd., 11 Community Centre, Panchsheel Park,
New Delhi - 110 017, India
Penguin Group (NZ), cnr Airborne and Rosedale Roads, Albany,
Auckland 1310, New Zealand (a division of Pearson New Zealand Ltd.)
Penguin Books (South Africa) (Pty.) Ltd., 24 Sturdee Avenue,
Rosebank, Johannesburg 2196, South Africa

Penguin Books Ltd., Registered Offices:
80 Strand, London WC2R 0RL, England

Published by Signet Classics, an imprint of New American Library,
a division of Penguin Group (USA) Inc.

First Signet Classics Printing, September 1961
First Signet Classics Printing (Mulford Afterword), September 2001
20 19 18 17 16 15 14 13 12 11 10

OTHER ACKNOWLEDGMENTS
The American Philosophical Society, Philadelphia, for permission to reprint Items
  1, 9, and 11 in Chapter V.
The Philip H. & A. S. Rosenbach Foundation, Philadelphia for Item 17 in Chapter V.
The Yale University Library, New Haven, for Item 6 in Chapter IV and Item 6
  in Chapter V. From the Franklin Collection.
The Yale University Press, for items 1–4 in Chapter I, Item 1 in Chapter II, Item
  3 in Chapter II, and Item 1 in Chapter VI.

Library of Congress Catalog Card Number: 2001041146
Printed in the United States of America

INTRODUCTION

"One does not dress for private company as for a public ball."

In the following pages we meet the many-sided Franklin. We see him through his own eyes and sometimes through the eyes of others: his wife, his son, Abigail Adams, fellow-scientist Joseph Priestley, to name a few. He is father, son, brother, husband, lover; he is scientist, inventor, educator, diplomat, propagandist, politician, humorist; he reveals his own ambition and advises us on the way to wealth and in the art of conversation; he explains his religion and tells us how he did good.

Franklin introduces himself to us in his *Memoirs*—as he always called his autobiography. We meet him at the punch bowl where, from time to time, he steps aside from the ball to hurriedly relate his reminiscences. He comes to a quiet corner of the hall and speaks candidly, but he is still dressed for a public ball. He tells us the truth but is careful to keep his distance: "Let all Men know thee, but no man know thee thoroughly," said Poor Richard; "Men freely ford that see the shallows." Himself a master of the motives of human conduct, Franklin did not set out to reveal himself in his autobiography. Rather he intended to tell us (insofar as we, the nation, are the "posterity" to whom he addressed himself) how life was to be lived, good done, and happiness achieved—how the ball was to be danced.

So the Franklin of the *Memoirs* and of Poor Richard is by no means the whole man. This Franklin is a *persona,* a conscious literary creation presented for our emulation. Perhaps he thought of this creation in much the same way that he thought of a house which he planned: "Regard is to be had chiefly to these particulars, Convenience, Security against Fire and cheapness; so that it may be considered a kind of Pattern House by future Builders, within the Power of Tradesmen and people of moderate Circumstances to imitate and follow." An older man, wisely aware of his own vanity and the deficiencies of memory, tried to make an imperfect dwelling into such a model house. But sometimes vanity or forgetfulness did alter the original situation, as when he recalled that, during his first visit to England, Sir Hans Sloane had heard of the asbestos which Franklin brought with him from America, came to see him, invited him to his house, and persuaded the young man to part with it. In fact, the earliest of Franklin's letters still extant (written in a hand as yet no more cultivated than that of the average American artisan of his day) shows greater aggressiveness than the autobiographer chose to remember: it was Franklin who wrote to Sloane, offering his asbestos for sale, and in a P. S. begged for "an immediate Answer." Here the passive voice used in the *Memoirs* covers real activity on Franklin's part. Again and again we find similar products of his attempt to create a self worthy of imitation.

If the artfully constructed *persona* of the *Memoirs* at times bowdlerizes Franklin's character, it also lessens his humanity. The real Franklin *was* real—a man, and a great one at that. We do him an injustice to idolize a parody of him when a more human sort of greatness emerges from an examination of his passionate struggle within himself to reconcile the prejudices of his intellectual heritage with life as he found it. The real Franklin was more complex, a man of more nuances than the "snuff-coloured little man" attacked in D. H. Lawrence's essay in his *Studies in Classic American Literature*. A man of many selves, of both public and private characters, he was, as Carl Van Doren put it in his biography, "a harmonious human multitude." And if any one trait held that multitude in harmony, it was his sense of humor. His ability to stand apart from himself and look at his various endeavors and enthusiasms and laugh sets Franklin apart.

Benjamin Franklin was born in Boston on January 17,

1706, the tenth and youngest son of Josiah Franklin, a candlemaker. His father intended him for the church and sent him to Boston Grammar School at the age of eight. But such an education was too expensive a tithe; Josiah withdrew Benjamin and sent him to George Brownell's school for writing and arithmetic. After another year, Franklin's formal education ended, and his father put him to work making candles. But Benjamin wanted to go to sea; to prevent this, his father saw to it that he was apprenticed to his brother James, a printer.

Franklin began reading early. He read Bunyan, Defoe, Cotton Mather, Shaftesbury, Locke, Addison and Steele. He trained himself in writing, and submitted some satirical items over the signature of an imaginary widow, "Silence Dogood." These "Dogood Papers" were printed in his brother's newspaper, the *New England Courant*. James Franklin had done his apprenticeship in England and had returned a radical; his newspaper was the focal point for Boston's rising young opposition. When James offended the authorities and was imprisoned for a time, young Benjamin brought out the *Courant*. James continued his radical activities and was forbidden to publish his paper. Benjamin then became the titular publisher, although still bound to his brother by secret indentures of apprenticeship. The younger brother had acquired some new ideas and disputatious habits. He could not get along with his brother, from whom he received too many beatings for what he later conceded was "too saucy and provoking" conduct, and presently took advantage of the secrecy of the indentures—unfairly, he later admitted—to demand his freedom. His plan to get work with some other Boston printer was forestalled by James; people were beginning to call him an atheist and an infidel; all in all, he thought it well to leave Boston. Since their father took James's side, Benjamin left secretly, with the connivance of a friend, on a sloop bound for New York. Unable to find work there, he proceeded by difficult stages to Philadelphia.

Franklin's entry into Philadelphia in the fall of 1723 has been likened to the beginning of Christian's ascent to the Heavenly City in *Pilgrim's Progress*. The seventeen-year-old boy, dirty and poorly dressed, part of his last dollar spent on "three great puffy rolls," walked—eating as he went—alone and unknown, through streets which witnessed his triumphs in later years. He found a job as a journeyman printer and, shortly thereafter, lodgings with the father of his future wife.

He had learned the trade well from James, and soon was able to gain the confidence of his employers and associates. It was not long before Franklin was recommended to the Governor of Pennsylvania, who was so impressed with the young man that he offered to set him up in business and underwrite the expenses of a trip to London to buy printing equipment.

Unfortunately, the governor's kindness proved to be a whim. Franklin got as far as London before he found out that he would receive no more official support, whether financial or moral. Alone and on his own again, in a strange city, Franklin found work at his trade.

During his stay he wrote—and printed—"A Dissertation on Liberty and Necessity, Pleasure and Pain" (1725), which brought him the acquaintance of a group of scientists and writers.

From Franklin's return to Philadelphia in 1726 until his retirement in 1748, his story is one of rapid ascent—remarkable even in the fluid society of eighteenth-century America. Returning to his old job, he soon formed a partnership with another journeyman, and in 1728 they set up their own business. By 1730 Franklin had his own newspaper, had become printer for Pennsylvania, and was sole owner of a growing business.

In 1727 he had gathered his friends together in the Junto, a club devoted to the improvement of the young tradesmen who were its members. Here Franklin perfected his techniques of persuasion and organization. These techniques brought dividends, both for himself and for the society around him, in a succession of offices and civic ventures. In 1731 he was instrumental in founding the first American subscription library; he became a Mason that year, and three years later Grand Master of the lodge. In 1736 he was chosen clerk to the Pennsylvania legislature, and in that same year he established the first fire company; in 1737 he was appointed postmaster of Philadelphia; in 1743 and 1744 he proposed and established the American Philosophical Society. Some of the virtues which brought Franklin success—frugality and industry—were celebrated in *Poor Richard's Almanack,* which he published annually from 1732 on.

In 1748 the enterprise, hard work, and careful planning of the past two decades enabled Franklin, at forty-two, to retire from business. His partner took over the management of the shop, from which Franklin received an average of five hundred pounds a year, and from this time on he divided his attention between science and politics. He performed his electrical experiments, corresponded with fellow scientists, and received many honors, both in America and in Great Britain. Concurrently, he advanced in Pennsylvania politics until, in 1757, the colonial legislature sent him to London to represent them in their dispute with the governor. He returned to America in 1762, but two years later was again sent to England by the Assembly, this time to petition the King to end the proprietary government of the colony. But his functions as agent of Pennsylvania became secondary as he emerged as the leading American spokesman in London against the chain of unconstitutional legislation beginning with the Stamp Act in 1765. He was subsequently appointed colonial agent for Georgia in 1768, for New Jersey in 1769, and for Massachusetts in 1770, holding all these positions concurrently.

His and his nation's relations with England became more and more difficult. He left England for America a month before Lexington and Concord. His countrymen had chosen him as a delegate to the second Continental Congress, which had, in turn, appointed him a member of the committee to draft the Declaration of Independence. Soon after the Revolution began, he was sent to France to negotiate an alliance with Louis XVI. Franklin stayed on as Minister and afterward to make peace with George III.

In 1784 the war was over. Franklin was almost seventy-eight, living in Passy, a suburb of Paris. He asked Congress to recall him, but he was not notified of his release until the spring of 1785.

Back in America, Franklin was chosen President of the Executive Council of Pennsylvania, an office he held for three years; in 1787 he was a delegate to the Constitutional Convention. Released from public affairs in 1788, and suffering severe pain most of the time, he still was able to work on his autobiography, to maintain his interests, and to enjoy his friends. He died on April 17, 1790, at the age of eighty-four.

After presenting Franklin as he saw himself in the autobiography, the present volume goes on and attempts to complete the picture—chronologically and also in greater depth for the years already covered in his *Memoirs*—by other selections from his writings. These are grouped according to various aspects of the many-sided man. First the rising young tradesman presents practical advice. Accounts of the organization and early history of some of his institutional projects—the Junto, the Library Company, the Union Fire Company, the American Philosophical Society, and the Pennsylvania Academy—follow. His primary interest in science—to which he turned on his retirement in 1748—his electrical experiments, and other inventions are described. The approaching conflict with Britain interfered with his scientific career, and he turned to diplomacy. A section dealing with his services in behalf of his country's independence contains some of his best propaganda pieces and his own accounts of the coming of the war and the negotiation of the peace. (Readers seeking a more detailed report on these events should read his *Account of the Negotiations in London for Effecting a Reconciliation between Great Britain and the American Colonies,* and *Journal of the Negotiation for Peace with Great Britain from March 21st to July 1st, 1782,* both too long for reprinting here.) Some indications of Franklin's close personal relationships with his family and others, the latter usually more successful, are presented in his own words and those of his wife and son. The final section shows the development of the religious beliefs of the man whom the sociologist Max Weber chose to exemplify the Protestant Ethic.

The text of the autobiography printed in this edition is that originally published in Max Farrand's *The Autobiography of Benjamin Franklin. A Restoration of a "Fair Copy"* (Berkeley: Univ. of Calif. Press, 1949). Confronted with interlineations and revisions in the original manuscript and lacking the revised copies which Franklin made—now lost—Farrand compared the original with other texts, in French and English, based on the lost copies. The result of this complex study is the only critical text extant of Franklin's *Memoirs*, the closest we will come to what the author intended as his final version.

The sources for the selections in Part Two are listed preceding the Notes on Sources (page 337). Each of the editors had his own system of textual reproduction. In this edition some items are transcribed directly from the original manuscript and many others have been taken from such reliable editions as those compiled by Leonard W. Labaree or Carl Van Doren. When the only available copy of an item was in an edition in which the original practice had been altered to conform with whatever was then "modern usage," no attempt has been made to re-create artificially an "original"; these altered versions have been let stand. But nothing has been done to force more accurate versions of other items into consistency. Thus most of the items in this book follow eighteenth-century spelling, punctuation, and capitalization.

PART ONE

The Autobiography

The *Memoirs,* as Franklin originally called these papers, were written over a period of eighteen years. The first section, which Franklin addressed to his son, and which carries his life to 1730, was written in less than two weeks during a visit to Bishop Shipley at Twyford in August, 1771. He was then sixty-five and in England on his second mission as agent of the Pennsylvania Assembly.

The great events of the years that followed kept him away from the *Memoirs* for more than a decade. While he was in Paris as peace commissioner, he received a letter from a Philadelphia merchant who had seen the manuscript of the first part and urged him to continue it. A friend to whom Franklin showed this letter and his outline for the *Memoirs*—he had no copy of the first installment in Paris—also wrote him to "solicit the history of your life." With this encouragement Franklin took up his narration in 1784, while he was at Passy awaiting release from his duties by Congress. This time he wrote directly for the public. The pages written at Passy contain perhaps the best-known part of the book, Franklin's account of "the bold and arduous project of arriving at moral perfection"—the list of the thirteen virtues (pp. 94–95).

Franklin returned to America in 1785 but public duties again deferred continuation of the *Memoirs.* In August, 1788, he took them up again, in spite of racking pain and the opiates needed for its relief, bringing the story up to 1757, and early the following year added a few more pages. More than thirty years of his life were still to be recorded when he died.

DEAR SON,

I HAVE ever had a pleasure in obtaining any little anecdotes of my ancestors. You may remember the enquiries I made among the remains of my relations when you were with me in England and the journey I undertook for that purpose. Imagining it may be equally agreeable to you to know the circumstances of *my* life—many of which you are yet unacquainted with—and expecting a week's uninterrupted leisure in my present country retirement, I sit down to write them for you. Besides, there are some other inducements that excite me to this undertaking. From the poverty and obscurity in which I was born and in which I passed my earliest years, I have raised myself to a state of affluence and some degree of celebrity in the world. As constant good fortune has accompanied me even to an advanced period of life, my posterity will perhaps be desirous of learning the means, which I employed, and which, thanks to Providence, so well succeeded with me. They may also deem them fit to be imitated, should any of them find themselves in similar circumstances. That good fortune, when I reflected on it, which is frequently the case, has induced me sometimes to say that were it left to my choice, I should have no objection to go over the same life from its beginning to the end, only asking the advantage authors have of correcting in a second edition some faults of the first. So would I also wish to change some incidents of it for others more favourable. Notwithstanding, if this condition were denied, I should still accept the offer. But as this repetition is not to be expected, that which resembles most living one's life over again, seems to be to recall all the circumstances of it; and, to render this remembrance more durable, to record them in writing. In thus employing myself I shall yield to the inclination so natural to old men of talking of themselves and their own actions, and I shall indulge it, without being tiresome to those who, from respect to my age, might conceive themselves obliged to listen to me, since they will be always free to read me or not. And lastly (I may as well confess it, as the denial of it would be believed by nobody) I shall perhaps not a little gratify my own vanity. Indeed, I never heard or saw the introductory words, "Without Vanity I may say," etc., but some vain thing immediately followed. Many people dislike vanity in others whatever share they have of it themselves, but I give it fair quarter wherever I meet with it, being persuaded that it is often productive of good to the possessor and to others who are within his sphere of action. And therefore, in many cases it would not be altogether absurd if a man were to thank God for his vanity among the other comforts of life.

And now I speak of thanking God, I desire with all humility to acknowledge that I owe the mentioned happiness of my past life to his divine providence, which led me to the means I used and gave them success. My belief of this induces me to *hope,* though I must not *presume,* that the same goodness will still be exercised towards me in continuing that happiness or in enabling me to bear a fatal reverse, which I may experience as others have done—the complexion of my future fortune being known to him only, and in whose power it is to bless to us even our afflictions.

Some notes one of my uncles (who had the same curiosity in collecting family anecdotes) once put into my hands furnished me with several particulars relating to our ancestors. From these notes I learned that they had lived in the same village, Ecton in Northamptonshire, on a freehold of about thirty acres, for at least three hundred years, and how much longer he knew not. Perhaps from the time when the name of Franklin, which before was the name of an order of people, was assumed by them as a surname, when others took surnames all over the kingdom.*

This small estate would not have sufficed for their maintenance without the business of a smith, which had continued in the family down to my uncle's time, the eldest son being always brought up to that business—a custom which he and my father followed with regard to their eldest sons. When I searched the register at Ecton, I found an account of their births, marriages, and burials from the year 1555 only, there being no register kept in that parish previous thereto. By that register I learned that I was the youngest son of the youngest son for five generations back. My grandfather Thomas, who was born in 1598, lived at Ecton till he was too old to continue his business, when he retired to Banbury in Oxfordshire to the house of his son John, a dyer, with whom my father served an apprenticeship. There my grandfather died and lies buried. We saw his gravestone in 1758. His eldest son Thomas lived in the house at Ecton and left it with the land to his only daughter, who with her husband, one Fisher of Wallingborough, sold it to Mr. Isted, now lord of the manor there. My grandfather had four sons that grew up; viz., Thomas, John, Benjamin, and Josiah. Being at a distance from my papers, I will give you what account I can of them from memory, and if they are not

---

*As a proof that Franklin was anciently the common name of an order or rank in England, see Judge Fortescue, *De laudibus Legum Anglioe,* written about the year 1412, in which is the following passage, to show that good juries might easily be formed in any part of England.

"Regio etiam illa, ita respersa refertaque est *possessoribus terrarum* et agrorum, quod in ea, villula tam parva reperiri non poterit, in qua non est *miles, armiger,* vel paterfamilias, qualis ibidem *Franklin* vulgariter nuncupatur, magnis ditatus posessionibus, nec non libere tenentes et alii *valecti* plurimi, suis partimoniis sufficientes ad faciendum juratum, in forma prænotata."

"Moreover, the same country is so filled and replenished with landed menne, that therein so small a Thorpe cannot be found wherein dweleth not a knight, an esquire, or such a house-holder, as is there commonly called a *Franklin,* enriched with great possessions; and also other freeholders and many yeomen able for their livelihoods to make a jury in form aforementioned." (Old translation.)

lost in my absence, you will find among them many more particulars.

Thomas was bred a smith under his father, but being ingenious and encouraged in learning (as all his brothers were) by an Esquire Palmer, then the principal inhabitant of that parish, he qualified himself for the business of scrivener, became a considerable man in the county affairs, was a chief mover of all public-spirited enterprizes for the county or town of Northampton and his own village, of which many instances were told us at Ecton, and he was much taken notice of and patronized by Lord Halifax. He died in 1702, the 6th of January, four years to a day before I was born. The recital which elderly people made to us of his life and character, I remember, struck you as something extraordinary from its similarity with what you knew of me. "Had he died," said you, "four years later, on the same day, one might have supposed a transmigration." John was bred a dyer, I believe of wool. Benjamin was bred a silk dyer, serving an apprenticeship at London. He was an ingenious man. I remember him well, for when I was a boy he came to my father's in Boston and lived in the house with us some years. There was always a particular affection between my father and him, and I was his godson. He lived to a great age. He left behind him two quarto volumes of manuscript of his own poetry, consisting of fugitive pieces addressed to his friends and relations, of which the following, sent to me, is a specimen.

To my Namesake upon a Report of his Inclination to
    Martial Affairs, July 7th, 1710

Believe me, Ben, war is a dangerous trade.
The sword has many marred as well as made;
By it do many fall, not many rise—
Makes many poor, few rich, and fewer wise;
Fills towns with ruin, fields with blood; beside
'Tis Sloth's maintainer and the shield of Pride.
Fair cities, rich today in plenty flow,
War fills with want tomorrow, and with woe.
Ruined estates, vice, broken limbs, and scars
Are the effects of desolating wars.

ACROSTIC

B-e to thy parents an obedient son,
E-ach day let duty constantly be done.
N-ever give way to sloth or lust or pride,
I-f free you'd be from thousand ills beside;
A-bove all ills, be sure avoid the shelf;
M-an's danger lies in Satan, sin, and self.
I-n virtue, learning, wisdom progress make,
N-e'er shrink at suffering for thy Saviour's sake.
F-raud and all falsehood in thy dealings flee,
R-eligious always in thy station be,
A-dore the maker of thy inward part.
N-ow's the accepted time; give God thy heart.
K-eep a good conscience, 'tis a constant friend;
L-ike judge and witness this thy act attend.
I-n heart, with bended knee, alone, adore
N-one but the Three-in-One forevermore.

He had invented a shorthand of his own, which he taught me, but not having practised it, I have now forgot it. He was very pious, an assiduous attendant at the sermons of the best preachers, which he reduced to writing according to his method, and had thus collected several volumes of them. He was also a good deal of a politician—too much so, perhaps, for his station. There fell lately into my hands in London a collection he had made of all the principal pamphlets relating to public affairs from 1641 to 1717. Many of the volumes are wanting, as appears by the numbering, eight volumes in folio, and twenty-four in quarto and in octavo. A dealer in old books met with them, and knowing me by my sometimes buying books of him, he brought them to me. It would appear that my uncle must have left them here when he went to America, which was about fifty years ago. I have found many of his notes in the margins. His grandson, Samuel Franklin, is still living in Boston.

Our humble family early embraced the Reformation. Our forefathers continued Protestants through the reign of Mary, when they were sometimes in danger of persecution on account of their zeal against popery. They had an English Bible, and to conceal it and place it in safety, it was fastened open with tapes under and within the cover of a joint stool. When my great-great-grandfather wished to read it to his family, he turned up the joint stool upon his knees and then turned over the leaves under the tapes. One of the children stood at the door to give notice if he saw the apparitor coming, who was an officer of the spiritual court. In that case the stool was turned down again upon its feet, when the Bible remained concealed under it as before. This anecdote I had from my uncle Benjamin. The family continued all of the Church of England, till about the end of Charles the Second's reign, when some of the ministers that had been outed for nonconformity holding conventicles in Northamptonshire, Benjamin and Josiah adhered to them and so continued all their lives. The rest of the family remained with the Episcopal church.

Josiah, my father, married young and carried his wife with three children to New England about 1682. The conventicles being at that time forbidden by law and frequently disturbed, some considerable men of his acquaintance determined to go to that country; and he was prevailed with to accompany them thither, where they expected to enjoy the exercise of their religion with freedom. By the same wife, my father had four children more born there, and by a second wife ten others—in all seventeen, of which I remember often to have seen thirteen sitting together at his table, who all grew up to years of maturity and married. I was the youngest son and the youngest of all the children except two daughters. I was born in Boston, in New England.

My mother, the second wife, was Abiah Folger, daughter of Peter Folger, one of the first settlers of New England, of whom honourable mention is made by Cotton Mather in his ecclesiastical history of that country, entitled *Magnalia Christi Americana,* as a ''godly and learned Englishman,'' if I remember the words rightly. I have heard that he wrote several small occasional pieces, but only one of them was printed, which I saw many years since. It was written in 1675, in familiar verse according to the taste of the time and people, and addressed to those then concerned in the government there. It asserts the liberty of conscience, and in behalf of the Anabaptists, Quakers, and other sectaries that had been persecuted. He attributes to this persecution the Indian Wars and other calamities that had befallen the country, regarding them as so many judgments of God to punish so heinous an offence, and exhorting a repeal of those laws, so contrary to charity. This piece appeared to me as written with manly freedom and a pleasing simplicity. The six last lines I remember, though I have forgotten the two first; the purport of them was that his censures proceeded from good will, and therefore he would be known to be the author.

> Because to be a libeller (says he),
>   I hate it with my heart.
> From Sherburne Town* where now I dwell,
>   My name I do put here,
> Without offence, your real friend,
>   It is Peter Folgier.

My elder brothers were all put apprentices to different trades. I was put to the grammar school at eight years of age, my father intending to devote me as the tithe of his sons to the service of the church. My early readiness in learning to read (which must have been very early, as I do not remember when I could not read) and the opinion of all his friends that I should certainly make a good scholar, encouraged him in this purpose of his. My uncle Benjamin, too, approved of it and proposed to give me all his shorthand volumes of sermons to set up with, if I would learn his shorthand. I continued, however, at the grammar school rather less than a year, though in that time I had risen gradually from the middle of the class of that year to be at the head of the same class, and was removed into the next class, whence I was to be placed in the third at the end of the year. But my father, burdened with a numerous family, was unable without inconvenience to support the expence of a college education, considering, moreover, as he said to one of his friends in my presence, the little encouragement that line of life afforded to those educated for it. He gave up his first intentions, took me from the grammar school,

*In the island of Nantucket.

and sent me to a school for writing and arithmetic kept by a then famous man, Mr. Geo. Brownell. He was a skillful master, and successful in his profession, employing the mildest and most encouraging methods. Under him I learned to write a good hand pretty soon, but I failed in the arithmetic and made no progress in it. At ten years old, I was taken home to help my father in his business, which was that of a tallow chandler and soap boiler—a business he was not bred to but had assumed on his arrival in New England, because he found his dyeing trade, being in little request, would not maintain his family. Accordingly, I was employed in cutting wick for the candles, filling the molds for cast candles, attending the shop, going of errands, etc.

I disliked the trade and had a strong inclination to go to sea, but my father declared against it; however, living near the water, I was much in it and on it. I learned early to swim well and to manage boats; and when embarked with other boys, I was commonly allowed to govern, especially in any case of difficulty; and upon other occasions I was generally the leader among the boys and sometimes led them into scrapes, of which I will mention one instance as it shows an early projecting public spirit, tho' not then justly conducted.

There was a salt marsh that bounded part of the mill pond, on the edge of which at high water, we used to stand to fish for minnows. By much trampling we had made it a mere quagmire. My proposal was to build a wharf there for us to stand upon, and I showed my comrades a large heap of stones which were intended for a new house near the marsh and which would very well suit our purpose. Accordingly, in the evening when the workmen were gone home, I assembled a number of my playfellows, and we worked diligently like so many emmets, sometimes two or three to a stone, 'till we brought them all to make our little wharf. The next morning the workmen were surprised at missing the stones, which had formed our wharf; enquiry was made after the authors of this transfer; we were discovered, complained of; several of us were corrected by our fathers, and tho' I demonstrated the utility of our work, mine convinced me that that which was not honest could not be truly useful.

I suppose you may like to know what kind of a man my father was. He had an excellent constitution, was of middle stature, but well set and very strong. He was ingenious, could draw prettily, was skilled a little in music; his voice was sonorous and agreeable, so that when he played Psalm tunes on his violin and sung withal as he sometimes did in an evening after the business of the day was over, it was extremely agreeable to hear. He had some knowledge of mechanics, too, and on occasion was very handy with other tradesmen's tools. But his great excellence was a sound understanding and a solid judgment in prudential matters, both in private and public affairs. It is true he was never employed in the latter, the numerous family he had to educate and the straitness of his circumstances keeping him close to his trade; but I remember well his being frequently visited by leading men who consulted him for his opinion in affairs of the town or of the church he belonged to, and who showed a good deal of respect for his judgment and advice. He was also much consulted by private persons about their affairs when any difficulty occurred, and frequently chose an arbitrator between contending parties. At his table he liked to have, as often as he could, some sensible friend or neighbour to converse with, and always took care to start some ingenious or useful topic for discourse which might tend to improve the minds of his children. By this means he turned our attention to what was good, just, and prudent in the conduct of life; and little or no notice was ever taken of what related to the victuals on the table—whether it was well or ill dressed, in or out of season, of good or bad flavour, preferable or inferior to this or that other thing of the kind; so that I was brought up in such a perfect inattention to those matters as to be quite indifferent what kind of food was set before me, and so unobservant of it, that to this day I can scarce tell a few hours after dinner of what dishes it consisted. This has been a great convenience to me in travelling, where my companions have been sometimes very unhappy for want of a suitable gratification of their more delicate, because better instructed, tastes and appetites.

My mother had likewise an excellent constitution. She suckled all her ten children. I never knew either my father or mother to have any sickness but that of which they died, he at eighty-nine and she at eighty-five years of age. They lie buried together at Boston, where I some years since placed a marble stone over their grave with this inscription:

Josiah Franklin
And Abiah his wife
Lie here interred.
They lived lovingly together in wedlock
Fifty-five years.
Without an estate or any gainful employment,
By constant labour and industry,
With God's blessing,
They maintained a large family
Comfortably;
And brought up thirteen children,
And seven grandchildren
Reputably.
From this instance, Reader,
Be encouraged to diligence in thy calling,
And distrust not Providence.
He was a pious and prudent man,
She a discreet and virtuous woman.
Their youngest son,
In filial regard to their memory,
Places this stone.
J. F. born 1655—Died 1744—AEtat. 89.
A. F. born 1667—Died 1752——85.

By my rambling digressions I perceive myself to be grown old. I used to write more methodically. But one does not dress for private company as for a public ball. Perhaps 'tis only negligence.

To return: I continued thus employed in my father's business for two years, that is, till I was twelve years old; and my brother John, who was bred to that business, having left my father, married and set up for himself at Rhode Island, there was every appearance that I was destined to supply his place and be a tallow chandler. But my dislike to the trade continuing, my father had apprehensions that if he did not put me to one more agreeable,

I should break loose and go to sea, as my brother Josiah had done, to his great vexation. In consequence he sometimes took me to walk with him and see joiners, bricklayers, turners, braziers, etc., at their work that he might observe my inclination and endeavour to fix it on some trade that would keep me on land. It has ever since been a pleasure to me to see good workmen handle their tools; and it has been useful to me to have learned so much by it as to be able to do little jobs myself in my house, when a workman could not readily be got, and to construct little machines for my experiments when the intention of making these was warm in my mind. My father determined at last for the cutler's trade, and placed me for some days on trial with Samuel, son of my uncle Benjamin, who was bred to that trade in London and had just established himself in Boston. But the sum he exacted as a fee for my apprenticeship displeased my father, and I was taken home again.

From my infancy I was passionately fond of reading, and all the little money that came into my hands was laid out in the purchasing of books. I was very fond of voyages. My first acquisition was Bunyan's works in separate little volumes. I afterwards sold them to enable me to buy R. Burton's historical collections; they were small chapmen's books and cheap, forty or fifty in all. My father's little library consisted chiefly of books in polemic divinity, most of which I read. I have since often regretted that at a time when I had such a thirst for knowledge, more proper books had not fallen in my way, since it was now resolved I should not be bred to divinity. There was among them Plutarch's *Lives,* in which I read abundantly, and I still think that time spent to great advantage. There was also a book of Defoe's called an *Essay on Projects* and another of Dr. Mather's called *Essays to do Good,* which perhaps gave me a turn of thinking that had an influence on some of the principal future events of my life.

This bookish inclination at length determined my father to make me a printer, though he had already one son (James) of that profession. In 1717 my brother, James, returned from England with a press and letters to set up his business in Boston. I liked it much better than that of my father, but still had a hankering for the sea. To prevent the apprehended effect of such an inclination, my father was impatient to have me bound to my brother. I stood out some time, but at last was persuaded and signed the indenture, when I was yet but twelve years old. I was to serve as apprentice till I was twenty-one years of age, only I was to be allowed journeyman's wages during the last year. In a little time I made a great progress in the business and became a useful hand to my brother. I now had access to better books. An acquaintance with the apprentices of booksellers enabled me sometimes to borrow a small one, which I was careful to return soon and clean. Often I sat up in my room reading the greatest part of the night, when the book was borrowed in the evening and to be returned early in the morning, lest it should be found missing or wanted.

After some time a merchant, an ingenious, sensible man, Mr. Matthew Adams, who had a pretty collection of books and who frequented our printing house, took notice of me, invited me to see his library, and very kindly proposed to lend me such books as I chose to read. I now took a fancy to poetry and made some little pieces. My brother, supposing it might turn to account, encouraged me and induced me to compose two occasional ballads. One was called the "Lighthouse Tragedy," and contained an account of the shipwreck of Capt. Worthilake with his two daughters; the other was a "Sailor's Song on the Taking of the Famous *Teach*, or Blackbeard, the Pirate." They were wretched stuff, in street ballad style; and when they were printed, he sent me about the town to sell them. The first sold prodigiously, the event being recent and having made a great noise. This success flattered my vanity, but my father discouraged me by ridiculing my performances and telling me verse-makers were generally beggars. Thus I escaped being a poet and probably a very bad one. But as prose writing has been of great use to me in the course of my life and was a principal means of my advancement, I shall tell you how in such a situation I acquired what little ability I may be supposed to have in that way.

There was another bookish lad in the town, John Collins by name, with whom I was intimately acquainted.

We sometimes disputed, and very fond we were of argument, and very desirous of confuting one another—which disputatious turn, by the way, is apt to become a very bad habit, making people often extremely disagreeable in company, by the contradiction that is necessary to bring it into practice; and thence besides souring and spoiling the conversation, it is productive of disgusts and perhaps enmities where you may have occasion for friendship. I had caught it by reading my father's books of dispute on religion. Persons of good sense, I have since observed, seldom fall into it, except lawyers, university men, and men of all sorts who have been bred at Edinburgh. A question was once somehow or other started between Collins and me on the propriety of educating the female sex in learning and their abilities for study. He was of opinion that it was improper and that they were naturally unequal to it. I took the contrary side, perhaps a little for dispute sake. He was naturally more eloquent, having a greater plenty of words, and sometimes, as I thought, I was vanquished more by his fluency than by the strength of his reasons. As we parted without settling the point and were not to see one another again for some time, I sat down to put my arguments in writing, which I copied fair and sent to him. He answered and I replied. Three or four letters on a side had passed, when my father happened to find my papers and read them. Without entering into the subject in dispute, he took occasion to talk with me about my manner of writing, observed that though I had the advantage of my antagonist in correct spelling and pointing (which I owed to the printing house) I fell far short in elegance of expression, in method, and in perspicuity—of which he convinced me by several instances. I saw the justice of his remarks and thence grew more attentive to my manner of writing, and determined to endeavour to improve my style.

About this time I met with an odd volume of the *Spectator*. It was the third. I had never before seen any of them. I bought it, read it over and over, and was much delighted with it. I thought the writing excellent and wished if possible to imitate it. With that view, I took some of the papers, and making short hints of the sentiment in each sentence, laid them by a few days, and then without looking at the book, tried to complete the papers again by expressing each hinted sentiment at length and as fully as it had been expressed before, in any suitable words that should occur to me. Then I compared my *Spectator* with the original, discovered some of my faults, and corrected them. But I found I wanted a stock of words or a readiness in recollecting and using them, which I thought I should have acquired before that time if I had gone on making verses; since the continual search for words of the same import but of different length to suit the measure, or of different sound for the rhyme would have laid me under a constant necessity of searching for variety, and also have tended to fix that variety in my mind, and make me master of it. Therefore I took some of the tales in the *Spectator* and turned them into verse, and after a time, when I had pretty well forgotten the prose, turned them back again. I also sometimes jumbled my collections of hints into confusion, and after some weeks endeavoured to reduce them into the best order before I began to form the full sentences and complete the paper. This was to teach me method in the arrangement of the thoughts. By comparing my work afterwards with the original, I discovered many faults and corrected them; but I sometimes had the pleasure of fancying that in certain particulars of small import I had been lucky enough to improve the method or the language, and this encouraged me to think that I might possibly in time come to be a tolerable English writer, of which I was extremely ambitious.

The time I allotted for these exercises and for reading, was at night after work, or before it began in the morning, or on Sundays, when I contrived to be in the printing house alone, avoiding as much as I could the common attendance on public worship which my father used to exact of me when I was under his care—and which, indeed, I still thought a duty, though I could not, as it seemed to me, afford the time to practise it.

When about sixteen years of age I happened to meet with a book written by one Tryon, recommending a vegetable diet. I determined to go into it. My brother, being yet unmarried, did not keep house but boarded himself and his apprentices in another family. My refusing to eat flesh occasioned an inconveniency, and I was frequently chid for my singularity. I made myself acquainted with Tryon's manner of preparing some of his dishes, such as boiling potatoes or rice, making hasty pudding, and a few others; and then proposed to my brother that if he would give me weekly half the money he paid for my board, I would board myself. He instantly agreed to it, and I presently found that I could save half what he paid me. This was an additional fund for buying of books. But I had another advantage in it. My brother and the rest going from the printing house to their meals, I remained there alone, and dispatching presently my light repast (which often was no more than a biscuit or a slice of bread, a handful of raisins or a tart from the pastry cook's, and a glass of water) had the rest of the time till their return for study, in which I made the greater progress from that greater clearness of head and quicker apprehension which generally attend temperance in eating and drinking. Now it was that being on some occasion made ashamed of my ignorance in figures, which I had twice failed in learning when at school, I took Cocker's book of arithmetic, and went through the whole by myself with the greatest ease. I also read Seller's and Sturmy's book on navigation and became acquainted with the little geometry it contains, but I never proceeded far in that science. I read about this time Locke *On Human Understanding,* and *The Art of Thinking* by Messrs. du Port Royal.

While I was intent on improving my language, I met with an English grammar (I think it was Greenwood's) at the end of which there were two little sketches on the arts of rhetoric and logic, the latter finishing with a dispute in the Socratic method. And soon after I procured Xenophon's *Memorable Things of Socrates,* wherein there are many examples of the same method. I was charmed with it, adopted it, dropped my abrupt contradiction and positive argumentation, and put on the humble enquirer. And being then, from reading Shaftsbury and Collins, made a doubter, as I already was in many points of our religious doctrines, I found this method the safest for myself and very embarrassing to those against whom I used it; therefore, I took a delight in it, practised it continually, and grew very artful and expert in drawing people, even of superior knowledge, into concessions the consequences of which they did not foresee, entangling them in difficulties out of which they could not extricate themselves, and so obtaining victories that neither myself nor my cause always deserved. I continued this method some few years but gradually left it, retaining only the habit of expressing myself in terms of modest diffidence, never using when I advance anything that may possibly be disputed the words, "certainly," "undoubtedly," or any others that give the air of positiveness to an opinion; but rather say, "I conceive or apprehend a thing to be so or so," "It appears to me," or "I should think it so or so, for such and such reasons," or "I imagine it to be so," or "It is so if I am not mistaken." This habit, I believe, has been of great advantage to me when I have had occasion to inculcate my opinions and persuade men into measures that I have been from time to time engaged in promoting. And as the chief ends of conversation are to *inform,* or to *be informed,* to *please* or to *persuade,* I wish well-meaning and sensible men would not lessen their power of doing good by a positive, assuming manner that seldom fails to disgust, tends to create opposition, and to defeat every one of those purposes for which speech was given to us. In fact, if you wish to instruct others, a positive, dogmatical manner in advancing your sentiments may provoke contradiction and prevent a candid attention. If you desire instruction and improvement from the knowledge of others, you should not at the same time express yourself as firmly fixed in your present opinions; modest and sensible men, who do not love disputation, will probably leave you undisturbed in the possession of your error. In adopting such a manner you can seldom expect to please your hearers, or to persuade those whose concurrence you desire. Pope judiciously observes,

> Men must be taught as if you taught them not,
> And things unknown propos'd as things forgot.

He also recommends it to us,

> To speak, though sure, with seeming diffidence.

And he might have joined with this line that which he has coupled with another, I think less properly,

> For want of modesty is want of sense.

If you ask why *less properly,* I must repeat the lines,

> Immodest words admit of *no defence,*
> *For* want of modesty is want of sense.

Now is not the "want of sense" (where a man is so unfortunate as to want it) some apology for his "want of modesty"? and would not the lines stand more justly thus?

> Immodest words admit *but* this defense
> That want of modesty is want of sense.

This, however, I should submit to better judgments.

My brother had in 1720 or '21 begun to print a newspaper. It was the second that appeared in America and was called *The New England Courant.* The only one before it was *The Boston Newsletter.* I remember his being dissuaded by some of his friends from the undertaking as not likely to succeed, one newspaper being in their judgment enough for America. At this time, 1771, there are not less than five-and-twenty. He went on, however, with the undertaking; I was employed to carry the papers to the customers, after having worked in composing the types and printing off the sheets. He had some ingenious men among his friends who amused themselves by writing little pieces for this paper, which gained it credit and made it more in demand; and these gentlemen often visited us. Hearing their conversations and their accounts of the approbation their papers were received with, I was excited to try my hand among them. But being still a boy and suspecting that my brother would object to printing anything of mine in his paper if he knew it to be mine, I contrived to disguise my hand; and writing an anonymous paper, I put it at night under the door of the printing house. It was found in the morning and communicated to his writing friends when they called in as usual. They read it, commented on it in my hearing, and I had the exquisite pleasure of finding it met with their approbation, and that in their different guesses at the author, none were named but men of some character among us for learning and ingenuity. I suppose now that I was rather lucky in my judges and that perhaps they were not really so very good as I then believed them to be. Encouraged, however, by this attempt, I wrote and sent in the same way to the press several other pieces, which were equally approved, and I kept my secret till my small fund of sense for such performances was pretty well exhausted, and then I discovered it, when I began to be considered a little more by my brother's acquaintance. However, that did not quite please him as he thought that it tended to make me too vain.

This might be one occasion of the differences we began to have about this time. Though a brother, he considered himself as my master and me as his apprentice, and accordingly expected the same services from me as he would from another; while I thought he degraded me too much in some he required of me, who from a brother expected more indulgence. Our disputes were often brought before our father, and I fancy I was either generally in the right or else a better pleader, because the judgment was generally in my favour. But my brother was passionate and had often beaten me, which I took extremely amiss. I fancy his harsh and tyrannical treatment of me might be a means of impressing me with that aversion to arbitrary power that has stuck to me through my whole life. Thinking my apprenticeship very tedious, I was continually wishing for some opportunity of shortening it, which at length offered in a manner unexpected.

One of the pieces in our newspaper on some political point which I have now forgotten, gave offence to the Assembly. He was taken up, censured, and imprisoned for a month by the Speaker's warrant, I suppose because he would not discover the author. I, too, was taken up and examined before the Council; but though I did not give them any satisfaction, they contented themselves with admonishing me and dismissed me, considering me, perhaps, as an apprentice who was bound to keep his master's secrets. During my brother's confinement, which

I resented a good deal notwithstanding our private differences, I had the management of the paper, and I made bold to give our rulers some rubs in it, which my brother took very kindly, while others began to consider me in an unfavourable light as a young genius that had a turn for libelling and satire. My brother's discharge was accompanied with an order from the House (a very odd one) that "James Franklin should no longer print the paper called the *New England Courant*." There was a consultation held in our printing house amongst his friends in this conjuncture. Some proposed to elude the order by changing the name of the paper; but my brother seeing inconveniences in that, it was finally concluded on as a better way to let it be printed for the future under the name of "Benjamin Franklin"; and to avoid the censure of the Assembly that might fall on him as still printing it by his apprentice, the contrivance was that my old indenture should be returned to me with a full discharge on the back of it, to show in case of necessity; but to secure to him the benefit of my service, I should sign new indentures for the remainder of the term, which were to be kept private. A very flimsy scheme it was, but, however, it was immediately executed, and the paper went on accordingly under my name for several months. At length a fresh difference arising between my brother and me, I took upon me to assert my freedom, presuming that he would not venture to produce the new indentures. It was not fair in me to take this advantage, and this I therefore reckon one of the first errata of my life. But the unfairness of it weighed little with me, when under the impressions of resentment for the blows his passion too often urged him to bestow upon me, though he was otherwise not an ill-natured man. Perhaps I was too saucy and provoking.

When he found I would leave him, he took care to prevent my getting employment in any other printing house of the town by going round and speaking to every master, who accordingly refused to give me work. I then thought of going to New York as the nearest place where there was a printer; and I was the rather inclined to leave Boston when I reflected that I had already made myself a little obnoxious to the governing party; and from the arbitrary proceedings of the Assembly in my brother's case, it was likely I might if I stayed soon bring myself into scrapes, and further that my indiscreet disputations about religion began to make me pointed at with horror by good people as an infidel or atheist. I determined on the point, but my father now siding with my brother, I was sensible that if I attempted to go openly, means would be used to prevent me. My friend Collins therefore undertook to manage my flight. He agreed with the captain of a New York sloop for my passage, under pretence of my being a young man of his acquaintance that had had an intrigue with a girl of bad character,[1] whose parents would compel me to marry her and therefore I could not appear or come away publicly. I sold some of my books to raise a little money, was taken on board the sloop privately, had a fair wind, and in three days found myself at New York, near three hundred miles from my home, at the age of seventeen, without the least recommendation to or knowledge of any person in the place, and with very little money in my pocket.

The inclination I had had for the sea was by this time done away, or I might now have gratified it. But having another profession and conceiving myself a pretty good workman, I offered my services to the printer of the place, old Mr. Wm. Bradford (who had been the first printer in Pennsylvania, but had removed thence in consequence of a quarrel with the Governor, Geo. Keith). He could give me no employment, having little to do and hands enough already. "But," says he, "my son at Philadelphia has lately lost his principal hand, Aquila Rose, by death. If you go thither I believe he may employ you."

Philadelphia was a hundred miles farther. I set out, however, in a boat for Amboy, leaving my chest and things to follow me round by sea. In crossing the bay we met with a squall that tore our rotten sails to pieces, prevented our getting into the kill, and drove us upon Long Island. In our way a drunken Dutchman, who was a passenger, too, fell overboard; when he was sinking, I reached through the water to his shock pate and drew

[1]Franklin originally wrote: "that had got a naughty girl with child."

him up so that we got him in again. His ducking sobered him a little, and he went to sleep, taking first out of his pocket a book which he desired I would dry for him. It proved to be my old favourite author Bunyan's *Pilgrim's Progress* in Dutch, finely printed on good paper with copper cuts, a dress better than I had ever seen it wear in its own language. I have since found that it has been translated into most of the languages of Europe, and suppose it has been more generally read than any other book except, perhaps, the Bible. Honest John was the first that I know of who mixes narration and dialogue, a method of writing very engaging to the reader, who in the most interesting parts finds himself, as it were, admitted into the company and present at the conversation. Defoe has imitated him successfully in his *Robinson Crusoe,* in his *Moll Flanders,* and other pieces; and Richardson has done the same in his *Pamela,* etc.

On approaching the island, we found it was in a place where there could be no landing, there being a great surf on the stony beach. So we dropped anchor and swung out our cable towards the shore. Some people came down to the water edge and hallooed to us, as we did to them, but the wind was so high and the surf so loud that we could not understand each other. There were some canoes on the shore, and we made signs and called to them to fetch us, but they either did not comprehend us or thought it impracticable, so they went off. Night approaching, we had no remedy but to have patience till the wind abated, and in the meantime the boatman and I concluded to sleep if we could, and so we crowded into the scuttle with the Dutchman who was still wet, and the spray breaking over the head of our boat leaked through to us, so that we were soon almost as wet as he. In this manner we lay all night with very little rest; but the wind abating the next day, we made a shift to reach Amboy before night, having been thirty hours on the water without victuals or any drink but a bottle of filthy rum, the water we sailed on being salt.

In the evening I found myself very feverish and went to bed; but having read somewhere that cold water drank plentifully was good for a fever, I followed the prescription, sweat plentifully most of the night, my fever left me, and in the morning crossing the ferry, I proceeded on my journey on foot, having fifty miles to Burlington, where I was told I should find boats that would carry me the rest of the way to Philadelphia.

It rained very hard that day, I was thoroughly soaked and by noon a good deal tired, so I stopped at a poor inn, where I stayed all night, beginning now to wish I had never left home. I made so miserable a figure, too, that I found by the questions asked me I was suspected to be some runaway servant, and in danger of being taken up on that suspicion. However, I proceeded the next day, and got in the evening to an inn within eight or ten miles of Burlington, kept by one Dr. Brown.

He entered into conversation with me while I took some refreshment and, finding I had read a little, became very sociable and friendly. Our acquaintance continued all the rest of his life. He had been, I imagine, an itinerant doctor, for there was no town in England or any country in Europe of which he could not give a very particular account. He had some letters and was ingenious, but he was an infidel and wickedly undertook some years after to travesty the Bible in doggerel verse as Cotton had done with Virgil. By this means he set many of the facts in a very ridiculous light and might have done mischief with weak minds if his work had been published, but it never was. At his house I lay that night, and the next morning reached Burlington, but had the mortification to find that the regular boats were gone a little before and no other expected to go before Tuesday, this being Saturday. Wherefore, I returned to an old woman in the town of whom I had bought some gingerbread to eat on the water and asked her advice; she invited me to lodge at her house till a passage by water should offer; and being tired with my foot travelling, I accepted the invitation. Understanding I was a printer, she would have had me remain in that town and follow my business, being ignorant of the stock necessary to begin with. She was very hospitable, gave me a dinner of ox cheek with great good will, accepting only of a pot of ale in return. And I thought myself fixed till Tuesday should come. However, walking in the evening by the side of the river, a boat came by, which I found was going towards Philadelphia with several people in her. They took me in, and as there was no wind, we rowed all the way; and about midnight, not having yet seen the city, some of the company were confident we must have passed it and would row no farther; the others knew not where we were, so we put towards the shore, got into a creek, landed near an old fence, with the rails of which we made a fire, the night being cold in October, and there we remained till daylight. Then one of the company knew the place to be Cooper's Creek, a little above Philadelphia, which we saw as soon as we got out of the creek, and arrived there about eight or nine o'clock, on the Sunday morning and landed at the Market Street wharf.

I have been the more particular in this description of my journey, and shall be so of my first entry into that city, that you may in your mind compare such unlikely beginnings with the figure I have since made there. I was in my working dress, my best clothes being to come round by sea. I was dirty from my journey; my pockets were stuffed out with shirts and stockings; I knew no soul, nor where to look for lodging. Fatigued with walking, rowing, and want of sleep, I was very hungry, and my whole stock of cash consisted of a Dutch dollar and about a shilling in copper coin, which I gave to the boatmen for my passage. At first they refused it on account of my having rowed, but I insisted on their taking it. A man is sometimes more generous when he has little money than when he has plenty, perhaps through fear of being thought to have but little. I walked towards the top of the street, gazing about till near Market Street, where I met a boy with bread. I have often made a meal of dry bread, and inquiring where he had bought it, I went immediately to the baker's he directed me to. I asked for biscuit, meaning such as we had in Boston, but that sort, it seems, was not made in Philadelphia. I then asked for a threepenny loaf and was told they had none such. Not knowing the different prices nor the names of the different sorts of bread, I told him to give me three pennyworth of any sort. He gave me accordingly three great puffy rolls. I was surprized at the quantity but took it, and having no room in my pockets, walked off with a roll under each arm and eating the other. Thus I went up

Market Street as far as Fourth Street, passing by the door of Mr. Read, my future wife's father, when she, standing at the door, saw me, and thought I made—as I certainly did—a most awkward, ridiculous appearance. Then I turned and went down Chestnut Street and part of Walnut Street, eating my roll all the way, and coming round, found myself again at Market Street wharf near the boat I came in, to which I went for a draught of the river water, and being filled with one of my rolls, gave the other two to a woman and her child that came down the river in the boat with us and were waiting to go farther. Thus refreshed, I walked again up the street, which by this time had many clean dressed people in it who were all walking the same way; I joined them, and thereby was led into the great meetinghouse of the Quakers near the market. I sat down among them, and after looking round awhile and hearing nothing said, being very drowsy through labour and want of rest the preceding night, I fell fast asleep and continued so till the meeting broke up, when someone was kind enough to rouse me. This was therefore the first house I was in or slept in, in Philadelphia.

I then walked down again towards the river, and looking in the faces of everyone, I met a young Quaker man whose countenance pleased me, and accosting him requested he would tell me where a stranger could get a lodging. We were then near the Sign of the Three Mariners. "Here," says he, "is a house where they receive strangers, but it is not a reputable one; if thee wilt walk with me, I'll show thee a better one." He conducted me to the Crooked Billet in Water Street. There I got a dinner. And while I was eating, several sly questions were asked me, as from my youth and appearance I was suspected of being a runaway. After dinner my sleepiness returned; and being shown to a bed, I lay down without undressing and slept till six in the evening, when I was called to supper. I went to bed again very early and slept soundly till next morning. Then I dressed myself as neat as I could, and went to Andrew Bradford, the printer's. I found in the shop the old man his father, whom I had seen at New York, and who travelling on horseback, had got to Philadelphia before me. He introduced me to his son, who received me civilly, gave me a breakfast, but told me he did not at present want a hand, being lately supplied with one. But there was another printer in town lately set up, one Keimer, who perhaps might employ me; if not, I should be welcome to lodge at his house, and he would give me a little work to do now and then till fuller business should offer.

The old gentleman said he would go with me to the new printer. And when we found him, "Neighbour," says Bradford, "I have brought to see you a young man of your business; perhaps you may want such a one." He asked me a few questions, put a composing stick in my hand to see how I worked, and then said he would employ me soon, though he had just then nothing for me to do. And taking old Bradford, whom he had never seen before, to be one of the townspeople that had a good will for him, entered into a conversation on his present undertaking and prospects; while Bradford, not discovering that he was the other printer's father, on Keimer's saying he expected soon to get the greatest part of the business into his own hands, drew him on by artful questions and starting little doubts to explain all his views, what influence he relied on, and in what manner he intended to proceed. I, who stood by and heard all, saw immediately that one of them was a crafty old sophister, and the other a true notice. Bradford left me with Keimer, who was greatly surprized when I told him who the old man was.

Keimer's printing house, I found, consisted of an old damaged press and a small worn-out fount of English types, which he was then using himself, composing an elegy on Aquila Rose, before-mentioned, an ingenious young man of excellent character, much respected in the town, secretary to the Assembly, and a pretty poet. Keimer made verses, too, but very indifferently. He could not be said to write them, for his method was to compose them in the types directly out of his head; so there being no copy but one pair of cases, and the elegy probably requiring all the letter, no one could help him. I endeavoured to put his press (which he had not yet used, and of which he understood nothing) into order fit to be worked with; and promising to come and print off his elegy as soon as he should have got it ready, I returned to Bradford's, who gave me a little job to do for the present, and there I lodged and dieted. A few days after Keimer sent for me to print off the elegy. And now he had got another pair of cases, and a pamphlet to reprint on which he set me to work.

These two printers I found poorly qualified for their business. Bradford had not been bred to it and was very illiterate; and Keimer, though something of a scholar, was a mere compositor, knowing nothing of presswork. He had been one of the French prophets and could act their enthusiastic agitations. At this time he did not profess any particular religion, but something of all on occasion, was very ignorant of the world, and had—as I afterwards found—a good deal of the knave in his composition. He did not like my lodging at Bradford's while I worked with him. He had a house, indeed, but without furniture, so he could not lodge me; but he got me a lodging at Mr. Read's, before-mentioned, who was the owner of his house. And my chest and clothes being come by this time, I made rather a more respectable appearance in the eyes of Miss Read than I had done when she first happened to see me eating my roll in the street.

I began now to have some acquaintance among the young people of the town that were lovers of reading, with whom I spent my evenings very pleasantly and gained money by my industry and frugality. I lived very contented, and forgot Boston as much as I could, and did not wish it should be known where I resided except to my friend Collins, who was in my secret and kept it when I wrote to him. At length an incident happened that sent me back again much sooner than I had intended.

I had a brother-in-law, Robert Holmes,[2] master of a sloop that traded between Boston and Delaware. He being at New Castle, forty miles below Philadelphia, heard there of me and wrote me a letter mentioning the concern of my relations and friends in Boston at my abrupt departure, assuring me of their good will to me, and that every thing would be accommodated to my mind if I would return, to which he exhorted me very earnestly. I wrote an answer to his letter, thanked him for his advice,

---

[2]Franklin later spells the name correctly—"Homes."

but stated my reasons for quitting Boston so fully and in such a light as to convince him that I was not so much in the wrong as he had apprehended.

Sir William Keith, Governor of the province, was then at New Castle, and Captain Holmes happening to be in company with him when my letter came to hand, spoke to him of me, and showed him the letter. The Governor read it, and seemed surprized when he was told my age. He said I appeared a young man of promising parts and therefore should be encouraged. The printers at Philadelphia were wretched ones, and if I would set up there, he made no doubt I should succeed; for his part, he would procure me the public business, and do me every other service in his power. This my brother-in-law afterwards told me in Boston. But I knew as yet nothing of it; when one day Keimer and I being at work together near the window, we saw the Governor and another gentleman (who proved to be Colonel French of New Castle) finely dressed, come directly across the street to our house and heard them at the door. Keimer ran down immediately, thinking it a visit to him; but the Governor enquired for me, came up, and with a condescension and politeness I had been quite unused to, made me many compliments, desired to be acquainted with me, blamed me kindly for not having made myself known to him when I first came to the place, and would have me away with him to the tavern where he was going with Colonel French to taste, as he said, some excellent Madeira. I was not a little surprized, and Keimer stared with astonishment.[3] I went, however, with the Governor and Colonel French, to a tavern the corner of Third Street, and over the Madeira he proposed my setting up my business. He stated the probabilities of success, and both he and Colonel French assured me I should have their interest and influence to obtain for me the public business of both governments. On my doubting whether my father would assist me in it, Sir William said he would give me a letter to him in which he would set forth the advantages, and he did not doubt he should determine him to comply. So it was concluded I should return to Boston by the first vessel with

[3]Franklin originally wrote: "Keimer stared like a pig poisoned."

the Governor's letter of recommendation to my father. In the meantime the intention was to be kept secret, and I went on working with Keimer as usual. The Governor sent for me now and then to dine with him, which I considered a great honour, more particularly as he conversed with me in the most affable, familiar, and friendly manner imaginable.

About the end of April, 1724, a little vessel offered for Boston. I took leave of Keimer as going to see my friends. The Governor gave me an ample letter, saying many flattering things of me to my father and strongly recommending the project of my setting up at Philadelphia as a thing that would make my fortune. We struck on a shoal in going down the bay and sprung a leak; we had a blustering time at sea and were obliged to pump almost continually, at which I took my turn. We arrived safe, however, at Boston in about a fortnight. I had been absent seven months, and my friends had heard nothing of me, for my brother Homes was not yet returned and had not written about me. My unexpected appearance surprized the family; all were, however, very glad to see me and made me welcome, except my brother. I went to see him at his printing house. I was better dressed than ever while in his service, having a genteel new suit from head to foot, a watch, and my pockets lined with near five pounds sterling in silver. He received me not very frankly, looked me all over, and turned to his work again. The journeymen were inquisitive where I had been, what sort of a country it was, and how I liked it. I praised it much and the happy life I led in it, expressing strongly my intention of returning to it; and one of them asking what kind of money we had there, I produced a handful of silver and spread it before them, which was a kind of raree show they had not been used to, paper being the money of Boston. Then I took an opportunity of letting them see my watch, and lastly (my brother still grum and sullen) I gave them a piece of eight to drink and took my leave. This visit of mine offended him extremely. For when my mother sometime after spoke to him of a reconciliation, and of her wish to see us on good terms together, and that we might live for the future as brothers, he said I had insulted him in such a manner before his people that he could never forget or forgive it. In this, however, he was mistaken.

My father received the Governor's letter with some surprize but said little of it to me for some days. Captain Homes returning, he showed it to him, and asked him if he knew Keith and what kind of a man he was, adding his opinion that he must be of small discretion to think of setting a boy up in business who wanted yet three years to arrive at man's estate. Homes said what he could in favour of the project; but my father was clear in the impropriety of it, and at last gave a flat denial. Then he wrote a civil letter to Sir William, thanking him for the patronage he had so kindly offered me, and declining to assist me as yet in setting up, I being in his opinion too young to be trusted with the management of an undertaking so important, and for which the preparation required a considerable expenditure.

My old companion Collins, who was a clerk in the post office, pleased with the account I gave him of my new country, determined to go thither also. And while I waited for my father's determination, he set out before me by land to Rhode Island, leaving his books, which were a pretty collection of mathematics and natural philosophy, to come with mine and me to New York, where he proposed to wait for me.

My father, though he did not approve Sir William's proposition, was yet pleased that I had been able to obtain so advantageous a character from a person of such note where I had resided, and that I had been so industrious and careful as to equip myself so handsomely in so short a time. Therefore, seeing no prospect of an accommodation between my brother and me, he gave his consent to my returning again to Philadelphia, advised me to behave respectfully to the people there, endeavour to obtain the general esteem, and avoid lampooning and libelling, to which he thought I had too much inclination—telling me that by steady industry and a prudent parsimony I might save enough by the time I was one-and-twenty to set me up, and that if I came near the matter he would help me out with the rest. This was all I could obtain, except some small gifts as tokens of his and my mother's love, when I embarked again for New

York, now with their approbation and their blessing. The sloop putting in at Newport, Rhode Island, I visited my brother John, who had been married and settled there some years. He received me very affectionately, for he always loved me. A friend of him, one Vernon, having some money due to him in Pennsylvania, about thirty-five pounds currency, desired I would recover it for him, and keep it till I had his directions what to employ it in. Accordingly he gave me an order. This business afterwards occasioned me a good deal of uneasiness.

At Newport we took in a number of passengers—among which were two young women travelling together and a grave, sensible, matron-like Quaker lady with her servants. I had shown an obliging readiness to render her some little services, which impressed her, I suppose, with a degree of good will towards me; for when she saw a daily growing familiarity between me and the two young women, which they appeared to encourage, she took me aside and said, "Young man, I am concerned for thee, as thou hast no friend with thee and seems not to know much of the world or of the snares youth is exposed to; depend upon it, those are very bad women; I can see it by all their actions; and if thee art not upon thy guard, they will draw thee into some danger; they are strangers to thee, and I advise thee, in a friendly concern for thy welfare, to have no acquaintance with them." As I seemed at first not to think so ill of them as she did, she mentioned some things she had observed and heard that had escaped my notice, but now convinced me she was right. I thanked her for her kind advice and promised to follow it. When we arrived at New York, they told me where they lived and invited me to come and see them; but I avoided it. And it was well I did; for the next day the captain missed a silver spoon and some other things that had been taken out of his cabin; and knowing that these were a couple of strumpets, he got a warrant to search their lodgings, found the stolen goods, and had the thieves punished. So though we escaped a sunken rock which we scraped upon in the passage, I thought this escape of rather more importance to me.

At New York I found my friend Collins, who had arrived there sometime before me. We had been intimate from children and had read the same books together, but he had the advantage of more time for reading and studying and a wonderful genius for mathematical learning, in which he far outstripped me. While I lived in Boston, most of my hours of leisure for conversation were spent with him; and he continued a sober as well as an industrious lad, was much respected for his learning by several of the clergy and other gentlemen, and seemed to promise making a good figure in life. But during my absence he had acquired a habit of sotting with brandy, and I found by his own account, as well as that of others, that he had been drunk every day since his arrival at New York, and behaved himself in a very extravagant manner. He had gamed, too, and lost his money, so that I was obliged to discharge his lodgings and defray his expenses on the road and at Philadelphia—which proved a great burden to me. The then Governor of New York, Burnet, son of Bishop Burnet, hearing from the captain that a young man, one of his passengers, had a great many books, desired him to bring me to see him. I waited upon him and should have taken Collins with me, had he been sober. The Governor received me with great civility, showed me his library, which was a very considerable one, and we had a good deal of conversation about books and authors. This was the second governor who had done me the honour to take notice of me, and for a poor boy like me was very pleasing.

We proceeded to Philadelphia. I received on the way Vernon's money, without which we could hardly have finished our journey. Collins wished to be employed in some countinghouse; but whether they discovered his dramming by his breath or by his behaviour, though he had some recommendations, he met with no success in any application and continued lodging and boarding at the same house with me and at my expense. Knowing I had that money of Vernon's, he was continually borrowing of me, still promising repayment as soon as he should be in business. At length he had got so much of it, that I was distressed to think what I should do in case of being called on to remit it. His drinking continued, about which we sometimes quarreled, for when a little intoxicated he was very fractious. Once in a boat on the Delaware with some other young men, he refused to row in his turn.

"I will be rowed home," says he.

"We will not row you," says I.

"You must," says he, "or stay all night on the water, just as you please."

The others said, "Let us row; what signifies it?"

But my mind being soured with his other conduct, I continued to refuse. So he swore he would make me row or throw me overboard; and coming along stepping on the thwarts towards me, when he came up and struck at me, I clapped my hand under his crutch and rising pitched him head-foremost into the river. I knew he was a good swimmer and so was under little concern about him; but before he could get round to lay hold of the boat, we had with a few strokes pulled her out of his reach. And ever when he drew near the boat, we asked if he would row, striking a few strokes to slide her away from him. He was ready to stifle with vexation, and obstinately would not promise to row; however, seeing him at last beginning to tire, we drew him into the boat and brought him home dripping wet in the evening. We hardly exchanged a civil word after this adventure. At length a West India captain who had a commission to procure a tutor for the sons of a gentleman at Barbadoes, happening to meet with him, proposed to carry him thither to fill that situation. He accepted and left me, promising to remit me what he owed me out of the first money he should receive, but I never heard of him after.

The violation of my trust respecting Vernon's money was one of the first great errata of my life, and this affair showed that my father was not much out in his judgment when he supposed me too young to manage business of importance. But Sir William, on reading his letter, said he was too prudent, that there was a great difference in persons, and discretion did not always accompany years, nor was youth always without it. "And since he will not set you up," says he, "I will do it myself. Give me an inventory of the things necessary to be had from England, and I will send for them. You shall repay me when you are able; I am resolved to have a good printer here, and I am sure you must succeed." This was spoken with such an appearance of cordiality that I had not the least doubt of his meaning what he said. I had hitherto kept the proposition of my setting up a secret in Philadelphia, and I still kept it. Had it been known that I depended on the Governor, probably some friend that knew him better would have advised me not to rely on him, as I afterwards heard it as his known character to be liberal of promises which he never meant to keep. Yet unsolicited as he was by me, how could I think his generous offers insincere? I believed him one of the best men in the world.

I presented him an inventory of a little printing house, amounting by my computation to about £100 sterling. He liked it but asked me if my being on the spot in England to choose the types and see that everything was good of the kind might not be of some advantage. "Then," says he, "when there you may make acquaintances and establish correspondences in the bookselling and stationery way." I agreed that this might be advantageous. "Then," says he, "get yourself ready to go with *Annis*," which was the annual ship and the only one at that time usually passing between London and Philadelphia. But it would be some months before *Annis* sailed, so I continued working with Keimer, fretting extremely about the money Collins had got from me, and in daily apprehensions of being called upon for it by Vernon—which, however, did not happen for some years after.

I believe I have omitted mentioning that in my first voyage from Boston to Philadelphia, being becalmed off Block Island, our crew employed themselves catching cod and hauled up a great number. 'Till then I had stuck to my resolution to eat nothing that had had life; and on this occasion I considered, according to my Master Tryon, the taking every fish as a kind of unprovoked murder, since none of them had or ever could do us any injury that might justify this massacre. All this seemed very reasonable. But I had formerly been a great lover of fish, and when this came hot out of the frying pan, it smelled admirably well. I balanced some time between principle and inclination till I recollected that when the fish were opened, I saw smaller fish taken out of their stomachs. "Then," thought I, "if you eat one another, I don't see why we mayn't eat you.'' So I dined upon cod very heartily and have since continued to eat as other people, returning only now and then occasionally to a vegetable diet. So convenient a thing it is to be a *reasonable creature,* since it enables one to find or make a reason for everything one has a mind to do.

Keimer and I lived on a pretty good familiar footing and agreed tolerably well, for he suspected nothing of my setting up. He retained a great deal of his old enthusiasm and loved argumentation. We therefore had many disputations. I used to work him so with my Socratic method and had trapanned him so often by questions apparently so distant from any point we had in hand, and yet by degrees leading to the point and bringing him into difficulties and contradictions, that at last he grew ridiculously cautious and would hardly answer the most common question without asking first, ''What do you intend to infer from that?'' However, it gave him so high an opinion of my abilities in the confuting way that he seriously proposed my being his colleague in a project he had of setting up a new sect. He was to preach the doctrines, and I was to confound all opponents. When he came to explain with me upon the doctrines, I found several conundrums which I objected to, unless I might have my way a little, too, and introduce some of mine. Keimer wore his beard at full length, because somewhere in the Mosaic Law it is said, ''Thou shalt not mar the corners of thy beard.'' He likewise kept the seventh day Sabbath, and these two points were essentials with him. I disliked both but agreed to admit them upon condition of his adopting the doctrine of not using animal food. ''I doubt,'' says he, ''my constitution will bear it.'' I assured him it would and that he would be the better for it. He was usually a great glutton, and I wished to give myself some diversion in half-starving him. He consented to try the practice if I would keep him company; I did so, and we held it for three months. Our provisions were purchased, cooked, and brought to us regularly by a woman in the neighbourhood who had from me a list of forty dishes to be prepared for us at different times, in which there entered neither fish, flesh, nor fowl. This whim suited me better at this time from the cheapness of it, not costing us above eighteen pence sterling each per week. I have since kept several Lents most strictly, leaving the common diet for that, and that for common, abruptly, without the least inconvenience, so that I think there is little in the advice of making those changes by easy gradations. I went on pleasantly, but poor Keimer suffered grievously, tired of the project, longed for the flesh pots of Egypt, and ordered a roast pig. He invited me and two women friends to dine with him, but it being brought too soon upon table, he could not resist the temptation and ate it all up before we came.

I had made some courtship during this time to Miss Read. I had a great respect and affection for her, and had some reasons to believe she had the same for me; but as I was about to take a long voyage and we were both very young, only a little above eighteen, it was thought most prudent by her mother to prevent our going too far at present, as a marriage, if it was to take place, would be more convenient after my return, when I should be as I hoped set up in my business. Perhaps, too, she thought my expectations not so well founded as I imagined them to be.

My chief acquaintances at this time were Charles Osborne, Joseph Watson, and James Ralph—all lovers of reading. The two first were clerks to an eminent scrivener or conveyancer in the town, Charles Brogden; the other was clerk to a merchant. Watson was a pious, sensible young man of great integrity. The others [were] rather more lax in their principles of religion, particularly Ralph, who as well as Collins had been unsettled by me, for which they both made me suffer. Osborne was sensible, candid, frank—sincere and affectionate to his friends—but in literary matters too fond of criticism. Ralph was ingenious, genteel in his manners, and extremely eloquent; I think I never knew a prettier talker. Both were great admirers of poetry and began to try their hands in little pieces. Many pleasant walks we four had together on Sundays in the woods on the banks of the Schuylkill, when we read to one another and conferred on what we read. Ralph was inclined to give himself up entirely to poetry, not doubting but he might make great proficiency in it and even make his fortune by it. He pretended that the greatest poets must, when they first began to write, have committed as many faults as he did. Osborne endeavoured to dissuade him, assured him he had no genius for poetry, and advised him to think of nothing beyond the business he was bred to: "That in the mercantile way, though he had no stock, he might by his diligence and punctuality recommend himself to employment as a factor and in time acquire wherewith to trade on his own account." I approved for my part the amusing one's self with poetry now and then, so far as to improve one's language, but no farther. On this it was proposed that we should each of us at our next meeting produce a piece of our own composing in order to improve by our mutual observations, criticisms, and corrections. As language and expression was what we had in view, we excluded all considerations of invention, by agreeing that the task should be a version of the eighteenth Psalm, which describes the descent of a deity. When the time of our meeting drew nigh, Ralph called on me first and let me know his piece was ready; I told him I had been busy and, having little inclination, had done nothing. He then showed me his piece for my opinion; and I much approved it, as it appeared to have great merit. "Now," says he, "Osborne never will allow the least merit in anything of mine but makes a thousand criticisms out of mere envy. He is not so jealous of you. I wish therefore you would take this piece and produce it as yours. I will pretend not to have had time, and so produce nothing. We shall then see what he will say to it." It was agreed, and I immediately transcribed it that it might appear in my own hand. We met. Watson's performance was read; there were some beauties in it, but many defects. Osborne's was read; it was much better. Ralph did it justice, remarked some faults, but applauded the beauties. He himself had nothing to produce. I was backward, seemed desirous of being excused, had not had sufficient time to correct, etc.; but no excuse could be admitted, produce I must. It was read and repeated; Watson and Osborne gave up the contest and joined in applauding it. Ralph only made some criticisms and proposed some amendments, but I defended my text. Osborne was against Ralph, and told him he was no better able to criticise than compose verses. As these two were returning home together, Osborne expressed himself still more strongly in favour of what he thought my production, having before refrained, as he said, lest I should think he meant to flatter me. "But who would have imagined," says he, "that Franklin had been capable of such a performance—such painting, such force, such fire! He has even improved the original. In his common conversation, he seems to have no choice of words; he hesitates and blunders; and yet, good God, how he writes!" When we next met, Ralph discovered the trick we had played him, and Osborne was a little laughed at. This transaction fixed Ralph in his resolution of becoming a poet. I did all I could to dissuade him from it, but he continued scribbling verses till Pope cured him.* He became, however, a pretty good prose writer. More of him hereafter. But as I may not have occasion to mention the other two, I shall just remark here that Watson died in my arms a few years after, much lamented, being the best of our set. Osborne went to the West Indies, where he became an eminent lawyer and made money but died young. He and I had made a serious agreement that the one who happened first to die should, if possible, make a friendly visit to the other and acquaint him how he found things in that separate state. But he never fulfilled his promise.

The Governor, seeming to like my company, had me frequently to his house; and his setting me up was always mentioned as a fixed thing. I was to take with me letters recommendatory to a number of his friends, besides the letter of credit, to furnish me with the necessary money for purchasing the press, types, paper, etc. For these letters I was appointed to call at different times, when they were to be ready, but a future time was still named. Thus we went on till the ship (whose departure, too, had been several times postponed) was on the point of sailing. Then when I called to take my leave and receive the letters, his secretary, Dr. Bard, came out to me and said the Governor was extremely busy in writing but would

---

*"Silence ye wolves, while Ralph to Cynthia howls,
    And makes night hideous:—answer him ye owls!"
                                    (Pope's *Dunciad*)

be down at New Castle before the ship, and there the letters would be delivered to me.

Ralph, though married and having one child, had determined to accompany me in this voyage. It was thought he intended to establish a correspondence and obtain goods to sell on commission. But I found afterwards that having some cause of discontent with his wife's relations, he proposed to leave her on their hands and never to return to America. Having taken leave of my friends and exchanged promises with Miss Read, I quitted Philadelphia in the ship, which anchored at New Castle. The Governor was there, but when I went to his lodging, his secretary came to me from him with expressions of the greatest regret that he could not then see me, being engaged in business of the utmost importance, but that he would send the letters to me on board, wished me heartily a good voyage and a speedy return, etc. I returned on board a little puzzled but still not doubting.

Mr. Andrew Hamilton, a famous lawyer of Philadelphia, had taken passage in the same ship for himself and son, and with Mr. Denham, a Quaker merchant, and Messrs. Onion and Russel, masters of an iron work in Maryland, had engaged the great cabin, so that Ralph and I were forced to take up with a berth in the steerage—and none on board knowing us, were considered as ordinary persons. But Mr. Hamilton and his son (it was James, since Governor) returned from New Castle to Philadelphia, the father being recalled by a great fee to plead for a seized ship. And just before we sailed Col. French coming on board, and showing me great respect, I was more taken notice of and with my friend Ralph invited by the other gentlemen to come into the cabin, there being now room. Accordingly, we removed thither.

Understanding that Col. French had brought on board the Governor's dispatches, I asked the captain for those letters that were to be under my care. He said all were put into the bag together; and he could not then come at them, but before we landed in England I should have an opportunity of picking them out. So I was satisfied for the present, and we proceeded on our voyage. We had a sociable company in the cabin and lived uncommonly well, having the addition of all Mr. Hamilton's stores, who had laid in plentifully. In this passage, Mr. Denham contracted a friendship for me that continued during his life. The voyage was otherwise not a pleasant one, as we had a great deal of bad weather.

When we came into the channel, the captain kept his word with me and gave me an opportunity of examining the bag for the Governor's letters. I found none upon which my name was put as under my care; I picked out six or seven that by the handwriting I thought might be the promised letters, especially as one of them was addressed to Basket, the King's printer, another to some stationer. We arrived in London the 24th of December, 1724. I waited upon the stationer who came first in my way, delivering the letter as from Gov. Keith. "I don't know such a person," says he, but opening the letter, "Oh, this is from Riddlesden; I have lately found him to be a complete rascal, and I will have nothing to do with him, nor receive any letters from him." So putting the letter into my hand, he turned on his heel and left me to serve some customer. I was surprized to find these were not the Governor's letters; and after recollecting and comparing circumstances, I began to doubt his sincerity. I found my friend Denham and opened the whole affair to him. He let me into Keith's character, told me there was not the least probability that he had written any letters for me, that no one who knew him had the smallest dependence on him, and he laughed at the idea of the Governor's giving me a letter of credit, having, as he said, no credit to give. On my expressing some concern about what I should do, he advised me to endeavour getting some employment in the way of my business. "Among the printers here," says he, "you will improve yourself; and when you return to America, you will set up to greater advantage."

We both of us happened to know, as well as the stationer, that Riddlesden, the attorney, was a very knave. He had half ruined Miss Read's father by drawing him in to be bound for him. By his letter it appeared there was a secret scheme on foot to the prejudice of Mr. Hamilton (supposed to be then coming over with us) and that Keith was concerned in it with Riddlesden. Denham, who was a friend of Hamilton's, thought he ought to be acquainted with it. So when he arrived in England, which was soon after, partly from resentment and ill-will to Keith and Riddlesden, and partly from good will to him, I waited on him and gave him the letter. He thanked me cordially, the information being of importance to him. And from that time he became my friend, greatly to my advantage afterwards on many occasions.

But what shall we think of a Governor playing such pitiful tricks and imposing so grossly on a poor ignorant boy! It was a habit he had acquired. He wished to please everybody; and having little to give, he gave expectations. He was otherwise an ingenious, sensible man, a pretty good writer, and a good governor for the people, tho' not for his constituents, the Proprietaries, whose instructions he sometimes disregarded. Several of our best laws were of his planning and passed during his administration.

Ralph and I were inseparable companions. We took lodgings together in Little Britain at 3 *s.* 6 *d.* per week, as much as we could then afford. He found some relations, but they were poor and unable to assist him. He now let me know his intentions of remaining in London and that he never meant to return to Philadelphia. He had brought no money with him, the whole he could muster having been expended in paying his passage. I had fifteen pistoles, so he borrowed occasionally of me to subsist while he was looking out for business. He first endeavoured to get into the playhouse, believing himself qualified for an actor; but Wilkes to whom he applied, advised him candidly not to think of that employment, as it was impossible he should succeed in it. Then he proposed to Roberts, a publisher in Paternoster Row, to write for him a weekly paper like the *Spectator,* on certain conditions which Roberts did not approve. Then he endeavoured to get employment as a hackney writer to copy for the stationers and lawyers about the Temple, but could find no vacancy.

For myself, I immediately got into work at Palmer's, then a famous printing house in Bartholomew Close, and here I continued near a year. I was pretty diligent, but I spent with Ralph a good deal of my earnings in going to plays and other places of amusement. We had together consumed all my pistoles, and now just rubbed on from hand to mouth. He seemed quite to have forgotten his wife and child, and I by degrees my engagements with Miss Read, to whom I never wrote more than one letter, and that was to let her know I was not likely soon to return. This was another of the great errata of my life which I should wish to correct if I were to live it over again. In fact, by our expenses, I was constantly kept unable to pay my passage.

At Palmer's I was employed in composing for the second edition of Wollaston's *Religion of Nature*. Some of his reasonings not appearing to me well-founded, I wrote a little metaphysical piece in which I made remarks on them. It was entitled, "A Dissertation on Liberty and Necessity, Pleasure and Pain." I inscribed it to my friend Ralph; I printed a small number. It occasioned my being more considered by Mr. Palmer as a young man of some ingenuity, tho' he seriously expostulated with me upon the principles of my pamphlet, which to him appeared abominable. My printing this pamphlet was another erratum.

While I lodged in Little Britain I made an acquaintance with one Wilcox, a bookseller, whose shop was next door. He had an immense collection of second-hand books. Circulating libraries were not then in use; but we agreed that on certain reasonable terms, which I have now forgotten, I might take, read, and return any of his books. This I esteemed a great advantage, and I made as much use of it as I could.

My pamphlet by some means falling into the hands of one Lyons, a surgeon, author of a book entitled *The Infallibility of Human Judgment*, it occasioned an acquaintance between us; he took great notice of me, called on me often to converse on those subjects, carried me to the Horns, a pale ale house in —— Lane, Cheapside, and introduced me to Dr. Mandeville, author of *The Fable of the Bees* who had a club there, of which he was the soul, being a most facetious, entertaining companion. Lyons, too, introduced me to Dr. Pemberton at Batson's Coffee House, who promised to give me an opportunity sometime or other of seeing Sir Isaac Newton, of which I was extremely desirous; but this never happened.

I had brought over a few curiosities, among which the principal was a purse made of the asbestos, which purifies by fire. Sir Hans Sloane heard of it, came to see me, and invited me to his house in Bloomsbury Square, where he showed me all his curiosities and persuaded me to add that to the number, for which he paid me handsomely.

In our house there lodged a young woman, a milliner, who, I think, had a shop in the cloisters. She had been genteelly bred, was sensible, lively, and of a most pleasing conversation. Ralph read plays to her in the evenings, they grew intimate, she took another lodging, and he followed her. They lived together some time, but he being still out of business, and her income not sufficient to maintain them with her child, he took a resolution of going from London, to try for a country school, which he thought himself well qualified to undertake, as he wrote an excellent hand and was a master of arithmetic and accounts. This, however, he deemed a business below him, and confident of future better fortune when he should be unwilling to have it known that he was once so meanly employed, he changed his name and did me the honour to assume mine. For I soon after had a letter from him, acquainting me that he was settled in a small village in Berkshire, I think it was, where he taught reading and writing to ten or a dozen boys at sixpence per week, recommending Mrs. T. to my care and desiring me to write to him, directing for Mr. Franklin, schoolmaster at such a place. He continued to write to me frequently, sending me large specimens of an epic poem which he was then composing, and desiring my remarks and corrections. These I gave him from time to time, but endeavoured rather to discourage his proceeding. One of Young's satires was then just published. I copied and sent him a great part of it, which set in a strong light the folly of pursuing the Muses with any hope of advancement by them. All was in vain; sheets of the poem continued to come by every post. In the meantime Mrs. T., having on his account lost her friends and business, was often in distresses and used to send for me and borrow what I could spare to help her out of them. I grew fond of her company, and being at this time under no religious restraint, and presuming on my importance to her, I attempted familiarities (another erratum), which she repulsed with a proper resentment. She wrote to Ralph and acquainted him with my conduct; this occasioned a breach between us. And when he returned to London, he let me know he considered all the obligations he had been under to me as annulled—from which I concluded I was never to expect his repaying the money I had lent him or that I had advanced for him. This, however, was of little consequence, as he was totally unable; and by the loss of his friendship, I found myself relieved from a heavy burthen. I now began to think of getting a little money beforehand, and expecting better employment, I left Palmer's to work at Watts's near Lincoln's Inn Fields, a still greater printing house. Here I continued all the rest of my stay in London.

At my first admission into this printing house, I took to working at press, imagining I felt a want of the bodily exercise I had been used to in America, where press-work is mixed with the composing. I drank only water; the other workmen, near fifty in number, were great guzzlers of beer. On occasion I carried up and down stairs a large form of types in each hand, when others carried but one in both hands. They wondered to see from this and several instances that the "Water-American," as they called me, was *stronger* than themselves who drank *strong* beer. We had an alehouse boy who attended always in the house to supply the workmen. My companion at the press drank every day a pint before breakfast, a pint at breakfast with his bread and cheese, a pint between breakfast and dinner, a pint at dinner, a pint in the afternoon about six o'clock, and another when he had done his day's work. I thought it a detestable custom; but it was necessary, he supposed, to drink *strong* beer that he might be *strong* to labour. I endeavoured to convince him that the bodily strength afforded by beer could only be in proportion to the grain or flour of the barley dissolved in the water of which it was made, that there was more flour in a pennyworth of bread, and therefore if he would eat that with a pint of water, it would give him more strength than a quart of beer. He drank on, however, and had four of five shillings to pay out of his wages every Saturday night for that muddling liquor, an expence I was free from. And thus these poor devils keep themselves always under.

Watts after some weeks desiring to have me in the composing room, I left the pressmen. A new *bienvenu* for drink, being five shillings, was demanded of me by the compositors. I thought it an imposition, as I had paid below. The master thought so, too, and forbad my paying it. I stood out two or three weeks, was accordingly considered as an excommunicate, and had so many little pieces of private malice practised on me by mixing my sorts, transposing my pages, breaking my matter, etc., etc., if ever I stepped out of the room—and all ascribed to the Chapel Ghost, which they said ever haunted those not regularly admitted—that notwithstanding the master's protection, I found myself obliged to comply and pay the money, convinced of the folly of being on ill terms with those one is to live with continually. I was now on a fair footing with them and soon acquired considerable influence. I proposed some reasonable alterations in their chapel* laws, and carried them against all opposition. From my example, a great many of them left their muddling breakfast of beer, bread, and cheese, finding they could with me be supplied from a neighbouring house with a large porringer of hot water gruel, sprinkled with pepper, crumbled with bread, and a bit of butter in it, for the price of a pint of beer, viz., three halfpence. This was a more comfortable as well as a cheaper breakfast and kept their heads clearer. Those who continued sotting with beer all day were often, by not paying, out of credit at the ale-house and used to make interest with me to get beer, their "light," as they phrased it, "being out." I watched the paytable on Saturday night, and collected what I stood engaged for them, having to pay sometimes near thirty shillings a week on their accounts. This and my being esteemed a pretty good "riggite"; that is, a jocular, verbal satirist, supported my consequence in the society. My constant attendance (I never making a St. Monday), recommended me to the master; and my uncommon quickness at composing occasioned

*A printing house is always called a chapel by the workmen.

my being put upon all work of dispatch, which was generally better paid. So I went on now very agreeably.

My lodging in Little Britain being too remote, I found another in Duke Street opposite to the Romish chapel. It was up two pair of stairs backwards, at an Italian warehouse. A widow lady kept the house; she had a daughter and a maidservant and a journeyman, who attended the warehouse but lodged abroad. After sending to enquire my character at the house where I last lodged, she agreed to take me in at the same rate, 3 *s.* 6 *d.* per week, cheaper, as she said, from the protection she expected in having a man lodge in the house. She was a widow, an elderly woman, and had been bred a Protestant, (being a clergyman's daughter), but was converted to the Catholic religion by her husband, whose memory she much revered; had lived much among people of distinction and knew a thousand anecdotes of them as far back as the times of Charles the Second. She was lame in her knees with the gout and therefore seldom stirred out of her room, so sometimes wanted company; and hers was so highly amusing to me that I was sure to spend an evening with her whenever she desired it. Our supper was only half an anchovy each, on a very little slice of bread and butter, and half a pint of ale between us; but the entertainment was in her conversation. My always keeping good hours and giving little trouble in the family made her unwilling to part with me so that when I talked of a lodging I had heard of nearer my business for 2 *s.* a week, which, intent as I now was on saving money, made some difference, she bid me not think of it, for she would abate me two shillings a week for the future; so I remained with her at 1 *s.* 6 *d.* as long as I stayed in London.

In a garret of her house, there lived a maiden lady of seventy in the most retired manner, of whom my landlady gave me this account: that she was a Roman Catholic, had been sent abroad when young and lodged in a nunnery with an intent of becoming a nun; but the country not agreeing with her, she returned to England, where there being no nunnery, she had vowed to lead the life of a nun as near as might be done in those circumstances. Accordingly, she had given all her estate to charitable uses, reserving only twelve pounds a year to live on, and out of this sum she still gave a part in charity, living herself on water gruel only and using no fire but to boil it. She had lived many years in that garret, being permitted to remain there gratis by successive Catholic tenants of the house below, as they deemed it a blessing to have her there. A priest visited her, to confess her every day.

"I have asked her," says my landlady, "how she, as she lived, could possibly find so much employment for a confessor."

"O," says she, "it is impossible to avoid *vain thoughts.*" I was permitted once to visit her. She was cheerful and polite, and conversed pleasantly. The room was clean, but had no other furniture than a mattress, a table with a crucifix and book, a stool, which she gave me to sit on, and a picture over the chimney of St. Veronica, displaying her handkerchief, with the miraculous figure of Christ's bleeding face on it, which she explained to me with great seriousness. She looked pale but was never sick, and I give it as another instance on how small an income life and health may be supported.

At Watts's printing house I contracted an acquaintance with an ingenious young man, one Wygate, who having wealthy relations, had been better educated than most printers, was a tolerable Latinist, spoke French, and loved reading. I taught him, and a friend of his to swim, at twice going into the river, and they soon became good swimmers. They introduced me to some gentlemen from the country, who went to Chelsea by water to see the college and Don Saltero's curiosities. In our return, at the request of the company, whose curiosity Wygate had excited, I stripped and leaped into the river and swam from near Chelsea to Blackfriar's, performing on the way many feats of activity, both upon and under water, that surprized and pleased those to whom they were novelties. I had from a child been ever delighted with this exercise, had studied and practised all Thevenot's motions and positions, added some of my own, aiming at the graceful and easy as well as the useful. All these I took this occasion of exhibiting to the company and was much flattered by their admiration. And Wygate, who was desirous of becoming a master, grew more and more attached to me on that account, as well as from the similarity of our studies. He at length proposed to me travelling all over Europe together, supporting ourselves everywhere by working at our business. I was once inclined to it; but mentioning it to my good friend Mr. Denham, with whom I often spent an hour when I had leisure, he dissuaded me from it, advising me to think only of returning to Pennsylvania, which he was now about to do.

I must record one trait of this good man's character. He had formerly been in business at Bristol, but failed in debt to a number of people, compounded, and went to America. There, by a close application to business as a merchant, he acquired a plentiful fortune in a few years. Returning to England in the ship with me, he invited his old creditors to an entertainment, at which he thanked them for the easy composition they had favoured him with; and when they expected nothing but the treat, every man at the first remove found under his plate an order on a banker for the full amount of the unpaid remainder with interest.

He now told me he was about to return to Philadelphia and should carry over a great quantity of goods in order to open a store there. He proposed to take me over as his clerk to keep his books (in which he would instruct me), copy his letters, and attend the store. He added that as soon as I should be acquainted with mercantile business he would promote me by sending me with a cargo of flour and bread, etc., to the West Indies, and procure me commissions from others which would be profitable, and if I managed well, would establish me handsomely. The thing pleased me, for I was grown tired of London, remembered with pleasure the happy months I had spent in Pennsylvania, and wished again to see it. Therefore, I immediately agreed on the terms of fifty pounds a year, Pennsylvania money—less, indeed, than my then present gettings as a compositor but affording a better prospect.

I now took leave of printing, as I thought, forever, and was daily employed in my new business—going about with Mr. Denham among the tradesmen to purchase various articles and see them packed up, delivering messages, calling upon workmen to dispatch, etc.; and when all was on board, I had a few days' leisure. On one of these days I was, to my surprise, sent for by a great man I knew only by name, a Sir William Wyndham, and I waited upon him. He had heard by some means or other of my swimming from Chelsea to Blackfriar' and of my teaching Wygate and another young man to swim in a few hours. He had two sons about to set out on their travels; he wished to have them first taught swimming, and proposed to gratify me handsomely if I would teach them. They were not yet come to town, and my star was uncertain, so I could not undertake it. But from this incident I thought it likely that if I were to remain in England and open a swimming school, I might get a good deal of money; and it struck me so strongly that, had the overture been made me sooner, probably I should not so soon have returned to America. After many years, you and I had something of more importance to do with one of these sons of Sir William Wyndham, become Earl of Egremont, which I shall mention in its place.

Thus I passed about eighteen months in London. Most part of the time, I worked hard at my business, and spent but little upon myself except in seeing plays, and in books. My friend Ralph had kept me poor. He owed me about twenty-seven pounds, which I was now never likely to receive—a great sum out of my small earnings. I loved him notwithstanding, for he had many amiable qualities. I had improved my knowledge, however, though I had by no means improved my fortune. But I had made some very ingenious acquaintance, whose conversation was of great advantage to me, and I had read considerably.

We sailed from Gravesend on the 23rd of July, 1726. For the incidents of the voyage, I refer you to my Journal where you will find them all minutely related. Perhaps the most important part of that Journal is the *Plan* to be found in it, which I formed at sea, for regulating the future conduct of my life. It is the more remarkable as being formed when I was so young and yet being pretty faithfully adhered to quite thro' to old age.

We landed at Philadelphia the 11th of October, where I found sundry alterations. Keith was no longer Governor, being superceded by Major Gordon. I met him walking the streets as a common citizen. He seemed a little

ashamed at seeing me, but passed without saying anything. I should have been as much ashamed at seeing
Miss Read, had not her friends, despairing with reason
of my return after the receipt of my letter, persuaded her
to marry another, one Rogers, a potter, which was done
in my absence. With him, however, she was never happy,
and soon parted from him, refusing to cohabit with
him, or bear his name, it being now said he had another
wife. He was a worthless fellow, though an excellent
workman, which was the temptation to her friends. He
got into debt and ran away in 1727 or '28, went to the
West Indies, and died there. Keimer had got a better
house, a shop well supplied with stationery, plenty of
new types, and a number of hands, tho' none good, and
seemed to have a great deal of business.

Mr. Denham took a store in Water Street, where we
opened our goods. I attended the business diligently,
studied accounts, and grew in a little time expert at selling. We lodged and boarded together; he counselled me
as a father, having a sincere regard for me. I respected
and loved him, and we might have gone on together very
happily; but in the beginning of February, 1727, when I
had just passed my twenty-first year, we both were taken
ill. My distemper was a pleurisy, which very nearly carried me off. I suffered a good deal, gave up the point in
my own mind, and was rather disappointed when I found
myself recovering, regretting in some degree that I must
now sometime or other have all that disagreeable work
to go over again. I forget what Mr. Denham's distemper
was; it held him a long time and at length carried him
off. He left me a small legacy in a nuncupative will, as
a token of his kindness for me, and he left me once more
to the wide world; for the store was taken into the care
of his executors, and my employment under him ended.
My brother-in-law Homes, being now at Philadelphia,
advised my return to my business; and Keimer tempted
me with an offer of large wages by the year to come and
take the management of his printing house, that he might
better attend to his stationer's shop. I had heard a bad
character of him in London, from his wife and her
friends, and was not for having any more to do with him.

I tried for further employment as a merchant's clerk, but not readily meeting with any, I closed again with Keimer.

I found in his house these hands: Hugh Meredith, a Welsh Pennsylvanian, thirty years of age; bred to country work; he was honest, sensible, a man of experience, and fond of reading, but addicted to drinking. Stephen Potts, a young country man of full age, bred to the same, of uncommon natural parts, and great wit and humour, but a little idle. These he had agreed with at extreme low wages per week, to be raised a shilling every three months, as they would deserve by improving in their business, and the expectation of these high wages to come on hereafter was what he had drawn them in with. Meredith was to work at press, Potts at bookbinding, which he by agreement was to teach them, though he knew neither one nor t'other. John ——, a wild Irishman, brought up to no business, whose service for four years Keimer had purchased from the captain of a ship, he too was to be made a pressman. George Webb, an Oxford scholar, whose time for four years he had likewise bought, intending him for a compositor (of whom more presently); and David Harry, a country boy, whom he had taken apprentice.

I soon perceived that the intention of engaging me at wages so much higher than he had been used to give was to have these raw, cheap hands formed thro' me, and as soon as I had instructed them, then, they being all articled to him, he should be able to do without me. I went on, however, very cheerfully, put his printing house in order, which had been in great confusion, and brought his hands by degrees to mind their business and to do it better.

It was an odd thing to find an Oxford scholar in the situation of a bought servant. He was not more than eighteen years of age, and he gave me this account of himself: that he was born in Gloucester, educated at a grammar school there, and had been distinguished among the scholars for some apparent superiority in performing his part when they exhibited plays; belonged to the Witty Club there, and had written some pieces in prose and verse which were printed in the Gloucester newspapers; thence was sent to Oxford; there he continued about a year, but not well satisfied, wishing of all things to see London and become a player. At length receiving his quarterly allowance of fifteen guineas, instead of discharging his debts, he walked out of town, hid his gown in a furze bush, and footed it to London; where having no friend to advise him, he fell into bad company, soon spent his guineas, found no means of being introduced among the players, grew necessitous, pawned his clothes, and wanted bread. Walking the street very hungry and not knowing what to do with himself, a crimp's bill was put into his hand, offering immediate entertainment and encouragement to such as would bind themselves to serve in America. He went directly, signed the indentures, was put into the ship, and came over, never writing a line to acquaint his friends what was become of him. He was lively, witty, good-natured, and a pleasant companion; but idle, thoughtless, and imprudent to the last degree.

John, the Irishman, soon ran away. With the rest I began to live very agreeably; for they all respected me, the more as they found Keimer incapable of instructing them and that from me they learned something daily. We never worked on a Saturday, that being Keimer's Sabbath. So I had two days for reading. My acquaintance with ingenious people in the town increased. Keimer himself treated me with great civility and apparent regard; and nothing now made me uneasy but my debt to Vernon, which I was yet unable to pay, being hitherto but a poor economist. He, however, kindly made no demand of it.

Our printing house often wanted sorts, and there was no letter founder in America. I had seen types cast at James's in London, but without much attention to the manner. However, I now contrived a mould, made use of the letters we had, as puncheons, struck the matrices in lead, and thus supplied in a pretty tolerable way all deficiencies. I also engraved several things on occasion. I made the ink, I was warehouse man, and in short quite a factotum.

But however serviceable I might be, I found that my services became every day of less importance as the other hands improved in the business; and when Keimer paid me a second quarter's wages, he let me know that he felt them too heavy and thought I should make an abatement.

He grew by degrees less civil, put on more the airs of master, frequently found fault, was captious, and seemed ready for an outbreaking. I went on, nevertheless, with a good deal of patience, thinking that his incumbered circumstances were partly the cause. At length a trifle snapped our connection; for a great noise happening near the courthouse, I put my head out of the window to see what was the matter. Keimer being in the street, looked up and saw me, called out to me in a loud voice and angry tone to mind my business, adding some reproachful words that nettled me the more for their publicity, all the neighbours who were looking out on the same occasion being witnesses how I was treated. He came up immediately into the printing house, continued the quarrel; high words passed on both sides, he gave me the quarter's warning we had stipulated, expressing a wish that he had not been obliged to so long a warning. I told him his wish was unnecessary for I would leave him that instant, and so taking my hat, walked out of doors, desiring Meredith, whom I saw below, to take care of some things I left, and bring them to my lodging.

Meredith came accordingly in the evening, when we talked my affair over. He had conceived a great regard for me and was very unwilling that I should leave the house while he remained in it. He dissuaded me from returning to my native country, which I began to think of. He reminded me that Keimer was in debt for all he possessed, that his creditors began to be uneasy, that he kept his shop miserably, sold often without profit for ready money, and often trusted without keeping accounts; that he must therefore fail, which would make a vacancy I might profit of. I objected my want of money. He then let me know that his father had a high opinion of me, and from some discourse that had passed between them, he was sure would advance money to set us up, if I would enter into partnership with him. "My time," says he, "will be out with Keimer in the spring; by that time we may have our press and types in from London. I am sensible I am no workman. If you like it, your skill in the business shall be set against the stock I furnish; and we will share the profits equally." The proposal was agreeable to me, and I consented. His father was in town and approved of it—the more as he saw I had great influence with his son, had prevailed on him to abstain long from dramdrinking, and he hoped might break him of that wretched habit entirely, when we came to be so closely connected. I gave an inventory to the father, who carried it to a merchant; the things were sent for; the secret was to be kept till they should arrive, and in the meantime I was to get work if I could at the other printing house. But I found no vacancy there and so remained idle a few days, when Keimer, on a prospect of being employed to print some paper money in New Jersey which would require cuts and various types that I only could supply, and apprehending Bradford might engage me and get the job from him, sent me a very civil message that old friends should not part for a few words, the effect of sudden passion, and wishing me to return. Meredith persuaded me to comply, as it would give more opportunity for his improvement under my daily instructions. So I returned, and we went on more smoothly than for some time before. The New Jersey job was obtained. I contrived a copper-plate press for it, the first that had been seen in the country. I cut several ornaments and checks for the bills. We went together to Burlington, where I executed the whole to satisfaction; and he received so large a sum for the work as to be enabled thereby to keep his head much longer above water.

At Burlington I made an acquaintance with many principal people of the province. Several of them had been appointed by the Assembly a committee to attend the press and take care that no more bills were printed than the law directed. They were therefore by turns constantly with us, and generally he who attended brought with him a friend or two for company. My mind having been much more improved by reading than Keimer's, I suppose it was for that reason my conversation seemed to be more valued. They had me to their houses, introduced me to their friends, and showed me much civility; while he, tho' the master, was a little neglected. In truth he was an odd fish, ignorant of common life, fond of rudely opposing received opinions, slovenly to extreme dirtiness, enthusiastic in some points of religion, and a little knavish withal.

We continued there near three months, and by that time I could reckon among my acquired friends Judge Allen, Samuel Bustill, the Secretary of the province, Isaac Pearson, Joseph Cooper, and several of the Smiths, members of Assembly, and Isaac Decow, the Surveyor-General. The latter was a shrewd, sagacious, old man, who told me that he began for himself when young by wheeling clay for the brickmakers, learned to write after he was of age, carried the chain for surveyors, who taught him surveying, and he had now by his industry acquired a good estate; and says he, ''I foresee that you will soon work this man out of his business and make a fortune in it at Philadelphia.'' He had not then the least intimation of my intention to set up there or anywhere. These friends were afterwards of great use to me, as I occasionally was to some of them. They all continued their regard for me as long as they lived.

Before I enter upon my public appearance in business, it may be well to let you know the then state of my mind with regard to my principles and morals, that you may see how far those influenced the future events of my life. My parents had early given me religious impressions, and brought me through my childhood piously in the dissenting way. But I was scarce fifteen when, after doubting by turns of several points, as I found them disputed in the different books I read, I began to doubt of revelation itself. Some books against deism fell into my hands; they were said to be the substance of the sermons which had been preached at Boyle's lectures. It happened that they wrought an effect on me quite contrary to what was intended by them, for the arguments of the deists which were quoted to be refuted appeared to me much stronger than the refutations. In short, I soon became a thorough deist. My arguments perverted some others, particularly Collins and Ralph; but each of them having afterwards wronged me greatly without the least compunction, and recollecting Keith's conduct towards me (who was another freethinker) and my own towards Vernon and Miss Read (which at times gave me great trouble), I began to suspect that this doctrine, tho' it might be true, was not very useful. My London pamphlet which had for its motto these lines of Dryden

Whatever is, is right
Tho' purblind man
Sees but a part of the chain, the nearest link,
His eyes not carrying to the equal beam,
That poizes all above.

And which from the attributes of God, his infinite wisdom, goodness, and power, concludes that nothing could possibly be wrong in the world and that vice and virtue were empty distinctions, no such things existing, appeared now not so clever a performance as I once thought it; and I doubted whether some error had not insinuated itself unperceived into my argument so as to infect all that followed, as is common in metaphysical reasonings. I grew convinced that *truth, sincerity* and *integrity* in dealings between man and man were of the utmost importance to the felicity of life, and I formed written resolutions (which still remain in my Journal book) to practise them ever while I lived. Revelation had indeed no weight with me as such; but I entertained an opinion that tho' certain actions might not be bad *because* they were forbidden by it, or good *because* it commanded them, yet probably those actions might be forbidden *because* they were bad for us or commanded *because* they were beneficial to us, in their own natures, all the circumstances of things considered. And this persuasion, with the kind hand of Providence, or some guardian angel, or accidental favourable circumstances and situations, or all together, preserved me (thro' this dangerous time of youth and the hazardous situations I was sometimes in among strangers, remote from the eye and advice of my father) without any *wilful,* gross immorality or injustice that might have been expected from my want of religion. I say *wilful* because the instances I have mentioned had something of necessity in them, from my youth, inexperience, and the knavery of others. I had, therefore, a tolerable character to begin the world with; I valued it properly and determined to preserve it.

We had not been long returned to Philadelphia, before the new types arrived from London. We settled with Keimer and left him by his consent before he heard of it. We found a house to hire near the market and took it. To lessen the rent (which was then but £24 a year, tho' I have since known it let for seventy) we took in Thomas Godfrey, a glazier, and his family, who were to pay a considerable part of it to us, and we to board with them. We had scarce opened our letters and put our press in order before George House, an acquaintance of mine, brought a country man to us whom he had met in the street enquiring for a printer. All our cash was now expended in the variety of particulars we had been obliged to procure, and this country man's five shillings, being our first fruits and coming so seasonably, gave me more pleasure than any crown I have since earned, and from the gratitude I felt towards House, has made me often more ready than perhaps I should otherwise have been to assist young beginners.

There are croakers in every country always boding its ruin. Such a one then lived in Philadelphia, a person of note, an elderly man with a wise look and very grave manner of speaking. His name was Samuel Mickle. This gentleman, a stranger to me, stopped one day at my door and asked me if I was the young man who had lately opened a new printing house. Being answered in the affirmative, he said he was sorry for me because it was an expensive undertaking and the expence would be lost, for Philadelphia was a sinking place, the people already half bankrupts or near being so—all appearances of the contrary, such as new buildings and the rise of rents, being to his certain knowledge fallacious, for they were in fact among the things that would soon ruin us. And he gave me such a detail of misfortunes now existing, or that were soon to exist, that he left me half-melancholy. Had I known him before I engaged in this business, probably I never should have done it. This man continued to live in this decaying place and to declaim in the same strain, refusing for many years to buy a house there because all was going to destruction, and at last I had the pleasure of seeing him give five times as much for one as he might have bought it for when he first began his croaking.

I should have mentioned before that in the autumn of the preceding year I had formed most of my ingenious acquaintance into a club for mutual improvement which we called the Junto. We met on Friday evenings. The

rules I drew up required that every member in his turn
should produce one or more queries on any point of morals, politics, or natural philosophy, to be discussed by
the company, and once in three months produce and read
an essay of his own writing on any subject he pleased.
Our debates were to be under the direction of a president,
and to be conducted in the sincere spirit of enquiry after
truth, without fondness for dispute or desire of victory;
and to prevent warmth, all expressions of positiveness in
opinion or of direct contradiction were after some time
made contraband and prohibited under small pecuniary
penalties.

The first members were, Joseph Breintnal, a copier of
deeds for the scriveners, a good-natured, friendly,
middle-aged man, a great lover of poetry—reading all he
could meet with and writing some that was tolerable—
very ingenious in many little nicknackeries, and of sensible conversation.

Thomas Godfrey, a self-taught mathematician, great in
his way, and afterwards inventor of what is now called
Hadley's Quadrant. But he knew little out of his way and
was not a pleasing companion, as like most great math-
ematicians I have met with, he expected unusual preci-
sion in everything said, or was forever denying or
distinguishing upon trifles to the disturbance of all conversation. He soon left us.

Nicholas Scull, a surveyor, afterwards Surveyor-
General, who loved books, and sometimes made a few
verses.

William Parsons, bred a shoemaker, but loving reading, had acquired a considerable share of mathematics,
which he first studied with a view to astrology that he
afterwards laughed at. He also became Surveyor-General.

William Maugridge, a joiner, but a most exquisite mechanic, and a solid, sensible man.

Hugh Meredith, Stephen Potts, and George Webb I
have characterised before.

Robert Grace, a young gentleman of some fortune,
generous, lively, and witty, a lover of punning and of his
friends.

Lastly, William Coleman, then a merchant's clerk,
about my age, who had the coolest, clearest head, the

best heart, and the exactest morals of almost any man I ever met with. He became afterwards a merchant of great note, and one of our provincial judges. Our friendship continued without interruption to his death, upwards of forty years. And the club continued almost as long and was the best school of philosophy, and politics that then existed in the province; for our queries which were read the week preceding their discussion, put us on reading with attention upon the several subjects that we might speak more to the purpose; and here, too, we acquired better habits of conversation, everything being studied in our rules which might prevent our disgusting each other— from hence the long continuance of the club, which I shall have frequent occasion to speak further of hereafter. But my giving this account of it here is to show something of the interest I had, every one of these exerting themselves in recommending business to us. Breintnal particularly procured us from the Quakers the printing forty sheets of their history, the rest being to be done by Keimer; and upon this we worked exceeding hard, for the price was low. It was a folio, *pro patria* size, in pica with long primer notes. I composed of it a sheet a day, and Meredith worked it off at press. It was often eleven at night, and sometimes later, before I had finished my distribution for the next day's work. For the little jobs sent in by our other friends now and then put us back. But so determined I was to continue doing a sheet a day of the folio, that one night when having imposed my forms I thought my day's work over, one of them by accident was broken and two pages reduced to pie, I immediately distributed and composed it over again before I went to bed. And this industry visible to our neighbours began to give us character and credit—particularly, I was told, that mention being made of the new printing office at the merchants' Every-night Club, the general opinion was that it must fail, there being already two printers in the place, Keimer and Bradford; but Doctor Baird (whom you and I saw many years after at his native place, St. Andrew's in Scotland) gave a contrary opinion: "For the industry of that Franklin," says he, "is superior to anything I ever saw of the kind; I see him still at work when I go home from club, and he is at work again before his neighbours are out of bed.'' This struck the rest, and we soon after had offers from one of them to supply us with stationery; but as yet we did not choose to engage in shop business.

I mention this industry the more particularly and the more freely, tho' it seems to be talking in my own praise, that those of my posterity who shall read it may know the use of that virtue, when they see its effects in my favour throughout this relation.

George Webb, who had found a female friend that lent him wherewith to purchase his time of Keimer, now came to offer himself as a journeyman to us. We could not then imploy him, but I foolishly let him know, as a secret, that I soon intended to begin a newspaper and might then have work for him. My hopes of success, as I told him, were founded on this: that the then only newspaper, printed by Bradford, was a paltry thing, wretchedly managed, no way entertaining, and yet was profitable to him. I therefore thought a good paper could scarcely fail of good encouragement. I requested Webb not to mention it, but he told it to Keimer, who immediately, to be beforehand with me, published proposals for printing one himself, on which Webb was to be employed. I was vexed at this, and to counteract them, not being able to commence our paper, I wrote several amusing pieces for Bradford's paper under the title of the ''Busybody,'' which Breintnal continued some months. By this means the attention of the public was fixed on that paper, and Keimer's proposals, which we burlesqued and ridiculed, were disregarded. He began his paper, however, and after carrying it on three-quarters of a year with at most only ninety subscribers, he offered it to me for a trifle; and I, having been ready some time to go on with it, took it in hand directly, and it proved in a few years extremely profitable to me.

I perceive that I am apt to speak in the singular number, though our partnership still continued; it may be that in fact the whole management of the business lay upon me. Meredith was no compositor, a poor pressman, and seldom sober. My friends lamented my connection with him, but I was to make the best of it.

Our first papers made a quite different appearance from

any before in the province, a better type and better printed; but some spirited remarks of my writing on the dispute then going on between Governor Burnet and the Massachusetts Assembly struck the principal people, occasioned the paper and the manager of it to be much talked of, and in a few weeks brought them all to be our subscribers. Their example was followed by many, and our number went on growing continually. This was one of the first good effects of my having learned a little to scribble. Another was that the leading men, seeing a newspaper now in the hands of one who could also handle a pen, thought it convenient to oblige and encourage me. Bradford still printed the votes and laws and other public business. He had printed an address of the House to the Governor in a coarse blundering manner. We reprinted it elegantly and correctly, and sent one to every member. They were sensible of the difference, it strengthened the hands of our friends in the House, and they voted us their printers for the year ensuing.

Among my friends in the House I must not forget Mr. Hamilton before-mentioned, who was then returned from England and had a seat in it. He interested himself for me strongly in that instance, as he did in many others afterwards, continuing his patronage till his death.

Mr. Vernon, about this time, put me in mind of the debt I owed him, but did not press me. I wrote him an ingenuous letter of acknowledgment, craved his forbearance a little longer, which he allowed me; and as soon as I was able, I paid the principal with interest and many thanks; so that erratum was in some degree corrected.

But now another difficulty came upon me which I had never the least reason to expect. Mr. Meredith's father, who was to have paid for our printing house according to the expectations given me, was able to advance only one hundred pounds currency, which had been paid; and a hundred more was due to the merchant, who grew impatient and sued us all. We gave bail but saw that if the money could not be raised in time, the suit must come to a judgment and execution, and our hopeful prospects must with us be ruined, as the press and letters must be sold for payment, perhaps at half price. In this distress two true friends, whose kindness I have never forgotten nor ever shall forget while I can remember anything, came to me separately, unknown to each other, and without any application from me, offered each of them to advance me all the money that should be necessary to enable me to take the whole business upon myself if that should be practicable; but they did not like my continuing the partnership with Meredith, who, as they said, was often seen drunk in the streets and playing at low games in alehouses, much to our discredit. These two friends were *William Coleman* and *Robert Grace*. I told them I could not propose a separation while any prospect remained of the Merediths fulfilling their part of our agreement, because I thought myself under great obligations to them for what they had done and would do if they could. But if they finally failed in their performance and our partnership must be dissolved, I should then think myself at liberty to accept the assistance of my friends.

Thus the matter rested for some time; when I said to my partner, "Perhaps your father is dissatisfied at the part you have undertaken in this affair of ours and is unwilling to advance for you and me what he would for you alone. If that is the case, tell me, and I will resign the whole to you and go about my business."

"No," says he, "my father has really been disappointed and is really unable; and I am unwilling to distress him further. I see this is a business I am not fit for. I was bred a farmer, and it was a folly in me to come to town and put myself at thirty years of age an apprentice to learn a new trade. Many of our Welsh people are going to settle in North Carolina, where land is cheap. I am inclined to go with them and follow my old employment. You may find friends to assist you. If you will take the debts of the company upon you, return to my father the hundred pounds he has advanced, pay my little personal debts, and give me thirty pounds and a new saddle, I will relinquish the partnership and leave the whole in your hands."

I agreed to this proposal. It was drawn up in writing, signed and sealed immediately. I gave him what he demanded, and he went soon after to Carolina, from whence he sent me next year two long letters containing the best account that had been given of that country, the climate, soil, husbandry, etc., for in those matters he was very judicious. I printed them in the papers, and they gave great satisfaction to the public.

As soon as he was gone, I recurred to my two friends; and because I would not give an unkind preference to either, I took half what each had offered and I wanted of one, and half of the other, paid off the company's debts, and went on with the business in my own name, advertising that the partnership was dissolved. I think this was in or about the year 1729.

About this time there was a cry among the people for more paper money, only £15,000 being extant in the province and that soon to be sunk. The wealthy inhabitants opposed any addition, being against all paper currency, from the apprehension that it would depreciate as it had done in New England to the prejudice of all creditors. We had discussed this point in our Junto, where I was on the side of an addition, being persuaded that the first small sum struck in 1723 had done much good by increasing the trade, employment, and number of inhabitants in the province, since I now saw all the old houses inhabited and many new ones building where, as I remembered well that when I first walked about the streets of Philadelphia eating my roll, I saw most of the houses in Walnut Street between Second and Front Streets with bills on their doors, "To be Let," and many likewise in Chestnut Street and other streets—which made me then think the inhabitants of the city were one after another deserting it.

Our debates possessed me so fully of the subject that I wrote and printed an anonymous pamphlet on it entitled *The Nature and Necessity of a Paper Currency*. It was well received by the common people in general; but the rich men disliked it, for it increased and strengthened the clamour for more money; and they happening to have no writers among them that were able to answer it, their opposition slackened, and the point was carried by a majority in the House. My friends there, who considered I had been of some service, thought fit to reward me by employing me in printing the money—a very profitable job and a great help to me. This was another advantage gained by my being able to write.

The utility of this currency became by time and experience so evident, as never afterwards to be much disputed, so that it grew soon to £55,000 and in 1739 to £80,000 since which it arose during war to upwards of £350,000—trade, building, and inhabitants all the while increasing—though I now think there are limits beyond which the quantity may be hurtful.

I soon afterwards obtained, thro' my friend Hamilton, the printing of the New Castle paper money, another profitable job as I then thought it—small things appearing great to those in small circumstances—and these to me were really great advantages, as they were great encouragements. He procured me also the printing of the laws and votes of that government, which continued in my hands as long as I followed the business.

I now opened a small stationer's shop. I had in it blanks of all sorts the correctest that ever appeared among us. I was assisted in that by my friend Breintnal. I had also paper, parchment, chapmen's books, etc. One Whitemash, a compositor I had known in London, an excellent workman, now came to me and worked with me constantly and diligently; and I took an apprentice, the son of Aquila Rose.

I began now gradually to pay off the debt I was under for the printing house. In order to secure my credit and character as a tradesman, I took care not only to be in *reality* industrious and frugal, but to avoid all *appearances* of the contrary. I dressed plain and was seen at no places of idle diversion. I never went out a fishing or shooting; a book, indeed, sometimes debauched me from my work, but that was seldom, snug, and gave no scandal; and to show that I was not above my business, I sometimes brought home the paper I purchased at the stores, thro' the streets on a wheelbarrow. Thus being esteemed an industrious, thriving, young man, and paying duly for what I bought, the merchants who imported stationery solicited my custom; others proposed supplying me with books, and I went on swimmingly. In the meantime Keimer's credit and business declining daily, he was at last forced to sell his printing house to satisfy his creditors. He went to Barbadoes and there lived some years in very poor circumstances.

His apprentice, David Harry, whom I had instructed while I worked with him, set up his place at Philadelphia, having bought his materials. I was at first apprehensive of a powerful rival in Harry, as his friends were very able and had a good deal of interest. I therefore proposed a partnership to him, which he, fortunately for me, rejected with scorn. He was very proud, dressed like a gentleman, lived expensively, took much diversion and pleasure abroad, ran in debt, and neglected his business—upon which all business left him; and finding nothing to do, he followed Keimer to Barbadoes, taking the printing house with him. There this apprentice employed his former master as a journeyman. They quarrelled often, Harry went continually behind-hand and at length was forced to sell his types and return to his country work in Pennsylvania. The person who bought them employed Keimer to use them, but a few years after he died.

There remained now no other competitor with me at Philadelphia but the old one, Bradford, who was rich and easy, did a little printing now and then by straggling hands, but was not very anxious about the business. However, as he kept the Post Office, it was imagined he had better opportunities of obtaining news, his paper was thought a better distributor of advertisements than mine and therefore had many more—which was a profitable thing to him and a disadvantage to me. For tho' I did indeed receive and send papers by the post, yet the public opinion was otherwise; for what I did send was by bribing the riders, who took them privately—Bradford being unkind enough to forbid it, which occasioned some resentment on my part; and I thought so meanly of him for it that when I afterwards came into his situation, I took care never to imitate it.

I had hitherto continued to board with Godfrey, who lived in part of my house with his wife and children, and had one side of the shop for his glazier's business, tho' he worked little, being always absorbed in his mathematics. Mrs. Godfrey projected a match for me with a relation's daughter, took opportunities of bringing us often together, till a serious courtship on my part ensued, the girl being in herself very deserving. The old folks encouraged me by continued invitations to supper and by leaving us together, till at length it was time to explain. Mrs. Godfrey managed our little treaty. I let her know that I expected as much money with their daughter as would pay off my remaining debt for the printing house, which I believe was not then above a hundred pounds. She brought me word they had no such sum to spare. I said they might mortgage their house in the Loan Office. The answer to this after some days was that they did not approve the match; that on enquiry of Bradford they had been informed the printing business was not a profitable one, the types would soon be worn out and more wanted; that S. Keimer and D. Harry had failed one after the other, and I should probably soon follow them; and therefore I was forbidden the house, and the daughter shut up. Whether this was a real change of sentiment or only artifice, on a supposition of our being too far engaged in affection to retract and therefore that we should steal a marriage, which would leave them at liberty to give or withhold what they pleased, I know not. But I suspected the motive, resented it, and went no more. Mrs. Godfrey brought me afterwards some more favourable accounts of their disposition and would have drawn me on again, but I declared absolutely my resolution to have nothing more to do with that family. This was resented by the Godfreys, we differed, and they removed, leaving me the whole house, and I resolved to take no more inmates. But this affair having turned my thoughts to marriage, I looked around me and made overtures of acquaintance in other places, but soon found that the business of a printer being generally thought a poor one, I was not to expect money with a wife, unless with such a one as I should not otherwise think agreeable. In the meantime that hard-to-be-governed passion of youth had hurried me frequently into intrigues with low women that fell in my way, which were attended with some expense and great inconvenience, besides a continual risk to my health by a distemper, which of all things I dreaded, tho' by great good luck I escaped it.

A friendly correspondence as neighbours and old acquaintances had continued between me and Miss Read's family, who all had a regard for me from the time of my first lodging in their house. I was often invited there and consulted in their affairs, wherein I sometimes was of service. I pitied poor Miss Read's unfortunate situation, who was generally dejected, seldom cheerful, and avoided company. I considered my giddiness and inconstancy when in London as in a great degree the cause of her unhappiness, tho' the mother was good enough to think the fault more her own than mine, as she had prevented our marrying before I went thither and persuaded the match in my absence. Our mutual affection was revived, but there were now great objections to our union. That match was indeed looked upon as invalid, a preceding wife being said to be living in England; but this could not easily be proved because of the distance. And tho' there was a report of his death, it was not certain. Then, tho' it should be true, he had left many debts which his successor might be called upon to pay. We ventured, however, over all these difficulties, and I took her to wife, Sept. 1, 1730. None of the inconveniencies happened that we had apprehended; she proved a good and faithful helpmate, assisted me much by attending the shop; we throve together and ever mutually endeavoured to make each other happy. Thus I corrected that great erratum as well as I could.

About this time our club meeting, not at a tavern, but in a little room of Mr. Grace's set apart for that purpose, a proposition was made by me that since our books were often referred to in our disquisitions upon the queries, it might be convenient to us to have them all together where we met, that upon occasion they might be consulted; and by thus clubbing our books to a common library, we should, while we liked to keep them together, have each of us the advantage of using the books of all the other members, which would be nearly as beneficial as if each owned the whole. It was liked and agreed to, and we filled one end of the room with such books as we could best spare. The number was not so great as we expected; and tho' they had been of great use, yet some inconveniences occurring for want of due care of them, the collection after about a year was separated, and each took his books home again.

And now I set on foot my first project of a public nature, that for a subscription library. I drew up the proposals, got them put into form by our great scrivener, Brockden, and by the help of my friends in the Junto, procured fifty subscribers of forty shillings each to begin with, and ten shillings a year for fifty years—the term our company was to continue. We afterwards obtained a charter, the company being increased to one hundred. This was the mother of all the North American subscription libraries, now so numerous. It is become a great thing itself and continually increasing. These libraries have improved the general conversation of the Americans, made the common tradesmen and farmers as intelligent as most gentlemen from other countries, and perhaps have contributed in some degree to the stand so generally made throughout the Colonies in defence of their privileges.

Memo: Thus far was written with the intention expressed in the beginning and therefore contains several little family anecdotes of no importance to others. What follows was written many years after, in compliance with the advice contained in these letters, and accordingly intended for the public. The affairs of the Revolution occasioned the interruption.

II

[Ten years and more had passed since the writing of the first part of the Autobiography. Franklin had returned to America in 1775, and the following year was sent as one of a commission of three to negotiate a treaty with France. He was living at Passy, near Paris, where toward the close of 1782, or early in 1783, he received the following letter.—*Ed. Note.*]

My dear and honored friend:

I have often been desirous of writing to thee, but could not be reconciled to the thoughts that the letter might fall into the hands of the British, lest some printer or busybody should publish some part of the contents and give our friends pain and myself censure.

Sometime since there fell into my hands to my great joy about twenty-three sheets in thy own hand writing containing an account of the parentage and life of thyself, directed to thy son, ending in the year 1730, with which there were notes likewise in thy writing, a copy of which I enclose in hopes it may be a means, if thou continuedst it up to a later period, that the first and latter part may be put together; and if it is not yet continued, I hope thou wilt not delay it. Life is uncertain, as the preacher tells us, and what will the world say if kind, humane, and benevolent Ben Franklin should leave his friends and the world deprived of so pleasing and profitable a work, a work which would be useful and entertaining not only to a few but to millions?

The influence writings under that class have on the minds of youth is very great and has nowhere appeared so plain as in our public friend's Journal. It almost insensibly leads the youth into the resolution of endeavouring to become as good and as eminent as the journalist. Should thine, for instance, when published—and I think it could not fail of it—lead the youth to equal the industry and temperance of thy early youth, what a blessing with that class would such a work be! I know of no character living, nor many of them put together, who has so much in his power as thyself to promote a greater spirit of industry and early attention to business, frugality, and temperance with the American youth. Not that I think the work would have no other merit and use in the world—far from it—but the first is of such vast importance, and I know nothing that can equal it. . . .

I trust I need make no apology to my good friend for mentioning to him these matters, believing he continues a relish for every exertion of the sort, in confidence of which I rest with great truth and perfect esteem his

Very affectionate friend,
(Signed) Abel James

The foregoing letter and the minutes accompanying it being shown to a friend, I received from him the following:

Paris, January 31, 1783.

My dearest sir:

When I had read over your sheets of minutes of the principal incidents of your life, recovered for you by your Quaker acquaintance, I told you I would send you a letter expressing my reasons why I thought it would be useful to complete and publish it as he desired. Various concerns have for sometime past prevented this letter being written, and I do not know whether it was worth any expectation; happening to be at leisure, however, at present, I shall by writing at least interest and instruct myself; but as the terms I am inclined to use may tend to offend a person of your manners, I shall only tell you how I would address any other person who was as good and as great as yourself but less diffident. I would say to him, sir, I solicit the history of your life from the following motives: Your history is so remarkable that if you do not give it, somebody else will certainly give it; and perhaps so as nearly to do as much harm, as your own management of the thing might do good. It will, moreover, present a table of the internal circumstances of your country which will very much tend to invite to it settlers of virtuous and manly minds. And considering the eagerness with which such information is sought by them, and the extent of your reputation, I do not know of a more efficacious advertisement than your biography would give. All that has happened to you is also connected with the detail of the manners and situation of a rising people; and in this respect I do not think that the writings of Caesar and Tacitus can be more interesting to a true judge of human nature and society. But these, sir, are small reasons, in my opinion, compared with the chance which your life will give for the forming of future great men; and in conjunction with your Art of Virtue (which you deign to publish) of improving the features of private character, and consequently of aiding all happiness, both public and domestic. The two works I allude to, sir, will in particular give a noble rule and example of self-education. School and other education constantly proceed upon false principles and show a clumsy apparatus pointed at a false mark; but your apparatus is simple and the mark a true one; and while parents and young persons are left destitute of other just means of estimating and becoming prepared for a reasonable course in life, your discovery that the thing is in many a man's private power, will be invaluable! Influence upon the private character, late in life, is not only an influence late in life, but a weak influence. It is in youth that we plant our chief habits and prejudices; it is in youth that we take our party as to profession, pursuits, and matrimony. In youth, therefore, the turn is given; in youth the education even of the next generation is given; in youth the private and public character is determined; and the term of life extending but from youth to age, life ought to begin well from youth, and more especially before we take our party as to our principal objects. But your biography will not merely teach self-education, but the education of a wise man; and the wisest man will receive lights and improve his progress, by seeing detailed the conduct of another wise man. And why are weaker men to be deprived of such helps, when we see our race has been blundering on in the dark, almost without a guide in this particular, from the farthest trace of time? Show then, sir, how much is to be done, both to sons and fathers; and invite all wise men to become like yourself, and other men to become wise. When we see how cruel statesmen and warriors can be to the human race, and how absurd distinguished men can be to their acquaintance, it will be instructive to observe the instances multiply of pacific, acquiescing manners; and to find how compatible it is to be great and domestic, enviable and yet good-humored.

The little private incidents which you will also have to relate, will have considerable use, as we want, above all things, rules of prudence in ordinary affairs; and it will be curious to see how you have acted in these. It will be so far a sort of key to life, and explain many things that all men ought to have once explained to them, to give them a chance of becoming wise by foresight. The nearest thing to having experience of one's own, is to have other people's affairs brought before us in a shape that is interesting; this is sure to happen from your pen; our affairs and management will have an air of simplicity or importance that will not fail to strike; and I am convinced you have conducted them with as much originality as if you had been conducting discussions in politics or philosophy; and what more worthy of experiments and system (its importance and its errors considered) than human life?

Some men have been virtuous blindly, others have speculated fantastically, and others have been shrewd to bad purposes; but you, sir, I am sure, will give under your hand, nothing but what is at the same moment, wise, practical, and good. Your account of yourself (for I suppose the parallel I am drawing for Dr. Franklin, will hold not only in point of character but of private history) will show that you are ashamed of no origin—a thing the more important as you prove how little necessary all origin is to happiness, virtue, or greatness. As no end likewise happens without a means, so we shall find, sir, that even you yourself framed a plan by which you became considerable; but at the same time we may see that though the event is flattering, the means are as simple as wisdom could make them; that is, depending upon nature, virtue, thought, and habit. Another thing demonstrated will be the propriety of every man's waiting for his time for appearing upon the stage of the world. Our sensations being very much fixed to the moment, we are apt to forget that more moments are to follow the first, and consequently that man should arrange his conduct so as to suit the whole of a life. Your attribution appears to have been applied to your life, and the passing moments of it have been enlivened with content and enjoyment, instead of being tormented with foolish impatience or regrets. Such a conduct is easy for those who make virtue and themselves in countenance by examples of other truly great men, of whom patience is so often the characteristic. Your Quaker correspondent, sir (for here again I will suppose the subject of my letter resembling Dr. Franklin), praised your frugality, diligence, and temperance, which he considered as a pattern for all youth; but it is singular that he should have forgotten your modesty and your disinterestedness, without which you never could have waited for your advancement or found your situation in the meantime comfortable—which is a strong lesson to show the poverty of glory and the importance of regulating our minds. If this correspondent had known the nature of your reputation as well as I do, he would have said, Your former writings and measures would secure attention to your Biography, and Art of Virtue; and your Biography and Art of Virtue, in return, would secure attention to them. This is an advantage attendant upon a various character, and which brings all that belongs to it into greater play; and it is the more useful, as perhaps more persons are at a loss for the means of improving their minds and characters than they are for the time or the inclination to do it. But there is one concluding reflection, sir, that will shew the use of your life as a mere piece of biography. This style of writing seems a little gone out of vogue, and yet it is a very useful one; and your specimen of it may be particularly serviceable as it will make a subject of comparison with the lives of various public cut throats and intriguers, and with absurd monastic self-tormentors or vain literary triflers. If it encourages more writings of the same kind with your own and induces more men to spend lives fit to be written, it will be worth all Plutarch's *Lives* put together. But being tired of figuring to myself a character of which every feature suits only one man in the world, without giving him the praise of it, I shall end my letter, my dear Dr. Franklin, with a personal application to your proper self. I am earnestly desirous, then, my dear sir, that you should let the world into the traits of your genuine character, as civil broils may otherwise tend to disguise or traduce it. Considering your great age, the caution of your character, and your peculiar style of thinking, it is not likely that any one besides yourself can be sufficiently master of the facts of your life or the intentions of your mind. Besides all this, the immense Revolution of the present period, will necessarily turn our attention towards the author of it, and when virtuous principles have been pretended in it, it will be highly important to shew that such have really influenced; and, as your own character will be the principal one to receive a scrutiny, it is proper (even for its effects upon your vast and rising country, as well as upon England and upon Europe) that it should stand respectable and eternal. For the furtherance of human happiness, I have always maintained that it is necessary to prove that man is not even at present a vicious and detestable animal, and still more to prove that good management may greatly amend him; and it is for much the same reason that I am anxious to see the opinion established that there are fair characters existing among the individuals of the race; for the moment that all men, without exception, shall be conceived abandoned, good people will cease efforts deemed to be hopeless, and perhaps think of taking their share in the scramble of life, or at least of making it comfortable principally for themselves. Take then, my dear sir, this work most speedily into hand: shew yourself good as you are good; temperate as you are temperate; and above all things, prove yourself as one who from your infancy have loved justice, liberty, and concord, in a way that has made it natural and consistent for you to have acted as we have seen you act in the last seventeen years of your life. Let Englishmen be made not only to respect, but even to love you. When they think well of individuals in your native country, they will go nearer to thinking well of your country; and when your countrymen see themselves well thought of by Englishmen, they will go nearer to thinking well of England. Extend your views even further; do not stop at those who speak the English tongue, but after having settled so many points in nature and politics, think of bettering the whole race of men. As I have not read any part of the life in question, but know only the character that lived it, I write somewhat at hazard. I am sure, however, that the life and the treatise I allude to (on the Art of Virtue) will necessarily fulfil the chief of my expectations, and still more so if you take up the measure of suiting these performances to the several views above stated. Should they even prove unsuccessful in all that a sanguine admirer of yours hopes from them, you will at least have framed pieces to interest the human mind; and whoever gives a feeling of pleasure that is innocent to man has added so much to the fair side of a life otherwise too much darkened by anxiety and too much injured by pain. In the hope, therefore, that you will listen to the prayer addressed to you in this letter, I beg to subscribe myself, my dearest sir, etc., etc.,

(Signed) Benj. Vaughan

Continuation of the Account of my Life.
Begun at Passy, 1784

It is some time since I received the above letters, but I have been too busy till now to think of complying with the request they contain. It might, too, be much better done if I were at home among my papers, which would aid my memory, and help to ascertain dates; but my return being uncertain, and having just now a little leisure, I will endeavour to recollect and write what I can. If I live to get home, it may there be corrected and improved.

Not having any copy here of what is already written, I know not whether an account is given of the means I used to establish the Philadelphia public library, which from a small beginning is now become so considerable, though I remember to have come down to near the time of that transaction, 1730. I will therefore begin here with an account of it, which may be struck out if found to have been already given.

At the time I established myself in Pennsylvania, there was not a good bookseller's shop in any of the Colonies to the southward of Boston. In New York and Philadelphia the printers were indeed stationers; they sold only paper, etc., almanacs, ballads, and a few common schoolbooks. Those who loved reading were obliged to send for their books from England. The members of the Junto had each a few. We had left the alehouse where we first met and hired a room to hold our club in. I proposed that we should all of us bring our books to that room, where they would not only be ready to consult in our conferences but become a common benefit, each of us being at liberty to borrow such as he wished to read at home. This was accordingly done and for some time contented us. Finding the advantage of this little collection, I proposed to render the benefit from books more common by commencing a public subscription library. I drew a sketch of the plan and rules that would be necessary, and got a skillful conveyancer, Mr. Charles Brockden, to put the whole in form of articles of agreement to be subscribed, by which each subscriber engaged to pay a certain sum down for the first purchase of books and an annual contribution for encreasing them. So few were the readers at that time in Philadelphia and the majority of us so poor that I was not able with great industry to find more than fifty persons, mostly young tradesmen, willing to pay down for this purpose forty shillings each and ten shillings per annum. With this little fund we began. The books were imported. The library was open one day in the week for lending them to the subscribers, on their promissory notes to pay double the value if not duly returned. The institution soon manifested its utility, was imitated by other towns and in other provinces; the libraries were augmented by donations; reading became fashionable; and our people, having no public amusements to divert their attention from study, became better acquainted with books, and in a few years were observed by strangers to be better instructed and more intelligent than people of the same rank generally are in other countries.

When we were about to sign the above-mentioned articles, which were to be binding on us, our heirs, etc., for fifty years, Mr. Brockden, the scrivener, said to us, "You are young men, but it is scarce probable that any of you will live to see the expiration of the term fixed in this instrument." A number of us, however, are yet living; but the instrument was after a few years rendered null by a charter that incorporated and gave perpetuity to the company.

The objections and reluctances I met with in soliciting the subscriptions made me soon feel the impropriety of presenting one's self as the proposer of any useful project that might be supposed to raise one's reputation in the smallest degree above that of one's neighbours when one has need of their assistance to accomplish that project. I therefore put myself as much as I could out of sight, and stated it as a scheme of a "number of friends" who had requested me to go about and propose it to such as they thought lovers of reading. In this way my affair went on more smoothly, and I ever after practised it on such occasions, and from my frequent successes can heartily recommend it. The present little sacrifice of your vanity will afterwards be amply repaid. If it remains a while uncertain to whom the merit belongs, someone more vain than yourself will be encouraged to claim it, and then even envy will be disposed to do you justice by plucking those assumed feathers and restoring them to their right owner.

This library afforded me the means of improvement by

constant study, for which I set apart an hour or two each day, and thus repaired in some degree the loss of the learned education my father once intended for me. Reading was the only amusement I allowed myself. I spent no time in taverns, games, or frolics of any kind. And my industry in my business continued as indefatigable as it was necessary. I was in debt for my printing house, I had a young family coming on to be educated, and I had two competitors to contend with for business, who were established in the place before me. My circumstances, however, grew daily easier—my original habits of frugality continuing, and my father having among his instructions to me when a boy frequently repeated a proverb of Solomon, "Seest thou a man diligent in his calling, he shall stand before kings, he shall not stand before mean men." I from thence considered industry as a means of obtaining wealth and distinction, which encouraged me, tho' I did not think that I should ever literally stand before kings, which, however, has since happened; for I have stood before five, and even had the honour of sitting down with one, the king of Denmark, to dinner.

We have an English proverb that says;

> He that would thrive
> Must ask his wife.

It was lucky for me that I had one as much disposed to industry and frugality as myself. She assisted me cheerfully in my business, folding and stitching pamphlets, tending shop, purchasing old linen rags for the papermakers, etc. We kept no idle servants, our table was plain and simple, our furniture of the cheapest. For instance, my breakfast was for a long time bread and milk, (no tea), and I ate it out of a twopenny earthen porringer with a pewter spoon. But mark how luxury will enter families and make a progress, in spite of principle. Being called one morning to breakfast, I found it in a china bowl, with a spoon of silver. They had been bought for me without my knowledge by my wife, and had cost her the enormous sum of three-and-twenty shillings, for which she had no other excuse or apology to make but that she thought *her* husband deserved a silver spoon and china bowl as well as any of his neighbours. This was the first appearance of plate and china in our house, which afterwards in a course of years as our wealth encreased, augmented gradually to several hundred pounds in value.

I had been religiously educated as a Presbyterian; and tho' some of the dogmas of the persuasion, such as the eternal decrees of God, election, reprobation, etc., appeared to me unintelligible, others doubtful, and I early absented myself from the public assemblies of the sect, Sunday being my studying-day, I never was without some religious principles. I never doubted, for instance, the existence of the Deity, that he made the world and governed it by his providence, that the most acceptable service of God was the doing good to man, that our souls are immortal, and that all crime will be punished and virtue rewarded either here or hereafter. These I esteemed the essentials of every religion, and being to be found in all the religions we had in our country, I respected them all, tho' with different degrees of respect as I found them more or less mixed with other articles which without any tendency to inspire, promote, or confirm morality, served principally to divide us and make us unfriendly to one another. This respect to all, with an opinion that the worst had some good effects, induced me to avoid all discourse that might tend to lessen the good opinion another might have of his own religion; and as our province increased in people and new places of worship were continually wanted and generally erected by voluntary contribution, my mite for such purpose, whatever might be the sect, was never refused.

Tho' I seldom attended any public worship, I had still an opinion of its propriety and of its utility when rightly conducted, and I regularly paid my annual subscription for the support of the only Presbyterian minister or meeting we had in Philadelphia. He used to visit me sometimes as a friend and admonish me to attend his administrations, and I was now and then prevailed on to do so, once for five Sundays successively. Had he been, *in my opinion,* a good preacher, perhaps I might have continued, notwithstanding the occasion I had for the Sunday's leisure in my course of study; but his discourses were chiefly either polemic arguments or explications of the peculiar doctrines of our sect, and were all to me very dry, uninteresting, and unedifying since not a single moral principle was inculcated or enforced, their aim seeming to be rather to make us Presbyterians than good citizens. At length he took for his text that verse of the fourth chapter of Philippians, "Finally, brethren, whatsoever things are true, honest, just, pure, lovely, or of good report, if there by any virtue, or any praise, think on these things"; and I imagined, in a sermon on such a text, we could not miss of having some morality. But he confined himself to five points only as meant by the apostle; viz., 1. Keeping holy the Sabbath day, 2. Being diligent in reading the Holy Scriptures, 3. Attending duly the public worship, 4. Partaking of the sacrament, 5. Paying a due respect to God's ministers. These might be all good things, but as they were not the kind of good things that I expected from that text, I despaired of ever meeting with them from any other, was disgusted, and attended his preaching no more. I had some years before composed a little liturgy or form of prayer for my own private use; viz., in 1728, entitled *Articles of Belief and Acts of Religion*. I returned to the use of this and went no more to the public assemblies. My conduct might be blamable, but I leave it without attempting further to excuse it, my present purpose being to relate facts and not to make apologies for them.

It was about this time I conceived the bold and arduous project of arriving at moral perfection. I wished to live without committing any fault at any time; I would conquer all that either natural inclination, custom, or company might lead me into. As I knew, or thought I knew, what was right and wrong, I did not see why I might not *always* do the one and avoid the other. But I soon found I had undertaken a task of more difficulty than I had imagined. While my attention was taken up and care employed in guarding against one fault, I was often surprized by another. Habit took the advantage of inattention. Inclination was sometimes too strong for reason. I concluded at length that the mere speculative conviction that it was our interest to be completely virtuous was not sufficient to prevent our slipping, and that the contrary habits must be broken and good ones acquired and established before we can have any dependence on a steady, uniform rectitude of conduct. For this purpose I therefore contrived the following method.

In the various enumerations of the moral virtues I had met with in my reading, I found the catalogue more or less numerous, as different writers included more or fewer ideas under the same name. Temperance, for example, was by some confined to eating and drinking, while by others it was extended to mean the moderating every other pleasure, appetite, inclination, or passion— bodily or mental, even to our avarice and ambition. I proposed to myself, for the sake of clearness, to use rather more names with fewer ideas annexed to each than a few names with more ideas; and I included under thirteen names of virtues all that at that time occurred to me as necessary or desirable, and annexed to each a short precept which fully expressed the extent I gave to its meaning.

These names of virtues with their precepts were

1. Temperance
Eat not to dulness. Drink not to elevation.

2. Silence
Speak not but what may benefit others or yourself. Avoid trifling conversation.

3. Order
Let all your things have their places. Let each part of your business have its time.

4. Resolution
Resolve to perform what you ought. Perform without fail what you resolve.

5. Frugality
Make no expence but to do good to others or yourself; i.e., waste nothing.

6. Industry
Lose no time. Be always employed in something useful. Cut off all unnecessary actions.

7. Sincerity
Use no hurtful deceit. Think innocently and justly; and, if you speak, speak accordingly.

8. Justice

Wrong none by doing injuries or omitting the benefits that are your duty.

9. Moderation

Avoid extremes. Forbear resenting injuries so much as you think they deserve.

10. Cleanliness

Tolerate no uncleanness in body, clothes or habitation.

11. Tranquillity

Be not disturbed at trifles or at accidents common or unavoidable.

12. Chastity

Rarely use venery but for health or offspring—never to dulness, weakness, or the injury of your own or another's peace or reputation.

13. Humility

Imitate Jesus and Socrates.

My intention being to acquire the *habitude* of all these virtues, I judged it would be well not to distract my attention by attempting the whole at once but to fix it on one of them at a time, and when I should be master of that, then to proceed to another, and so on till I should have gone thro' the thirteen. And as the previous acquisition of some might facilitate the acquisition of certain others, I arranged them with that view as they stand above. *Temperance* first, as it tends to procure that coolness and clearness of head which is so necessary where constant vigilance was to be kept up, and guard maintained, against the unremitting attraction of ancient habits, and the force of perpetual temptations. This being acquired and established, *Silence* would be more easy, and my desire being to gain knowledge at the same time that I improved in virtue, and considering that in conversation it was obtained rather by the use of the ear than of the tongue, and therefore wishing to break a habit I was getting into of prattling, punning, and joking, which only made me acceptable to trifling company, I gave *Silence* the second place. This and the next, *Order,* I expected would allow me more time for attending to my project and my studies. *Resolution,* once become habitual, would keep me firm in my endeavours to obtain all the subsequent virtues; *Frugality* and *Industry,* freeing me from my remaining debt and, producing affluence and independence, would make more easy the practice of *Sincerity* and *Justice,* etc., etc. Conceiving then that agreeable to the advice of Pythagoras in his golden verses, daily examination would be necessary, I contrived the following method for conducting that examination.

I made a little book in which I allotted a page for each of the virtues. I ruled each page with red ink so as to have seven columns, one for each day of the week, marking each column with a letter for the day. I crossed these columns with thirteen red lines, marking the beginning of each line with the first letter of one of the virtues, on which line and in its proper column I might mark by a little black spot every fault I found upon examination to have been committed respecting that virtue upon that day.

I determined to give a week's strict attention to each of the virtues successively. Thus in the first week my great guard was to avoid even the least offence against temperance, leaving the other virtues to their ordinary chance, only marking every evening the faults of the day. Thus if in the first week I could keep my first line marked "T." clear of spots, I supposed the habit of that virtue so much strengthened and its opposite weakened that I might venture extending my attention to include the next, and for the following week keep both lines clear of spots. Proceeding thus to the last, I could go thro' a course complete in thirteen weeks, and four courses in a year. And like him who, having a garden to weed, does not attempt to eradicate all the bad herbs at once, which would exceed his reach and his strength, but works on one of the beds at a time, and having accomplished the first, proceeds to a second; so I should have (I hoped) the encouraging pleasure of seeing on my pages the progress I made in virtue by clearing successively my lines of their spots, till in the end by a number of courses, I should be happy in viewing a clean book after a thirteen weeks' daily examination.

Thus my little book had for its motto these lines from Addison's *Cato;*

Here will I hold: if there is a power above us,
(And that there is, all Nature cries aloud
Thro' all her works) he must delight in virtue,
And that which he delights in must be happy.

FORM OF THE PAGES

	TEMPERANCE						
	Eat not to dulness.						
	Drink not to elevation.						
	S	M	T	W	T	F	S
T							
S	√√	√		√		√	
O	√	√	√		√	√	√
R			√			√	
F		√			√		
I			√				
S							
J							
M							
Cl.							
T							
Ch.							
H							

Another from Cicero,

> *O vitae philosophia dux! O virtutum indagatrix,*
> *expultrixque vitiorum! Unus dies bene et ex preceptis*
> *tuis actus, peccanti immortalitati est anteponendus.*

Another from the proverbs of Solomon speaking of wisdom or virtue;

> Length of days is in her right hand, and in her left hand riches and honours; her ways are ways of pleasantness, and all her paths are peace (III, 16, 17).

And conceiving God to be the fountain of wisdom, I thought it right and necessary to solicit his assistance for obtaining it; to this end I formed the following little prayer, which was prefixed to my tables of examination, for daily use.

> O powerful Goodness, bountiful Father, merciful Guide! Increase in me that wisdom which discovers my truest interests; strengthen my resolutions to perform what that wisdom dictates. Accept my kind offices to thy other children, as the only return in my power for thy continual favours to me.

I used also sometimes a little prayer which I took from Thomson's *Poems;* viz.,

> Father of light and life, thou Good supreme,
> Oh, teach me what is good, teach me thy self!
> Save me from folly, vanity and vice,
> From every low pursuit, and fill my soul
> With knowledge, conscious peace, and virtue pure,
> Sacred, substantial, never-fading bliss!

The precept of *Order* requiring that *every part of my business should have its allotted time,* one page in my little book contained the following scheme of employment for the twenty-four hours of a natural day.

The morning question, What good shall I do this day?	5	Rise, wash, and address *Powerful Goodness;* contrive day's business and take the resolution of the day; prosecute the present study; and breakfast.
	6	
	7	
	8	
	9	Work.
	10	
	11	
	12	Read or overlook my accounts, and dine.
	1	
	2	Work.
	3	
	4	
	5	
	6	Put things in their places, supper, music, or diversion, or conversation; examination of the day.
	7	
	8	
	9	
Evening question, What good have I done today?	10	
	11	
	12	
	1	Sleep.
	2	
	3	
	4	

I entered upon the execution of this plan for self-examination and continued it with occasional intermissions for some time. I was surprized to find myself so much fuller of faults than I had imagined, but I had the satisfaction of seeing them diminish. To avoid the trouble of renewing now and then my little book, which by scraping out the marks on the paper of old faults to make room for new ones in a new course became full of holes, I transferred my tables and precepts to the ivory leaves of a memorandum book on which the lines were drawn with red ink that made a durable stain, and on those lines I marked my faults with a black lead pencil, which marks I could easily wipe out with a wet sponge. After a while I went thro' one course only in a year, and afterwards only one in several years, till at length I omitted them entirely, being employed in voyages and business abroad with a multiplicity of affairs that interfered; but I always carried my little book with me. My scheme of *Order* gave me the most trouble, and I found that tho' it might be practicable where a man's business was such as to leave him the disposition of his time, that of a journeyman printer for instance, it was not possible to be exactly observed by a master, who must mix with the world and often receive people of business at their own hours. Order, too, with regard to places for things, papers, etc., I found extremely difficult to acquire. I had not been early accustomed to *method*, and having an exceeding good memory, I was not so sensible of the inconvenience attending want of method. This article therefore cost me so much painful attention, and my faults in it vexed me so much, and I made so little progress in amendment and had such frequent relapses, that I was almost ready to give up the attempt and content myself with a faulty character in that respect. Like the man who in buying an ax of a smith my neighbour, desired to have the whole of its surface as bright as the edge; the smith consented to grind it bright for him if he would turn the wheel. He turned while the smith pressed the broad face of the ax hard and heavily on the stone, which made the turning of it very fatiguing. The man came every now and then from the wheel to see how the work went on; and at length would take his ax as it was, without further grinding. "No," says the smith, "turn on, turn on; we shall have it bright by and by; as yet 'tis only speckled." "Yes," says the man, *"but I think I like a speckled ax best."* And I believe this may have been the case with many who having, for want of some such means as I employed, found the difficulty of obtaining good and breaking bad habits in other points of vice and virtue, have given up the struggle and concluded that "a speckled ax was best." For something that pretended to be reason was every now and then suggesting to me that such extreme nicety as I exacted of myself might be a kind of foppery in morals, which if it were known would make me ridiculous; that a perfect character might be attended with the inconvenience of being envied and hated; and that a benevolent man should allow a few faults in himself, to keep his friends in countenance. In truth, I found myself incorrigible with respect to *Order;* and now I am old and my memory bad, I feel very sensibly the want of it. But on the whole, tho' I never arrived at the perfection I had been so ambitious of obtaining but fell far short of it, yet I was by the endeavour a better and a happier man than I otherwise should have been if I had not attempted it; as those who aim at perfect writing by imitating the engraved copies, tho' they never reach the wished-for excellence of those copies, their hand is mended by the endeavour and is tolerable while it continues fair and legible.

It may be well my posterity should be informed that to this little artifice, with the blessing of God, their ancestor owed the constant felicity of his life down to his seventy-ninth year, in which this is written. What reverses may attend the remainder is in the hand of providence; but if they arrive, the reflection on past happiness enjoyed ought to help his bearing them with more resignation. To *Temperance* he ascribes his long-continued health and what is still left to him of a good constitution; to *Industry* and *Frugality,* the early easiness of his circumstances and acquisition of his fortune with all that knowledge which enabled him to be an useful citizen and obtained for him some degree of reputation among the learned. To *Sincerity* and *Justice,* the confidence of his country and the honourable employs it conferred upon him; and to the joint influence of the whole mass of the virtues, even in the imperfect state he was able to acquire them, all that evenness of temper and that cheerfulness in conversation which makes his company still sought for and agreeable even to his younger acquaintance. I hope, therefore, that some of my descendants may follow the example and reap the benefit.

It will be remarked that, tho' my scheme was not wholly without religion, there was in it no mark of any of the distinguishing tenets of any particular sect. I had purposely avoided them; for being fully persuaded of the utility and excellency of my method, and that it might be serviceable to people in all religions, and intending sometime or other to publish it, I would not have anything in it that should prejudice anyone of any sect against it. I purposed writing a little comment on each virtue, in which I would have shown the advantages of possessing it and the mischiefs attending its opposite vice; I should have called my book *The Art of Virtue* because it would have shown the means and manner of obtaining virtue, which would have distinguished it from the mere exhortation to be good, that does not instruct and indicate the means, but is like the apostle's man of verbal charity, who only, without showing to the naked and hungry how or where they might get clothes or victuals, exhorted them to be fed and clothed (*James* II: 15, 16).

But it so happened that my intention of writing and publishing this comment was never fulfilled. I did, indeed, from time to time put down short hints of the sentiments, reasonings, etc., to be made use of in it, some of which I have still by me; but the necessary close attention to private business in the earlier part of life and public business since, have occasioned my postponing it. For it being connected in my mind with *a great and extensive project* that required the whole man to execute, and which an unforeseen succession of employs prevented my attending to, it has hitherto remained unfinished.

In this piece it was my design to explain and enforce this doctrine: That vicious actions are not hurtful because they are forbidden, but forbidden because they are hurtful, the nature of man alone considered; that it was therefore everyone's interest to be virtuous who wished to be happy even in this world. And I should from this circumstance, there being always in the world a number of rich merchants, nobility, states, and princes who have need of honest instruments for the management of their affairs, and such being so rare have endeavoured to convince young persons, that no qualities are so likely to make a poor man's fortune as those of probity and integrity.

My list of virtues contained at first but twelve. But a Quaker friend having kindly informed me that I was generally thought proud, that my pride showed itself frequently in conversation, that I was not content with being in the right when discussing any point, but was overbearing and rather insolent—of which he convinced me by mentioning several instances—I determined endeavouring to cure myself if I could of this vice or folly among the rest, and I added *Humility* to my list, giving an extensive meaning to the word. I cannot boast of much success in acquiring the *reality* of this virtue, but I had a good deal with regard to the *appearance* of it. I made it a rule to forbear all direct contradiction to the sentiments of others and all positive assertion of my own. I even forbade myself agreeable to the old laws of our Junto, the use of every word or expression in the language that imported a fixed opinion, such as "certainly," "undoubtedly," etc.; and I adopted instead of them, "I conceive," "I apprehend," or "I imagine" a thing to be so or so, or "It so appears to me at present." When another asserted something that I thought an error, I denied myself the pleasure of contradicting him abruptly and of showing immediately some absurdity in his proposition; and in answering I began by observing that in certain cases or circumstances his opinion would be right, but that in the present case there "appeared" or "seemed to me" some difference, etc. I soon found the advantage of this change in my manners: The conversations I engaged in went on more pleasantly; the modest way in which I proposed my opinions procured them a readier reception and less contradiction; I had less mortification when I was found to be in the wrong, and I more easily prevailed with others to give up their mistakes and join with me when I happened to be in the right. And this mode, which I at first put on with some violence to natural inclination, became at length so easy and so habitual to me that perhaps for these fifty years past no one has ever heard a dogmatical expression escape me. And to this habit (after my character of integrity) I think it principally owing that I had early so much weight with my fellow citizens when I proposed new institutions or alterations in the old, and so much influence in public councils when I became a member. For I was but a bad speaker, never eloquent, subject to much hesitation in my choice of words, hardly correct in language, and yet I generally carried my point.

In reality there is perhaps no one of our natural passions so hard to subdue as *pride;* disguise it, struggle with it, beat it down, stifle it, mortify it as much as one pleases, it is still alive and will every now and then peep out and show itself. You will see it perhaps often in this history. For even if I could conceive that I had completely overcome it, I should probably be proud of my humility.

[Thus far written at Passy, 1784][5]

I am now about to write at home (Philadelphia), August 1788, but cannot have the help expected from my papers, many of them being lost in the war. I have, however, found the following.

Having mentioned *a great and extensive project* which I had conceived, it seems proper that some account should be here given of that project and its object. Its first rise in my mind appears in the following little paper, accidentally preserved, viz.,

Observations on my Reading History in Library,

May 9, 1731.

''That the great affairs of the world, the wars, revolutions, etc., are carried on and effected by parties.

[5]Square brackets are Franklin's.

"That the view of these parties is their present general interest, or what they take to be such.

"That the different views of these different parties occasion all confusion.

"That while a party is carrying on a general design, each man has his particular private interest in view.

"That as soon as a party has gained its general point, each member becomes intent upon his particular interest, which thwarting others, breaks that party into divisions and occasions more confusion.

"That few in public affairs act from a mere view of the good of their country, whatever they may pretend; and tho' their actings bring real good to their country, yet men primarily considered that their own and their country's interest was united and did not act from a principle of benevolence.

"That fewer still in public affairs act with a view to the good of mankind.

"There seems to me at present to be great occasion for raising a united party for virtue, by forming the virtuous and good men of all nations into a regular body, to be governed by suitable good and wise rules, which good and wise men may probably be more unanimous in their obedience to than common people are to common laws.

"I at present think that whoever attempts this aright and is well qualified, cannot fail of pleasing God and of meeting with success.   B.F."

Revolving this project in my mind, as to be undertaken hereafter when my circumstances should afford me the necessary leisure, I put down from time to time on pieces of paper such thoughts as occurred to me respecting it. Most of these are lost, but I find one purporting to be the substance of an intended creed, containing, as I thought, the essentials of every known religion and being free of everything that might shock the professors of any religion. It is expressed in these words, viz.,

"That there is one God who made all things.

"That he governs the world by his providence.

"That he ought to be worshipped by adoration, prayer, and thanksgiving.

"But that the most acceptable service to God is doing good to man.

"That the soul is immortal.

"And that God will certainly reward virtue and punish vice, either here or hereafter."

My ideas at that time were that the sect should be begun and spread at first among young and single men only; that each person to be initiated should not only declare his assent to such creed but should have exercised himself with the thirteen weeks' examination and practice of the virtues, as in the before-mentioned model; that the existence of such a society should be kept a secret till it was become considerable, to prevent solicitations for the admission of improper persons; but that the members should each of them search among his acquaintance for ingenuous, well-disposed youths to whom, with prudent caution, the scheme should be gradually communicated; that the members should engage to afford their advice, assistance, and support to each other in promoting one another's interest, business, and advancement in life; that for distinction we should be called the Society of the Free and Easy: free, as being by the general practice and habit of the virtues; free from the dominion of vice, and particularly by the practice of industry and frugality; free from debt, which exposes a man to confinement and a species of slavery to his creditors. This is as much as I can now recollect of the project, except that I communicated it in part to two young men who adopted it with some enthusiasm. But my then narrow circumstances and the necessity I was under of sticking close to my business occasioned my postponing the further prosecution of it at that time, and my multifarious occupations public and private induced me to continue postponing, so that it has been omitted till I have no longer strength or activity left sufficient for such an enterprize, tho' I am still of opinion that it was a practicable scheme and might have been very useful by forming a great number of good citizens. And I was not discouraged by the seeming magnitude of the undertaking, as I have always thought that one man of tolerable abilities may work great changes and accomplish great affairs among mankind if he first forms a good plan, and, cutting off all amusements or other employments that would divert his attention, makes the execution of that same plan his sole study and business.

In 1732 I first published my *Almanac,* under the name of Richard Saunders; it was continued by me about twenty-five years, commonly called *Poor Richard's Almanac.* I endeavoured to make it both entertaining and useful, and it accordingly came to be in such demand that I reaped considerable profit from it, vending annually near ten thousand. And observing that it was generally read, scarce any neighbourhood in the province being without it, I considered it as a proper vehicle for conveying instruction among the common people, who bought scarce any other books. I therefore filled all the little spaces that occurred between the remarkable days in the calendar with proverbial sentences, chiefly such as inculcated industry and frugality as the means of procuring wealth and thereby securing virtue—it being more difficult for a man in want to act always honestly, as (to use here one of those proverbs) "it is hard for an empty sack to stand upright." These proverbs, which contained the wisdom of many ages and nations, I assembled and formed into a connected discourse prefixed to the *Almanac* of 1757, as the harangue of a wise old man to the people attending an auction. The bringing all these scattered counsels thus into a focus enabled them to make greater impression. The piece, being universally approved, was copied in all the newspapers of the Continent, reprinted in Britain on a broadside to be stuck up in houses, two translations were made of it in French, and great numbers bought by the clergy and gentry to distribute gratis among their poor parishioners and tenants. In Pennsylvania, as it discouraged useless expence in foreign superfluities, some thought it had its share of influence in producing that growing plenty of money which was observable for several years after its publication.

I considered my newspaper also as another means of communicating instruction, and in that view frequently reprinted in it extracts from the *Spectator* and other moral writers, and sometimes published little pieces of my own which had been first composed for reading in our Junto. Of these are a Socratic dialogue tending to prove that whatever might be his parts and abilities, a vicious man could not properly be called a man of sense; and a discourse on self-denial showing that virtue was not secure till its practice became a habitude and was free from the opposition of contrary inclinations. These may be found in the papers about the beginning of 1735. In the conduct of my newspaper I carefully excluded all libelling and personal abuse, which is of late years become so disgraceful to our country. Whenever I was solicited to insert anything of that kind and the writers pleaded, as they generally did, the liberty of the press and that a newspaper was like a stagecoach in which any one who would pay had a right to a place, my answer was that I would print the piece separately if desired, and the author might have as many copies as he pleased to distribute himself, but that I would not take upon me to spread his detraction, and that having contracted with my subscribers to furnish them with what might be either useful or entertaining. I could not fill their papers with private altercation in which they had no concern without doing them manifest injustice. Now many of our printers make no scruple of gratifying the malice of individuals by false accusations of the fairest characters among ourselves, augmenting animosity even to the producing of duels, and are moreover so indiscreet as to print scurrilous reflections on the government of neighbouring states and even on the conduct of our best national allies, which may be attended with the most pernicious consequences. These things I mention as a caution to young printers, that they may be encouraged not to pollute their presses and disgrace their profession by such infamous practices but refuse steadily, as they may see by my example that such a course of conduct will not on the whole be injurious to their interests.

In 1733, I sent one of my journeymen to Charlestown, South Carolina, where a printer was wanting. I furnished him with a press and letters on an agreement of partnership, by which I was to receive one-third of the profits of the business, paying one-third of the expence. He was a man of learning and honest, but ignorant in matters of account; and tho' he sometimes made me remittances, I could get no account from him nor any satisfactory state of our partnership while he lived. On his decease, the business was continued by his widow, who being born and bred in Holland, where, as I have been informed, the knowledge of accompts makes a part of female education, she not only sent me as clear a state as she could find of the transactions past, but continued to account with the greatest regularity and exactitude every quarter afterwards, and managed the business with such success that she not only brought up reputably a family of children but at the expiration of the term was able to purchase of me the printing house and establish her son in it. I mention this affair chiefly for the sake of recommending that branch of education for our young females as likely to be of more use to them and their children in case of widowhood than either music or dancing, by preserving them from losses by imposition of crafty men, and enabling them to continue perhaps a profitable mercantile house with established correspondence till a son is grown up fit to undertake and go on with it, to the lasting advantage and enriching of the family.

About the year 1734 there arrived among us from Ireland a young Presbyterian preacher named Hemphill, who delivered with a good voice, and apparently extempore, most excellent discourses, which drew together considerable numbers of different persuasions, who joined in admiring them. Among the rest I became one of his constant hearers, his sermons pleasing me as they had little of the dogmatical kind but inculcated strongly the practice of virtue, or what in the religious style are called "good works." Those, however, of our congregation who considered themselves as orthodox Presbyterians disapproved his doctrine and were joined by most of the old clergy, who arraigned him of heterodoxy before the synod in order to have him silenced. I became his zealous partisan and contributed all I could to raise a party in his favour, and we combated for him awhile with some hopes of success. There was much scribbling pro and con upon the occasion; and finding that tho' an elegant preacher he was but a poor writer, I lent him my pen and wrote for him two or three pamphlets, and one piece in the *Gazette* of April 1735. Those pamphlets, as is generally the case with controversial writings, tho' eagerly read at the time, were soon out of vogue, and I question whether a single copy of them now exists.

During the contest an unlucky occurrence hurt his cause exceedingly. One of our adversaries, having heard him preach a sermon that was much admired, thought he had somewhere read that sermon before, or at least a part of it. On search he found that part quoted at length in one of the British reviews, from a discourse of Dr. Foster's. This detection gave many of our party disgust, who accordingly abandoned his cause and occasioned our more speedy discomfiture in the synod. I stuck by him, however, as I rather approved his giving us good sermons composed by others than bad ones of his own manufacture, tho' the latter was the practice of our common teachers. He afterwards acknowledged to me that none of those he preached were his own; adding that his memory was such as enabled him to retain and repeat any sermon after one reading only. On our defeat he left us in search elsewhere of better fortune, and I quitted the congregation, never joining it after, tho' I continued many years my subscription for the support of its ministers.

I had begun in 1733 to study languages. I soon made myself so much a master of the French as to be able to read the books with ease. I then undertook the Italian. An acquaintance who was also learning it used often to tempt me to play chess with him. Finding this took up too much of the time I had to spare for study, I at length refused to play any more unless on this condition—that the victor in every game should have a right to impose a task, either in parts of the grammar to be got by heart, or in translation, etc., which tasks the vanquished was to perform upon honour before our next meeting. As we played pretty equally, we thus beat one another into that language. I afterwards with a little painstaking acquired as much of the Spanish as to read their books also. I have already mentioned that I had only one year's instruction in a Latin school, and that when very young, after which I neglected that language entirely. But when I had attained an acquaintance with the French, Italian, and Spanish, I was surprized to find, on looking over a Latin Testament, that I understood so much more of that language than I had imagined—which encouraged me to apply myself again to the study of it; and I met with the more success, as those preceding languages had greatly smoothed my way. From these circumstances I have thought that there is some inconsistency in our common mode of teaching languages. We are told that it is proper to begin first with the Latin, and having acquired that, it will be more easy to attain those modern languages which are derived from it; and yet we do not begin with the Greek in order more easily to acquire the Latin. It is true that if you can clamber and get to the top of a staircase without using the steps, you will more easily gain them in descending; but certainly if you begin with the lowest, you will with more ease ascend to the top. And I would therefore offer it to the consideration of those who superintend the educating of our youth, whether, since many of those who begin with the Latin quit the same after spending some years without having made any great proficiency, and what they have learned becomes almost useless so that their time has been lost, it would not have been better to have begun them with the French, proceeding to the Italian, etc., for tho' after spending the same time they should quit the study of languages and never arrive at the Latin, they would, however, have acquired another tongue or two that being in modern use might be serviceable to them in common life.

After ten years' absence from Boston and having become more easy in my circumstances, I made a journey thither to visit my relations, which I could not sooner well afford. In returning I called at Newport to see my brother then settled there with his printing house. Our former differences were forgotten, and our meeting was very cordial and affectionate. He was fast declining in his health and requested of me that in case of his death, which he apprehended not far distant, I would take home his son, then but ten years of age, and bring him up to the printing business. This I accordingly performed, sending him a few years to school before I took him into the office. His mother carried on the business till he was grown up, when I assisted him with an assortment of new types, those of his father being in a manner worn out.

Thus it was that I made my brother ample amends for the service I had deprived him of by leaving him so early.

In 1736, I lost one of my sons, a fine boy of four years old, by the smallpox taken in the common way. I long regretted bitterly, and still regret, that I had not given it to him by inoculation. This I mention for the sake of parents who omit that operation on the supposition that they should never forgive themselves if a child died under it—my example showing that the regret may be the same either way, and that therefore the safer should be chosen.

Our club, the Junto, was found so useful and afforded such satisfaction to the members that several were desirous of introducing their friends, which could not well be done without exceeding what we had settled as a convenient number, viz., twelve. We had from the beginning made it a rule to keep our institution a secret, which was pretty well observed. The intention was to avoid applications of improper persons for admittance, some of whom perhaps we might find it difficult to refuse. I was one of those who were against any addition to our number, but instead of it made in writing a proposal that every member separately should endeavour to form a subordinate club with the same rules respecting queries, etc., and without informing them of the connection with the Junto. The advantages proposed were the improvement of so many more young citizens by the use of our institutions; our better acquaintance with the general sentiments of the inhabitants on any occasion, as the Junto member might propose what queries we should desire and was to report to the Junto what passed in his separate club; the promotion of our particular interests in business by more extensive recommendations; and the increase of our influence in public affairs and our power of doing good by spreading thro' the several clubs the sentiments of the Junto. The project was approved, and every member undertook to form his club, but they did not all succeed. Five or six only were completed, which were called by different names, as the Vine, the Union, the Band, etc. They were useful to themselves, and afforded us a good deal of amusement, information, and instruction, besides answering in some considerable degree our views of influencing the public opinion on particular occasions, of which I shall give some instances in course of time as they happened.

My first promotion was my being chosen in 1736 clerk of the General Assembly. The choice was made that year without opposition; but the year following when I was again proposed (the choice, like that of the members, being annual), a new member made a long speech against me in order to favour some other candidate. I was, however, chosen, which was the more agreeable to me, as besides the pay for immediate service as clerk, the place gave me a better opportunity of keeping up an interest among the members, which secured to me the business of printing the votes, laws, paper money, and other occasional jobs for the public, that, on the whole, were very profitable. I therefore did not like the opposition of this new member, who was a gentleman of fortune and education with talents that were likely to give him in time great influence in the House, which, indeed, afterwards happened. I did not, however, aim at gaining his favour by paying any servile respect to him, but after some time took this other method. Having heard that he had in his library a certain very scarce and curious book, I wrote a note to him expressing my desire of perusing that book and requesting he would do me the favour of lending it to me for a few days. He sent it immediately; and I returned it in about a week with another note expressing strongly my sense of the favour. When we next met in the House, he spoke to me (which he had never done before), and with great civility. And he ever afterwards manifested a readiness to serve me on all occasions, so that we became great friends, and our friendship continued to his death. This is another instance of the truth of an old maxim I had learned, which says, "He that has once done you a kindness will be more ready to do you another than he whom you yourself have obliged." And it shows how much more profitable it is prudently to remove, than to resent, return, and continue inimical proceedings.

In 1737, Col. Spotswood, late Governor of Virginia, and then Postmaster-General, being dissatisfied with the conduct of his deputy at Philadelphia respecting some negligence in rendering and want of exactness in framing his accounts, took from him the commission and offered it to me. I accepted it readily and found it of great advantage; for tho' the salary was small, it facilitated the correspondence that improved my newspaper, increased the number demanded as well as the advertisements to be inserted, so that it came to afford me a considerable income. My old competitor's newspaper declined proportionably, and I was satisfied without retaliating his refusal, while Postmaster, to permit my papers being carried by the riders. Thus he suffered greatly from his neglect in due accounting; and I mention it as a lesson to those young men who may be employed in managing affairs for others that they should always render accounts with great clearness and punctuality. The character of observing such a conduct is the most powerful of all recommendations to new employments and increase of business.

I began now to turn my thoughts a little to public affairs, beginning, however, with small matters. The city watch was one of the first things that I conceived to want regulation. It was managed by the constables of the respective wards in turn; the constable warned a number of housekeepers to attend him for the night. Those who chose never to attend paid him six shillings a year to be excused, which was supposed to be for hiring substitutes, but was in reality much more than was necessary for that purpose and made the constableship a place of profit; and the constable for a little drink often got such ragamuffins about him as a watch that respectable housekeepers did not choose to mix with. Walking the rounds, too, was often neglected, and most of the nights spent in tippling. I thereupon wrote a paper to be read in Junto representing these irregularities but insisting more particularly on the inequality of this six-shilling tax of the constables, respecting the circumstances of those who paid it, since a poor widow housekeeper, all whose property to be guarded by the watch did not, perhaps, exceed the value of fifty pounds, paid as much as the wealthiest merchant who had thousands of pounds'-worth of goods in his stores. On the whole, I proposed as a more effectual watch the hiring of proper men to serve constantly in that business; and as a more equitable way of supporting the charge, the levying a tax that should be proportioned to the property. This idea, being approved by the Junto, was communicated to the other clubs, but as arising in each of them. And tho' the plan was not immediately carried into execution, yet by preparing the minds of people for the change, it paved the way for the law obtained a few years after, when the members of our clubs were grown into more influence.

About this time I wrote a paper (first to be read in Junto, but it was afterwards published) on the different accidents and carelessness by which houses were set on fire, with cautions against them and means proposed of avoiding them. This was much spoken of as a useful piece, and gave rise to a project which soon followed it of forming a company for the more ready extinguishing of fires, and mutual assistance in removing and securing of goods when in danger. Associates in this scheme were presently found amounting to thirty. Our articles of agreement obliged every member to keep always in good order and fit for use a certain number of leather buckets with strong bags and baskets (for packing and transporting of goods) which were to be brought to every fire; and we agreed to meet once a month and spend a social evening together in discoursing and communicating such ideas as occurred to us upon the subject of fires as might be useful in our conduct on such occasions. The utility of this institution soon appeared, and many more desiring to be admitted than we thought convenient for one company, they were advised to form another, which was accordingly done. And this went on, one new company being formed after another till they became so numerous as to include most of the inhabitants who were men of property; and now at the time of my writing this, tho' upwards of fifty years since its establishment, that which I first formed, called the Union Fire Company, still subsists and flourishes, tho' the first members are all deceased but myself and one, who is older by a year than I am. The small fines that have been paid by members for absence at the monthly meetings have been applied to the purchase of fire engines, ladders, firehooks, and other useful implements for each company, so that I question whether there is a city in the world better provided with the means of putting a stop to beginning conflagrations; and in fact since those institutions, the city has never lost by fire more than one or two houses at a time, and the flames have often been extinguished before the house in which they began has been half consumed.

In 1739 arrived among us from England the Rev. Mr. Whitfield, who had made himself remarkable there as an itinerant preacher. He was at first permitted to preach in some of our churches; but the clergy, taking a dislike to him, soon refused him their pulpits, and he was obliged to preach in the fields. The multitudes of all sects and denominations that attended his sermons were enormous, and it was matter of speculation to me, who was one of the number, to observe the extraordinary influence of his oratory on his hearers and how much they admired and respected him, notwithstanding his common abuse of them, by assuring them they were naturally "half beasts and half devils." It was wonderful to see the change soon made in the manners of our inhabitants; from being thoughtless or indifferent about religion, it seemed as if all the world were growing religious, so that one could not walk thro' the town in an evening without hearing psalms sung in different families of every street. And it being found inconvenient to assemble in the open air subject to its inclemencies, the building of a house to meet in was no sooner proposed and persons appointed to receive contributions, but sufficient sums were soon received to procure the ground and erect the building which was one hundred feet long and seventy broad, about the size of Westminster Hall; and the work was carried on with such spirit as to be finished in a much shorter time than could have been expected. Both house and ground were vested in trustees expressly for the use of any preacher of any religious persuasion who might desire to say something to the people of Philadelphia, the design in building not being to accommodate any particular sect but the inhabitants in general, so that even if the Mufti of Constantinople were to send a missionary to preach Mahometanism to us, he would find a pulpit at his service.

Mr. Whitfield, in leaving us, went preaching all the way thro' the Colonies to Georgia. The settlement of that province had lately been begun; but instead of being made with hardy, industrious husbandmen accustomed to labour, the only people fit for such an enterprise, it was with families of broken shopkeepers and other insolvent debtors, many of indolent and idle habits, taken out of the gaols—who, being set down in the woods, unqualified for clearing land and unable to endure the hardships of a new settlement, perished in numbers, leaving many helpless children unprovided for. The sight of their miserable situation inspired the benevolent heart of Mr. Whitfield with the idea of building an orphan house there in which they might be supported and educated. Returning northward he preached up this charity and made large collections; for his eloquence had a wonderful power over the hearts and purses of his hearers, of which I myself was an instance. I did not disapprove of the design, but as Georgia was then destitute of materials and workmen and it was proposed to send them from Philadelphia at a great expence, I thought it would have been better to have built the house here and brought the children to it. This I advised, but he was resolute in his first project and rejected my counsel, and I thereupon refused to contribute. I happened soon after to attend one of his sermons, in the course of which I perceived he intended to finish with a collection, and I silently resolved he should get nothing from me. I had in my pocket a handful of copper money, three or four silver dollars, and five pistoles in gold. As he proceeded, I began to soften and concluded to give the coppers. Another stroke of his oratory made me ashamed of that and determined me to give the silver; and he finished so admirably that I emptied my pocket wholly into the collector's dish, gold and all. At this sermon there was also one of our club, who being of my sentiments respecting the building in Georgia and suspecting a collection might be intended, had by precaution emptied his pockets before he came from home; towards the conclusion of the discourse, however, he felt a strong desire to give and applied to a neighbour who stood near him to borrow some money for the purpose. The application was unfortunately made to perhaps the only man in the company who had the firmness not to be affected by the preacher. His answer was, "At any other time,

Friend Hopkinson, I would lend to thee freely, but not now; for thee seems to be out of thy right senses.''

Some of Mr. Whitfield's enemies affected to suppose that he would apply these collections to his own private emolument, but I who was intimately acquainted with him (being employed in printing his sermons and journals, etc.) never had the least suspicion of his integrity, but am to this day decidedly of opinion that he was in all his conduct a perfectly *honest man*. And methinks my testimony in his favour ought to have the more weight as we had no religious connection. He used, indeed, sometimes to pray for my conversion but never had the satisfaction of believing that his prayers were heard. Ours was a mere civil friendship, sincere on both sides, and lasted to his death.

The following instance will show something of the terms on which we stood. Upon one of his arrivals from England to Boston, he wrote to me that he should come soon to Philadelphia but knew not where he could lodge when there, as he understood his old, kind host, Mr. Benezet, was removed to Germantown. My answer was, ''You know my house; if you can make shift with its scanty accommodations, you will be most heartily welcome.'' He replied that if I made that kind offer for Christ's sake, I should not miss of a reward. And I returned, ''Don't let me be mistaken; it was not for Christ's sake but for your sake.'' One of our common acquaintance jocosely remarked that knowing it to be the custom of the saints when they received any favour to shift the burthen of the obligation from off their own shoulders and place it in Heaven, I had contrived to fix it on earth.

The last time I saw Mr. Whitfield was in London, when he consulted me about his orphan house concern and his purpose of appropriating it to the establishment of a college.

He had a loud and clear voice, and articulated his words and sentences so perfectly that he might be heard and understood at a great distance, especially as his auditories, however numerous, observed the most exact silence. He preached one evening from the top of the courthouse steps, which are in the middle of Market Street and on the west side of Second Street, which crosses it at right angles. Both streets were filled with his hearers to a considerable distance. Being among the hindmost in Market Street, I had the curiosity to learn how far he could be heard by retiring backwards down the street towards the river, and I found his voice distinct till I came near Front Street, when some noise in that street obscured it. Imagining then a semicircle, of which my distance should be the radius, and that it were filled with auditors, to each of whom I allowed two square feet, I computed that he might well be heard by more than thirty thousand. This reconciled me to the newspaper accounts of his having preached to twenty-five thousand people in the fields, and to the antient histories of generals haranguing whole armies, of which I had sometimes doubted.

By hearing him often I came to distinguish easily between sermons newly composed and those which he had often preached in the course of his travels. His delivery of the latter was so improved by frequent repetitions that every accent, every emphasis, every modulation of voice was so perfectly well turned and well placed that, without being interested in the subject, one could not help being pleased with the discourse, a pleasure of much the same kind with that received from an excellent piece of music. This is an advantage itinerant preachers have over those who are stationary, as the latter cannot well improve their delivery of a sermon by so many rehearsals.

His writing and printing from time to time gave great advantage to his enemies. Unguarded expressions and even erroneous opinions delivered in preaching might have been afterwards explained or qualified by supposing others that might have accompanied them, or they might have been denied, but *litera scripta manet*. Critics attacked his writings violently and with so much appearance of reason as to diminish the number of his votaries and prevent their encrease; so that I am of opinion if he had never written anything, he would have left behind him a much more numerous and important sect. And his reputation might in that case have been still growing, even after his death; as there being nothing of his writing on which to found a censure and give him a lower character, his proselytes would be left at liberty to feign for him as great a variety of excellencies as their enthusiastic admiration might wish him to have possessed.

My business was now continually augmenting and my circumstances growing daily easier, my newspaper having become very profitable, as being for a time almost the only one in this and the neighbouring provinces. I experienced, too, the truth of the observation that "after getting the first hundred pound, it is more easy to get the second:"—money itself being of a prolific nature.

The partnership at Carolina having succeeded, I was encouraged to engage in others and to promote several of my workmen who had behaved well, by establishing them with printing houses in different colonies on the same terms with that in Carolina. Most of them did well, being enabled at the end of our term, six years, to purchase the types of me and go on working for themselves, by which means several families were raised. Partnerships often finish in quarrels, but I was happy in this, that mine were all carried on and ended amicably, owing, I think, a good deal to the precaution of having very explicitly settled in our articles everything to be done by or expected from each partner, so that there was nothing to dispute—which precaution I would therefore recommend to all who enter into partnerships, for whatever esteem partners may have for and confidence in each other at the time of the contract, little jealousies and disgusts may arise, with ideas of inequality in the care and burthen of the business, etc., which are attended often with breach of friendship and of the connection, perhaps with lawsuits and other disagreeable consequences.

I had on the whole abundant reason to be satisfied with my being established in Pennsylvania. There were, however, two things that I regretted: there being no provision for defence nor for a complete education of youth, no militia nor any college. I therefore in 1743 drew up a proposal for establishing an academy; and at that time thinking the Reverend Mr. Peters, who was out of employ, a fit person to superintend such an institution, I communicated the project to him. But he, having more profitable views in the service of the Proprietors, which succeeded, declined the undertaking. And not knowing another at that time suitable for such a trust, I let the scheme lie awhile dormant. I succeeded better the next year, 1744, in proposing and establishing a philosophical society. The paper I wrote for that purpose will be found among my writings when collected.

With respect to defence, Spain having been several years at war against Britain and being at length joined by France, which brought us into greater danger, and the laboured and long-continued endeavours of our Governor Thomas to prevail with our Quaker Assembly to pass a militia law and make other provisions for the security of the province having proved abortive, I determined to try what might be done by a voluntary association of the people. To promote this, I first wrote and published a pamphlet, intitled *Plain Truth,* in which I stated our defenceless situation in strong lights, with the necessity of union and discipline for our defence, and promised to propose in a few days an association to be generally signed for that purpose. The pamphlet had a sudden and surprizing effect. I was called upon for the instrument of association; and having settled the draft of it with a few friends, I appointed a meeting of the citizens in the large building before-mentioned. The house was pretty full. I had prepared a number of printed copies, and provided pens and ink dispersed all over the room. I harangued them a little on the subject, read the paper, and explained it, and then distributed the copies, which were eagerly signed, not the least objection being made. When the company separated and the papers were collected, we found about twelve hundred hands; and other copies being dispersed in the country, the subscribers amounted at length to upwards of ten thousand. These all furnished themselves as soon as they could with arms, formed themselves into companies and regiments, chose their own officers, and met every week to be instructed in the manual exercise and other parts of military discipline. The women, by subscriptions among themselves, provided silk colours, which they presented to the companies, painted with different devices and mottos which I supplied. The officers of the companies composing the Philadelphia regiment being met, chose me for their colonel: but conceiving myself unfit, I declined that station and recommended Mr. Lawrence, a fine person and man of influence, who was accordingly appointed. I then proposed a lottery to defray the expence of building a battery below the town and furnishing it with cannon. It filled expeditiously, and the battery was soon erected, the merlons being framed of logs and filled with earth. We bought some old cannon from Boston, but these not being sufficient, we wrote to England for more, soliciting at the same time our Proprietaries for some assistance, tho' without much expectation of obtaining it. Meanwhile Colonel Lawrence, William Allen, Abraham Taylor, Esquires, and myself were sent to New York by the associators, commissioned to borrow some cannon of Governor Clinton. He at first refused us peremptorily; but at a dinner with his council where there was great drinking of Madeira wine, as the custom at that place then was, he softened by degrees and said he would lend us six. After a few more bumpers he advanced to ten. And at length he very good-naturedly conceded eighteen. They were fine cannon, eighteen-pounders, and their carriages, which we soon transported and mounted on our battery, where the associators kept a nightly guard while the war lasted. And among the rest I regularly took my turn of duty there as a common soldier.

My activity in these operations was agreeable to the Governor and Council; they took me into confidence, and I was consulted by them in every measure wherein their concurrence was thought useful to the association. Calling in the aid of religion, I proposed to them the proclaiming a fast to promote reformation and implore the blessing of Heaven on our undertaking. They embraced the motion, but as it was the first fast ever thought of in the province, the Secretary had no precedent from which to draw the proclamation. My education in New England, were a fast is proclaimed every year, was here of some advantage. I drew it in the accustomed style; it was translated into German, printed in both languages, and circulated thro' the province. This gave the clergy of the different sects an opportunity of influencing their congregations to join in the association; and it would probably have been general among all but Quakers if the peace had not soon intervened.

It was thought by some of my friends that by my activity in these affairs, I should offend that sect and thereby lose my interest in the Assembly, where they were a great majority. A young gentlemen who had likewise some friends in the House and wished to succeed me as their clerk, acquainted me that it was decided to displace me at the next election, and he therefore in good will advised me to resign, as more consistent with my honour than being turned out. My answer to him was that I had read or heard of some public man who made it a rule never to ask for an office and never to refuse one when offered to him. "I approve," says I, "of his rule and will practise it with a small addition; I shall never *ask*, never *refuse*, nor ever *resign* an office. If they will have my office of clerk to dispose of to another, they shall take it from me. I will not, by giving it up, lose my right of sometime or other making reprisals on my adversaries." I heard, however, no more of this. I was chosen again, unanimously as usual, at the next election. Possibly as they disliked my late intimacy with the members of Council who had joined the governors in all the disputes about military preparations with which the House had long been harassed, they might have been pleased if I would voluntarily have left them; but they did not care to displace me on account merely of my zeal for the association, and they could not well give another reason. Indeed, I had some cause to believe that the defence of the country was not disagreeable to any of them, provided they were not required to assist in it. And I found that a much greater number of them than I could have imagined, tho' against offensive war, were clearly for the defensive. Many pamphlets pro and con were published on the subject, and some by good Quakers in favour of defence, which I believe convinced most of their younger people. A transaction in our fire company gave me some insight into their prevailing sentiments. It had been proposed that we should encourage the scheme for building a battery by laying out the present stock, then about sixty pounds, in tickets of the lottery. By our rules no money could be disposed of till the next meeting after the proposal. The company consisted of thirty members, of which twenty-two were Quakers, and eight only of other persuasions. We eight punctually attended the meetings; but tho' we thought that some of the Quakers would join us, we were by no means sure of a majority. Only one Quaker, Mr. James Morris, appeared to oppose the measure. He expressed much sorrow that it had ever been proposed, as he said "Friends" were all against it, and I would create such discord as might break up the company. We told him that we saw no reason for that; we were the minority, and if "Friends" were against the measure and outvoted us, we must and should, agreeable to the usage of all societies, submit. When the hour for business arrived, it was moved to put the vote. He allowed we might then do it by the rules, but as he could assure us that a number of members intended to be present for the purpose of opposing it, it would be but candid to allow a little time for their appearing. While we were disputing this, a waiter came to tell me two gentlemen below desired to speak with me. I went down and found they were two of our Quaker members. They told me there were eight of them assembled at a tavern just by; that they were determined to come and vote with us if there should be occasion, which they hoped would not be the case; and desired we would not call for their assistance if we could do without it, as their voting for such a measure might embroil them with their elders and friends. Being thus secure of a majority, I went up, and after a little seeming hesitation, agreed to a delay of another hour. This Mr. Morris allowed to be extremely fair. Not one of his opposing friends appeared, at which he expressed great surprize; and at the expiration of the hour, we carried the resolution eight to one; and as of the twenty-two Quakers, eight were ready to vote with us and thirteen by their absence manifested that they were not inclined to oppose the measure, I afterwards estimated the proportion of Quakers sincerely against defence as one to twenty-one only. For these were all regular members of that society, and in good reputation among them, and had due notice of what was proposed at that meeting.

The honourable and learned Mr. Logan, who had always been of that sect, was one who wrote an address to them declaring his approbation of defensive war and supporting his opinion by many strong arguments. He put into my hands sixty pounds to be laid out in lottery tickets for the battery, with directions to apply what prizes might be drawn wholly to that service. He told me the following anecdote of his old master William Penn, respecting defence. He came over from England when a young man with that Proprietary, and as his secretary. It was war time, and their ship was chased by an armed vessel supposed to be an enemy. Their captain prepared for defence, but told William Penn and his company of Quakers that he did not expect their assistance and they might retire into the cabin, which they did, except James Logan, who chose to stay upon deck and was quartered to a gun. The supposed enemy proved a friend, so there was no fighting. But when the secretary went down to communicate the intelligence, William Penn rebuked him severely for staying upon deck and undertaking to assist in defending the vessel contrary to the principles of Friends, especially as it had not been required by the captain. This reproof being before all the company, piqued the secretary, who answered: "I being thy servant, why did thee not order me to come down? But thee was willing enough that I should stay and help to fight the ship when thee thought there was danger."

My being many years in the Assembly, the majority of which were constantly Quakers, gave me frequent opportunities of seeing the embarrassment given them by their principle against war whenever application was made to them by order of the Crown to grant aids for military purposes. They were unwilling to offend government, on the one hand, by a direct refusal and their Friends, the body of Quakers, on the other, by a compliance contrary to their principles—hence a variety of evasions to avoid complying and modes of disguising the compliance when it became unavoidable. The common mode at last was to grant money under the phrase of its being "for the King's use," and never to enquire how it was applied. But if the demand was not directly from the Crown, that phrase was found not so proper, and some other was to be invented. As when powder was wanting (I think it was for the garrison at Louisburg) and the government of New England solicited a grant of some from Pennsylvania (which was much urged on the House by Governor Thomas), they could not grant money to buy powder because that was an ingredient of war, but they voted an aid to New England of three thousand pounds, to be put into the hands of the Governor, and appropriated it for the purchasing of bread, flour, wheat, "or other grain." Some of the Council, desirous of giving the House still further embarrassment, advised the Governor not to accept provision as not being the thing he had demanded. But he replied, "I shall take the money, for I understand very well their meaning; 'other grain' is gunpowder"—which he accordingly bought, and they never objected to it. It was in allusion to this fact that when in our fire company we feared the success of our proposal in favour of the lottery and I had said to my friend Mr. Syng, one of our members, "If we fail, let us move the purchase of a fire engine with the money; the Quakers can have no objection to that. And then if you nominate me, and I you, as a committee for that purpose, we will buy a great gun, which is certainly a 'fire engine.' " "I see," says he, "you have improved by being so long in the Assembly; your equivocal project would be just a match for their wheat 'or other grain.' "

These embarrassments that the Quakers suffered from having established and published it as one of their principles that no kind of war was lawful, and which being once published, they could not afterwards, however they might change their minds, easily get rid of, reminds me of what I think a more prudent conduct in another sect among us, that of the Dunkers. I was acquainted with one of its founders, Michael Welfare, soon after it appeared. He complained to me that they were grievously calumniated by the zealots of other persuasions, and charged with abominable principles and practices to which they were utter strangers. I told him this had always been the case with new sects and that to put a stop to such abuse, I imagined it might be well to publish the articles of their belief and the rules of their discipline. He said that it had been proposed among them, but not agreed to for this reason: "When we were first drawn together as a society," says he, "it had pleased God to enlighten our minds so far as to see that some doctrines which we once esteemed truths were errors, and that others which we had esteemed errors were real truths. From time to time he has been pleased to afford us further light, and our principles have been improving and our errors diminishing. Now we are not sure that we are arrived at the end of this progression, and at the perfection of spiritual or theological knowledge; and we fear that if we should once print our confession of faith, we should feel ourselves as if bound and confined by it, and perhaps be unwilling to receive further improvement, and our successors still more so, as conceiving what their elders and founders had done to be something sacred, never to be departed from.'' This modesty in a sect is perhaps a singular instance in the history of mankind, every other sect supposing itself in possession of all truth, and that those who differ are so far in the wrong—like a man travelling in foggy weather: Those at some distance before him on the road he sees wrapped up in the fog, as well as those behind him, and also the people in the fields on each side; but near him all appears clear, tho' in truth he is as much in the fog as any of them. To avoid this kind of embarrassment, the Quakers have of late years been gradually declining the public service in the Assembly and in the magistracy, choosing rather to quit their power than their principle.

In order of time, I should have mentioned before that, having in 1742 invented an open stove for the better warming of rooms and at the same time saving fuel, as the fresh air admitted was warmed in entering, I made a present of the model to Mr. Robert Grace, one of my early friends, who having an iron furnace, found the casting of the plates for these stoves a profitable thing, as they were growing in demand. To promote that demand, I wrote and published a pamphlet entitled, *An Account of the New-Invented Pennsylvania Fireplaces: Wherein Their Construction and Manner of Operation is Particularly Explained, Their Advantages above Every Other Method of Warming Rooms Demonstrated; and All Objections That Have Been Raised against the Use of Them Answered and Obviated, etc.* This pamphlet had a good effect. Governor Thomas was so pleased with the construction of this stove as described in it that he offered to give me a patent for the sole vending of them for a term of years; but I declined it from a principle which as ever weighed with me on such occasions; viz., *that as we enjoy great advantages from the inventions of others, we should be glad of an opportunity to serve others by any invention of ours, and this we should do freely and generously.* An ironmonger in London, however, after assuming a good deal of my pamphlet, and working it up into his own, and making some small changes in the machine, which rather hurt its operation, got a patent for it there, and made, as I was told, a little fortune by it. And this is not the only instance of patents taken out for my inventions by others, tho' not always with the same success, which I never contested, as having no desire of profiting by patents myself and hating disputes. The use of these fireplaces in very many houses both of this and the neighbouring colonies, has been and is a great saving of wood to the inhabitants.

Peace being concluded and the association business therefore at an end, I turned my thoughts again to the affair of establishing an academy. The first step I took was to associate in the design a number of active friends, of whom the Junto furnished a good part, the next was to write and publish a pamphlet entitled *Proposals Relating to the Education of Youth in Pennsylvania.* This I distributed among the principal inhabitants gratis; and as soon as I could suppose their minds a little prepared by the perusal of it, I set on foot a subscription for opening and supporting an academy; it was to be paid in quotas yearly for five years; by so dividing it I judged the subscription might be larger, and I believe it was so, amounting to no less, if I remember right, than five thousand pounds.

In the introduction of these proposals, I stated their publication not as an act of mine, but of some "public-spirited gentlemen"; avoiding as much as I could, according to my usual rule, the presenting myself to the public as the author of any scheme for their benefit.

The subscribers, to carry the project into immediate execution, chose out of their number twenty-four trustees and appointed Mr. Francis, then Attorney-General, and myself to draw up constitutions for the government of the academy, which being done and signed, a house was hired, masters engaged, and the schools opened, I think, in the same year, 1749.

The scholars encreasing fast, the house was soon found too small, and we were looking out for a piece of ground properly situated, with intention to build, when Providence threw into our way a large house ready built, which with a few alterations might well serve our purpose. This was the building before-mentioned, erected by the hearers of Mr. Whitfield, and was obtained for us in the following manner.

' It is to be noted that the contributions to this building being made by people of different sects, care was taken in the nomination of trustees, in whom the building and ground were to be vested, that a predominancy should not be given to any sect, lest in time that predominancy might be a means of appropriating the whole to the use of such sect contrary to the original intention; it was for this reason that one of each sect was appointed, viz., one Church of England man, one Presbyterian, one Baptist, one Moravian, etc.; those in case of vacancy by death were to fill it by election from among the contributors. The Moravian happened not to please his colleagues, and on his death they resolved to have no other of that sect. The difficulty then was, how to avoid having two of some other sect by means of the new choice. Several persons were named and for that reason not agreed to. At length one mentioned me, with the observation that I was merely an honest man, and of *no sect* at all—which prevailed with them to choose me. The enthusiasm which existed when the house was built had long since abated, and its trustees had not been able to procure fresh contributions for paying the ground rent and discharging some other debts the building had occasioned, which embarrassed them greatly. Being now a member of both boards of trustees, that for the building and that for the academy, I had a good opportunity of negotiating with both, and brought them finally to an agreement by which the trustees for the building were to cede it to those of the academy, the latter undertaking to discharge the debt, to keep forever open in the building a large hall for occasional preachers according to the original intention, and maintain a free school for the instruction of poor children.

Writings were accordingly drawn, and on paying the debts the trustees of the academy were put in possession of the premises, and by dividing the great and lofty hall into stories, and different rooms above and below for the several schools, and purchasing some additional ground, the whole was soon made fit for our purpose, and the scholars removed into the building. The care and trouble of agreeing with the workmen, purchasing materials, and superintending the work fell upon me, and I went thro' it the more cheerfully, as it did not then interfere with my private business, having the year before taken a very able, industrious, and honest partner, Mr. David Hall, with those character I was well acquainted as he had worked for me four years. He took off my hands all care of the printing office, paying me punctually my share of the profits. This partnership continued eighteen years, successfully for us both.

The trustees of the academy after a while were incorporated by a charter from the Governor; their funds were increased by contributions in Britain and grants of land from the Proprietaries, to which the Assembly has since made considerable addition, and thus was established the present University of Philadelphia. I have been continued one of its trustees from the beginning, now near forty years, and have had the very great pleasure of seeing a number of the youth who have received their education in it distinguished by their improved abilities, serviceable in public stations, and ornaments to their country.

When I disengaged myself, as above mentioned, from private business, I flattered myself that, by the sufficient tho' moderate fortune I had acquired, I had secured leisure during the rest of my life for philosophical studies and amusements; I purchased all Dr. Spence's apparatus, who had come from England to lecture here; and I proceeded in my electrical experiments with great alacrity; but the public now considering me as a man of leisure, laid hold of me for their purposes—every part of our civil government, and almost at the same time, imposing some duty upon me. The Governor put me into the commission of the peace; the corporation of the city chose me of the common council and soon after an alderman; and the citizens at large elected me a burgess to represent them in Assembly. This latter station was the more agreeable to me, as I was at length tired with sitting there to hear debates in which as clerk I could take no part, and which were often so uninteresting that I was induced to amuse myself with making magic squares or circles or anything to avoid weariness. And I conceived my becoming a member would enlarge my power of doing good. I would not, however, insinuate that my ambition was not flattered by all these promotions. It certainly was. For considering my low beginning they were great things to me. And they were still more pleasing as being so many spontaneous testimonies of the public's good opinion, and by me entirely unsolicited.

The office of justice of the peace I tried a little, by attending a few courts and sitting on the bench to hear causes. But finding that more knowledge of the common law than I possessed was necessary to act in that station with credit, I gradually withdrew from it, excusing myself by my being obliged to attend the higher duties of a legislator in the Assembly. My election to this trust was repeated every year for ten years without my ever asking any elector for his vote or signifying either directly or indirectly any desire of being chosen. On taking my seat in the House, my son was appointed their clerk.

The year following, a treaty being to be held with the Indians at Carlisle, the Governor sent a message to the House proposing that they should nominate some of their members to be joined with some members of Council as commissioners for that purpose. The House named the Speaker (Mr. Norris) and myself; and being commissioned, we went to Carlisle and met the Indians accordingly. As those people are extremely apt to get drunk and when so are very quarrelsome and disorderly, we strictly forbade the selling any liquor to them; and when they complained of this restriction, we told them that if they would continue sober during the treaty, we would give them plenty of rum when business was over. They promised this, and they kept their promise because they could get no liquor, and the treaty was conducted very orderly and concluded to mutual satisfaction. Then they claimed and received the rum. This was in the afternoon. They were near one hundred men, women, and children, and were lodged in temporary cabins built in the form of a square, just without the town. In the evening, hearing a great noise among them, the commissioners walked out to see what was the matter. We found they had made a great bonfire in the middle of the square. They were all drunk, men and women, quarrelling and fighting. Their dark-coloured bodies, half naked, seen only by the gloomy light of the bonfire, running after and beating one another with firebrands, accompanied by their horrid yellings, formed a scene the most resembling our ideas of hell that could well be imagined. There was no appeasing the tumult, and we retired to our lodging. At midnight a number of them came thundering at our door demanding more rum—of which we took no notice. The next day, sensible they had misbehaved in giving us that disturbance, they sent three of their old counsellors to make their apology. The orator acknowledged the fault, but laid it upon the rum, and then endeavoured to excuse the rum by saying, ''The Great Spirit who made all things made everything for some use, and whatever use he designed anything for, that use it should always be put to. Now, when he made rum, he said, 'LET THIS BE FOR INDIANS TO GET DRUNK WITH.' And it must be so.'' And indeed if it be the design of Providence to extirpate these savages in order to make room for cultivators of the earth, it seems not improbable that rum may be the appointed means. It has already annihilated all the tribes who formerly inhabited the seacoast.

In 1751 Dr. Thomas Bond, a particular friend of mine, conceived the idea of establishing a hospital in Philadelphia for the reception and cure of poor, sick persons, whether the inhabitants of the province or strangers—a very beneficent design, which has been ascribed to me but was originally his. He was zealous and active in endeavouring to procure subscriptions for it; but the proposal being a novelty in America and at first not well understood, he met with small success. At length he came to me with the compliment that he found there was no such thing as carrying a public-spirited project through without my being concerned in it. ''For,'' says he, ''I am often asked by those to whom I propose subscribing, 'Have you consulted Franklin upon this business, and what does he think of it?' And when I tell them that I have not (supposing it rather out of your line), they do not subscribe but say they will consider of it.'' I enquired into the nature and probable utility of his scheme, and receiving from him a very satisfactory explanation, I not only subscribed to it myself but engaged heartily in the design of procuring subscriptions from others. Previous, however, to the solicitation, I endeavoured to prepare the minds of the people by writing on the subject in the newspapers, which was my usual custom in such cases, but which he had omitted. The subscriptions afterwards were more free and generous, but beginning to flag, I saw they would be insufficient without some assistance from the Assembly and therefore proposed to petition for it, which was done. The country members did not at first relish the project. They objected that it could only be serviceable to the city, and therefore the citizens should alone be at the expence of it; and they doubted whether the citizens themselves generally approved of it. My allegation on the contrary that it met with such approbation as to leave no doubt of our being able to raise £2000 by voluntary donations, they considered as a most extravagant supposition and utterly impossible. On this I formed my plan; and asking leave to bring in a bill for incorporating the contributors according to the prayer of their petition and granting them a blank sum of money, which leave was obtained chiefly on the consideration that the House could throw the bill out if they did not like it, I drew it so as to make the important clause a conditional one; viz., ''And be it enacted by the authority aforesaid that when the said contributors shall have met and chosen their managers and treasurer, *and shall have raised by their contributions a capital stock of £2000 value* (the yearly interest of which is to be applied to the accommodating of the sick poor in the said hospital, free of charge for diet, attendance, advice, and medicines) and *shall make the same appear to the satisfaction of the Speaker of the Assembly* for the time being, that *then* it shall and may be lawful for the said Speaker; and he is hereby required to sign an order on the provincial treasurer for the payment of £2000 in two yearly payments, to the treasurer of the said hospital, to be applied to the founding, building, and finishing of the same." This condition carried the bill through; for the members who had opposed the grant and now conceived they might have the credit of being charitable without the expence, agreed to its passage; and then in soliciting subscriptions among the people, we urged the conditional promise of the law as an additional motive to give, since every man's donation would be doubled. Thus the clause worked both ways. The subscriptions accordingly soon exceeded the requisite sum, and we claimed and received the public gift, which enabled us to carry the design into execution. A convenient and handsome building was soon erected, the institution has by constant experience been found useful and flourishes to this day. And I do not remember any of my political manoeuvres, the success of which gave me at the time more pleasure; or that in after-thinking of it, I more easily excused myself for having made use of cunning.

It was about this time that another projector, the Rev. Gilbert Tennent, came to me with a request that I would assist him in procuring a subscription for erecting a new meetinghouse. It was to be for the use of a congregation he had gathered among the Presbyterians who were originally disciples of Mr. Whitfield. Unwilling to make myself disagreeable to my fellow citizens by too frequently soliciting their contributions, I absolutely refused. He then desired I would furnish him with a list of the names of persons I knew by experience to be generous and public-spirited. I thought it would be unbecoming in me, after their kind compliance with my solicitations, to mark them out to be worried by other beggars, and therefore refused also to give such a list. He then desired I would at least give him my advice. "That I will readily do," said I, "and, in the first place, I advise you to apply to all those who you are uncertain whether they will give anything or not, and show them the list of those who have given; and lastly, do not neglect those who you are sure will give nothing, for in some of them you may be mistaken." He laughed and thanked me, and said he would take my advice. He did so, for he asked of *everybody;* and he obtained a much larger sum than he expected, with which he erected the capacious and very elegant meetinghouse that stands in Arch Street.

Our city, tho' laid out with a beautiful regularity, the streets large, straight, and crossing each other at right angles, had the disgrace of suffering those streets to remain long unpaved; and in wet weather the wheels of heavy carriages ploughed them into a quagmire so that it was difficult to cross them. And in dry weather the dust was offensive. I had lived near what was called the Jersey Market and saw with pain the inhabitants wading in mud while purchasing their provisions. A strip of ground down the middle of that market was at length paved with brick so that being once in the market they had firm footing, but were often over shoes in dirt to get there. By talking and writing on the subject, I was at length instrumental in getting the street paved with stone between the market and the bricked foot pavement that was on each side next the houses. This for some time gave an easy access to the market, dry-shod. But the rest of the street not being paved, whenever a carriage came out of the mud upon this pavement, it shook off and left its dirt upon it, and it was soon covered with mire, which was not removed, the city as yet having no scavengers. After some enquiry I found a poor, industrious man who was willing to undertake keeping the pavement clean by sweeping it twice a week and carrying off the dirt from before all the neighbours' doors, for the sum of sixpence per month, to be paid by each house. I then wrote and printed a paper, setting forth the advantages to the neighbourhood that might be obtained by this small expence: the greater ease in keeping our houses clean, so much dirt not being brought in by people's feet; the benefit to the shops by more custom, as buyers could more easily get at them; and by not having in windy weather the dust blown in upon their goods, etc., etc. I sent one of these papers to each house and in a day or two went round to see who would subscribe an agreement to pay these sixpences. It was unanimously signed and for a time well executed. All the inhabitants of the city were delighted with the cleanliness of the pavement that surrounded the market, it being a convenience to all; and this raised a general desire to have all the streets paved, and made the people more willing to submit to a tax for that purpose. After some time I drew a bill for paving the city and brought it into the Assembly. It was just before I went to England in 1757 and did not pass till I was gone, and then with an alteration in the mode of assessment, which I thought not for the better, but with an additional provision for lighting as well as paving the streets, which was a great improvement. It was by a private person, the late Mr. John Clifton, giving a sample of the utility of lamps by placing one at his door that the people were first impressed with the idea of lighting all the city. The honour of this public benefit has also been ascribed to me, but it belongs truly to that gentleman. I did but follow his example and have only some merit to claim respecting the form of our lamps as differing from the globe lamps we at first were supplied with from London. Those we found inconvenient in these respects: They admitted no air below; the smoke therefore did not readily go out above, but circulated in the globe, lodged on its inside, and soon obstructed the light they were intended to afford, giving, besides, the daily trouble of wiping them clean; and an accidental stroke on one of them would demolish it and render it totally useless. I therefore suggested the composing them of four flat panes, with a long funnel above, to draw up the smoke, and crevices admitting air below, to facilitate the ascent of the smoke. By this means they were kept clean, and did not grow dark in a few hours as the London lamps do, but continued bright till morning; and an accidental stroke would generally break but a single pane, easily repaired. I have sometimes wondered that the Londoners did not, from the effect holes in the bottom of the globe lamps used at Vauxhall have in keeping them clean, learn to have such holes in their street lamps. But those holes being made for another purpose, viz., to communicate flame more suddenly to the wick by a little flax hanging down thro' them, the other use of letting in air seems not to have been thought of. And therefore, after the lamps have been lit a few hours, the streets of London are very poorly illuminated.

The mention of these improvements puts me in mind of one I proposed when in London to Dr. Fothergill, who was among the best men I have known and a great promoter of useful projects. I had observed that the streets when dry were never swept and the light dust carried away, but it was suffered to accumulate till wet weather reduced it to mud; and then after lying some days so deep on the pavement that there was no crossing but in paths kept clean by poor people with brooms, it was with great labour raked together and thrown up into carts open above, the sides of which suffered some of the slush at every jolt on the pavement to shake out and fall, sometimes to the annoyance of foot passengers. The reason given for not sweeping the dusty streets was that the dust would fly into the windows of shops and houses. An accidental occurrence had instructed me how much sweeping might be done in a little time. I found at my door in Craven Street one morning a poor woman sweeping my pavement with a birch broom. She appeared very pale and feeble as just come out of a fit of sickness. I asked who employed her to sweep there. She said, "Nobody. But I am very poor and in distress, and I sweeps before gentlefolkses doors and hopes they will give me something." I bid her sweep the whole street clean and I would give her a shilling. This was at nine o'clock. At twelve she came for the shilling. From the slowness I saw at first in her working, I could scarce believe that the work was done so soon and sent my servant to examine it, who reported that the whole street was swept perfectly clean and all the dust placed in the gutter which was in the middle; and the next rain washed it quite away so that the pavement and even the kennel were perfectly clean. I then judged that if that feeble woman could sweep such a street in three hours, a strong, active man might have done it in half the time. And here let me remark the convenience of having but one gutter in such a narrow street running down its middle instead of two, one on each side near the footway. For where all the rain that falls on a street runs from the sides and meets in the middle, it forms there a current strong enough to wash away all the mud it meets with. But when divided into two channels, it is often too weak to cleanse either and only makes the mud it finds more fluid so that the wheels of carriages and feet of horses throw and dash it up on the foot pavement, which is thereby rendered foul and slippery, and sometimes splash it upon those who are walking. My proposal communicated to the good doctor was as follows:

"For the more effectual cleaning and keeping clean the streets of London and Westminster, it is proposed that the several watchmen be contracted with to have the dust swept up in dry seasons and the mud raked up at other times, each in the several streets and lanes of his round; that they be furnished with brooms and other proper instruments for these purposes, to be kept at their respective stands, ready to furnish the poor people they may employ in the service.

"That in the dry, summer months the dust be all swept up into heaps at proper distances before the shops and windows of houses are usually opened, when the scavengers with close-covered carts shall also carry it all away.

"That the mud when raked up be not left in heaps to be spread abroad again by the wheels of carriages and trampling of horses; but that the scavengers be provided with bodies of carts, not placed high upon wheels, but low upon sliders, with lattice bottoms, which being covered with straw, will retain the mud thrown into them and permit the water to drain from it, whereby it will become much lighter, water making the greatest part of its weight—these bodies of carts to be placed at convenient distances and the mud brought to them in wheelbarrows, they remaining where placed till the mud is drained, and then horses brought to draw them away."

I have since had doubts of the practicability of the latter part of this proposal, on account of the narrowness of some streets and the difficulty of placing the draining sleds so as not to encumber too much the passage. But I am still of opinion that the former, requiring the dust to be swept up and carried away before the shops are open, is very practicable in the summer when the days are long; for in walking thro' the Strand and Fleet Street one morning at seven o'clock, I observed there was not one shop open tho' it had been daylight and the sun up above three hours—the inhabitants of London choosing voluntarily to live much by candlelight and sleep by sunshine, and yet often complaining a little absurdly of the duty on candles and the high price of tallow.

Some may think these trifling matters not worth minding or relating. But when they consider that tho' dust blown into the eyes of a single person or into a single shop on a windy day is but of small importance, yet the great number of the instances in a populous city and its frequent repetitions give it weight and consequence; perhaps they will not censure very severely those who bestow some attention to affairs of this seemingly low nature. Human felicity is produced not so much by great advantages that occur every day. Thus, if you teach a poor young man to shave himself and keep his razor in order, you may contribute more to the happiness of his life than in giving him a thousand guineas. The money may be soon spent, the regret only remaining of having foolishly consumed it. But in the other case he escapes the frequent vexation of waiting for barbers and of their sometimes dirty fingers, offensive breaths, and dull razors. He shaves when most convenient to him and enjoys daily the pleasure of its being done with a good instrument. With these sentiments I have hazarded the few preceding pages, hoping they may afford hints which sometime or other may be useful to a city I love, having lived many years in it very happily—and perhaps to some of our towns in America.

Having been for some time employed by the Postmaster-General of America as his comptroller, in regulating the several offices and bringing the officers to account, I was upon his death in 1753 appointed jointly with Mr. William Hunter to succeed him by a commission from the Postmaster-General in England. The American office had never hitherto paid anything to that of Britain. We were to have £600 a year between us if we could make that sum out of the profits of the office. To do this, a variety of improvements were necessary; some of these were inevitably at first expensive, so that in the first four years the office became above £900 in debt to us. But it soon after began to repay us, and before I was displaced by a freak of the ministers, of which I shall speak hereafter, we had brought it to yield *three times* as much clear revenue to the Crown as the Post Office of

Ireland. Since that imprudent transaction, they have received from it—not one farthing.

The business of the Post Office occasioned my taking a journey this year to New England, where the College of Cambridge, of their own motion, presented me with the degree of Master of Arts. Yale College in Connecticut had before made me a similar compliment. Thus without studying in any college I came to partake of their honours. They were conferred in consideration of my improvements and discoveries in the electric branch of natural philosophy.

In 1754 war with France being again apprehended, a congress of commissioners from the different Colonies was by an order of the Lords of Trade to be assembled at Albany, there to confer with the chiefs of the six nations concerning the means of defending both their country and ours. Governor Hamilton having received this order, acquainted the House with it, requesting they would furnish proper presents for the Indians to be given on this occasion, and naming the Speaker (Mr. Norris) and myself to join Mr. Thomas Penn and Mr. Secretary Peters as commissioners to act for Pennsylvania. The House approved the nomination and provided the goods for the presents, tho' they did not much like treating out of the province, and we met the other commissioners at Albany about the middle of June. In our way thither, I projected and drew up a plan for the union of all the Colonies under one government, so far as might be necessary for defence and other important general purposes. As we passed thro' New York, I had there shown my project to Mr. James Alexander and Mr. Kennedy, two gentlemen of great knowledge in public affairs; and being fortified by their approbation, I ventured to lay it before the Congress. It then appeared that several of the commissioners had formed plans of the same kind. A previous question was first taken whether a union should be established, which passed in the affirmative unanimously. A committee was then appointed, one member from each colony, to consider the several plans and report. Mine happened to be preferred, and with a few amendments was accordingly reported. By this plan the general government was to be administered by a president-general appointed and supported by the Crown and a grand council to be chosen by the representatives of the people of the several Colonies met in their respective Assemblies. The debates upon it in Congress went on daily hand in hand with the Indian business. Many objections and difficulties were started, but at length they were all overcome, and the plan was unanimously agreed to, and copies ordered to be transmitted to the Board of Trade and to the Assemblies of the several provinces. Its fate was singular. The Assemblies did not adopt it, as they all thought there was too much *prerogative* in it; and in England it was judged to have too much of the *democratic*. The Board of Trade therefore did not approve of it; nor recommend it for the approbation of His Majesty; but another scheme was formed, supposed better to answer the same purpose, whereby the Governors of the provinces with some members of their respective Councils were to meet and order the raising of troops, building of forts, etc., and to draw on the Treasury of Great Britain for the expence, which was afterwards to be refunded by an act of Parliament laying a tax on America. My plan, with my reasons in support of it, is to be found among my political papers that are printed. Being the winter following in Boston, I had much conversation with Governor Shirley upon both the plans. Part of what passed between us on the occasion may also be seen among those papers. The different and contrary reasons of dislike to my plan make me suspect that it was really the true medium; and I am still of opinion it would have been happy for both sides the water if it had been adopted. The Colonies so united would have been sufficiently strong to have defended themselves; there would then have been no need of troops from England; of course the subsequent pretence for taxing America and the bloody contest it occasioned would have been avoided. But such mistakes are not new; history is full of the errors of states and princes.

> Look around the habitable world, how few
> Know their own good, or knowing it pursue.

Those who govern, having much business on their hands, do not generally like to take the trouble of considering and carrying into execution new projects. The best public measures are therefore seldom *adopted from previous wisdom, but forced by the occasion.*

The Governor of Pennsylvania in sending it down to the Assembly, expressed his approbation of the plan "as appearing to him to be drawn up with great clearness and strength of judgment, and therefore recommended it as well worthy their closest and most serious attention." The House, however, by the management of a certain member, took it up when I happened to be absent, which I thought not very fair, and reprobated it without paying any attention to it at all, to my no small mortification.

In my journey to Boston this year, I met at New York with our new Governor, Mr. Morris, just arrived there from England, with whom I had been before intimately acquainted. He brought a commission to supersede Mr. Hamilton, who, tired with the disputes his proprietary instructions subjected him to, had resigned. Mr. Morris asked me if I thought he must expect as uncomfortable an administration.

I said, "No, you may on the contrary have a very comfortable one, if you will only take care not to enter into any dispute with the Assembly."

"My dear friend," says he pleasantly, "how can you advise my avoiding disputes? You know I love disputing; it is one of my greatest pleasures. However, to show the regard I have for your counsel, I promise you I will, if possible, avoid them." He had some reason for loving to dispute, being eloquent, an acute sophister, and therefore generally successful in argumentative conversation. He had been brought up to it from a boy, his father, as I have heard, accustoming his children to dispute with one another for his diversion while sitting at table after dinner. But I think the practice was not wise, for in the course of my observation, these disputing, contradicting, and confuting people are generally unfortunate in their affairs. They get victory sometimes, but they never get good will, which would be of more use to them. We parted, he going to Philadelphia, and I to Boston. In returning I met at New York with the votes of the Assembly, by which it appeared that notwithstanding his promise to me, he and the House were already in high contention, and it was a continual battle between them as long as he retained the government. I had my share of it, for as soon as I got back to my seat in the Assembly, I was put on every committee for answering his speeches and messages, and by the committees always desired to make the drafts. Our answers as well as his messages were often tart, and sometimes indecently abusive. And as he knew I wrote for the Assembly, one might have imagined that when we met we could hardly avoid cutting throats. But he was so good-natured a man that no personal difference between him and me was occasioned by the contest, and we often dined together. One afternoon, in the height of this public quarrel, we met in the street. "Franklin," says he, "you must go home with me and spend the evening. I am to have some company that you will like"; and taking me by the arm, he led me to his house. In gay conversation over our wine after supper he told us jokingly that he much admired the idea of Sancho Panza, who, when it was proposed to give him a government, requested it might be a government of *blacks*, as then, if he could not agree with his people, he might sell them. One of his friends who sat next me says, "Franklin, why do you continue to side with these damned Quakers? Had not you better sell them? The Proprietor would give you a good price." "The Governor," says I, "has not yet *blacked* them enough." He had indeed laboured hard to blacken the Assembly in all his messages, but they wiped off his colouring as fast as he laid it on, and placed it in return thick upon his own face; so that finding he was likely to be negrofied himself, he, as well as Mr. Hamilton, grew tired of the contest and quitted the government.

These public quarrels were all at bottom owing to the Proprietaries, our hereditary governors, who when any expence was to be incurred for the defence of their province, with incredible meanness instructed their deputies to pass no act for levying the necessary taxes unless their vast estates were in the same act expressly excused; and they had even taken bonds of those deputies to observe such instructions. The Assemblies for three years held out against this injustice, tho' constrained to bend at last. At length Captain Denny, who was Governor Morris's successor, ventured to disobey those instructions; how that was brought about I shall show hereafter.

But I am got forward too fast with my story; there are still some transactions to be mentioned that happened during the administration of Governor Morris.

War being in a manner commenced with France, the government of Massachusetts Bay projected an attack upon Crown Point, and sent Mr. Quincy to Pennsylvania and Mr. Pownall, afterwards Governor Pownall, to New York to solicit assistance. As I was in the Assembly, knew its temper, and was Mr. Quincy's countryman, he applied to me for my influence and assistance. I dictated his address to them, which was well received. They voted an aid of £10,000, to be laid out in provisions. But the Governor refusing his assent to their bill (which included this with other sums granted for the use of the Crown) unless a clause were inserted exempting the proprietary estate from bearing any part of the tax that would be necessary, the Assembly, tho' very desirous of making their grant to New England effectual, were at a loss how to accomplish it. Mr. Quincy laboured hard with the Governor to obtain his assent, but he was obstinate. I then suggested a method of doing the business without the Governor, by orders on the Trustees of the Loan Office, which by law the Assembly had the right of drawing. There was indeed little or no money at that time in the office, and therefore I proposed that the orders should be payable in a year and to bear an interest of 5 per cent. With these orders I supposed the provisions might easily be purchased. The Assembly with very little hesitation adopted the proposal. The orders were immediately printed, and I was one of the committee directed to sign and dispose of them. The fund for paying them was the interest of all the paper currency then extant in the province upon loan, together with the revenue arising from the excise, which being known to be more than sufficient, they obtained instant credit, and were not only received in payment for the provisions, but many monied people who had cash lying by them vested it in those orders, which they found advantageous as they bore interest while upon hand and might on any occasion be used as money, so that they were eagerly all bought up, and in a few weeks none of them were to be seen. Thus this important affair was by my means completed. Mr. Quincy returned thanks to the Assembly in a handsome memorial, went home highly pleased with the success of his embassy, and ever after bore for me the most cordial and affectionate friendship.

The British government not choosing to permit the union of the Colonies as proposed at Albany and to trust that union with their defence, lest they should thereby grow too military and feel their own strength, suspicions, and jealousies at this time being entertained of them, sent over General Braddock with two regiments of regular English troops for that purpose. He landed at Alexandria in Virginia and thence marched to Frederick* in Maryland, where he halted for carriages. Our Assembly apprehending, from some information, that he had conceived violent prejudices against them, as averse to the service, wished me to wait upon him, not as from them, but as Postmaster-General, under the guise of proposing to settle with him the mode of conducting with most celerity and certainty the dispatches between him and the Governors of the several provinces, with whom he must necessarily have continual correspondence, and of which they proposed to pay the expence. My son accompanied me on this journey. We found the General at Frederick, waiting impatiently for the return of those he had sent thro' the back parts of Maryland and Virginia to collect waggons. I stayed with him several days, dined with him daily, and had full opportunity of removing all his prejudices by the information of what the Assembly had before his arrival actually done and were still willing to do to facilitate his operations. When I was about to depart, the returns of waggons to be obtained were brought in, by which it appeared that they amounted only to twenty-five, and not all of those were in serviceable condition. The General and all the officers were surprized, declared the expedition was then at an end, being impossible, and exclaimed against the ministers for ignorantly landing them in a country destitute of the means of conveying their stores, baggage, etc., not less than 150 waggons

*Franklin originally wrote ''Frederic Town.''

being necessary. I happened to say I thought it was pity they had not been landed rather in Pennsylvania, as in that country almost every farmer had his waggon. The General eagerly laid hold of my words and said, "Then you, sir, who are a man of interest there, can probably procure them for us; and I beg you will undertake it." I asked what terms were to be offered the owners of the waggons, and I was desired to put on paper the terms that appeared to me necessary. This I did, and they were agreed to, and a commission and instructions accordingly prepared immediately. What those terms were will appear in the advertisement I published as soon as I arrived at Lancaster; which being, from the great and sudden effect it produced, a piece of some curiosity, I shall insert it at length, as follows.

ADVERTISEMENT

Lancaster, April 26, 1753

Whereas, 150 waggons, with 4 horses to each waggon, and 1,500 saddles or pack horses are wanted for the service of His Majesty's forces, now about to rendezvous at Wills's Creek, and His Excellency, General Braddock, having been pleased to empower me to contract for the hire of the same; I hereby give notice that I shall attend for that purpose at Lancaster from this day to next Wednesday evening, and at York from next Thursday morning till Friday evening, where I shall be ready to agree for waggons and teams, or single horses, on the following terms; viz., 1. That there shall be paid for each waggon with 4 good horses and a driver, fifteen shillings per diem. And for each able horse with a pack-saddle or other saddle and furniture, two shillings per diem. And for each able horse without a saddle, eighteen pence per diem. 2. That the pay commence from the time of their joining the forces at Wills's Creek (which must be on or before the 20th May ensuing) and that a reasonable allowance be paid over and above for the time necessary for their travelling to Wills's Creek and home again after their discharge. 3. Each waggon and team, and every saddle or pack-horse is to be valued by indifferent persons chosen between me and the owner; and in case of the loss of any waggon, team, or other horse in the service; the price according to such valuation is to be allowed and paid. 4. Seven days' pay is to be advanced and paid in hand by me to the owner of each waggon and team, or horse, at the time of contracting, if required; and the remainder to be paid by General Braddock or by the paymaster of the army at the time of their discharge, or from time to time as it shall be demanded. 5. No drivers of waggons or persons taking care of the hired horses are on any account to be called upon to do the duty of soldiers, or be otherwise employed than in conducting or taking care of their carriages or horses. 6. All oats, Indian corn, or other forage that waggons or horses bring to the camp, more than is necessary for the subsistence of the horses, are to be taken for the use of the army, and a reasonable price paid for the same.

Note—My son, William Franklin, is empowered to enter into like contracts with any person in Cumberland County.

B. Franklin.

To the Inhabitants of the Counties of Lancaster, York, and Cumberland

Friends and Countrymen,

Being occasionally at the camp at Frederick, a few days since, I found the General and officers extremely exasperated on account of their not being supplied with horses and carriages, which had been expected from this province, as most able to furnish them; but through the dissensions between our Governor and Assembly, money had not been provided, nor any steps taken for that purpose.

It was proposed to send an armed force immediately into these counties to seize as many of the best carriages and horses as should be wanted and compel as many persons into the service as would be necessary to drive and take care of them.

I apprehended that the progress of British soldiers through these counties on such an occasion (especially considering the temper they are in and their resentment against us) would be attended with many and great inconveniences to the inhabitants, and therefore more willingly took the trouble of trying first what might be done by fair and equitable means. The people of these back counties have lately complained to the Assembly that a sufficient currency was wanting; you have opportunity of receiving and dividing among you a very considerable sum; for if the service of this expedition should continue (as it is more than probable it will) for 120 days, the hire of these waggons and horses will amount to upwards of £30,000, which will be paid you in silver and gold of the King's money.

The service will be light and easy, for the army will scarce march above twelve miles per day, and the waggons and baggage horses, as they carry those things that are absolutely necessary to the welfare of the army, must march with the army and no faster, and are, for the army's sake, always placed where they can be most secure, whether in a march or in a camp.

If you are really, as I believe you are, good and loyal subjects to His Majesty, you may now do a most acceptable service and make it easy to yourselves; for three or four of such as cannot separately spare from the business of their plantations a waggon and four horses and a driver, may do it together—one furnishing the waggon, another one or two horses, and another the driver—and divide the pay proportionally between you. But if you do not this service to your King and country voluntarily when such good pay and reasonable terms are offered to you, your loyalty will be strongly suspected. The King's business must be done; so many brave troops, come so far for your defence, must not stand idle through your backwardness to do what may be reasonably expected from you; waggons and horses must be had, violent measures will probably be used; and you will be to seek for a recompence where you can find it, and your case perhaps be little pitied or regarded.

I have no particular interest in this affair, as (except the satisfaction of endeavouring to do good) I shall have only my labour for my pains. If this method of obtaining the waggons and horses is not likely to succeed, I am obliged to send word to the General in fourteen days; and I suppose Sir John St. Clair, the hussar, with a body of soldiers, will immediately enter the province for the purpose—which I shall be sorry to hear because I am very sincerely and truly

> Your friend and well-wisher,
> B. Franklin

I received of the General about £800 to be disbursed in advance money to the waggon owners, etc.; but that sum being insufficient, I advanced upwards of £200 more, and in two weeks the 150 waggons with 259 carrying horses were on their march for the camp. The advertisement promised payment according to the valuation in case any waggon or horse should be lost. The owners, however, alleging they did not know General Braddock, or what dependence might be had on his promise, insisted on my bond for the performance, which I accordingly gave them.

While I was at the camp supping one evening with the officers of Col. Dunbar's regiment, he represented to me his concern for the subalterns, who he said were generally not in affluence, and could ill afford in this dear country to lay in the stores that might be necessary in so long a march thro' a wilderness where nothing was to be purchased. I commiserated their case and resolved to endeavour procuring them some relief. I said nothing, however, to him of my intention, but wrote the next morning to the Committee of Assembly, who had the disposition of some public money, warmly recommending the case of these officers to their consideration and proposing that a present should be sent them of necessaries and refreshments. My son, who had had some experience of a camp life and of its wants, drew up a list for me, which I enclosed in my letter. The Committee approved and used such diligence that, conducted by my son, the stores arrived at the camp as soon as the waggons. They consisted of twenty parcels, each containing

6 lb. loaf sugar
6 lb. good muscovado do
1 lb. good green tea
1 lb. good bohea do
6 lb. good ground coffee

6 lb. chocolate
1/2 cwt. best white biscuit
1/2 lb. pepper
1 quart best white wine vinegar
1 Gloucester cheese
1 keg containing 20 lb. good butter
2 doz. old Madeira wine
2 gallons Jamaica spirits
1 bottle flour of mustard
2 well-cured hams
1/2 doz. dried tongues
6 lb. rice
6 lb. raisins

These twenty parcels, well-packed, were placed on as many horses, each parcel with the horse being intended as a present for one officer. They were very thankfully received and the kindness acknowledged by letters to me from the colonels of both regiments in the most grateful terms. The General, too, was highly satisfied with my conduct in procuring him the waggons, etc., etc., and readily paid my account of disbursements, thanking me repeatedly and requesting my further assistance in sending provisions after him. I undertook this also and was busily employed in it till we heard of his defeat, advancing, for the service, of my own money upwards of £1,000 sterling, of which I sent him an account. It came to his hands, luckily for me, a few days before the battle, and he returned me immediately an order on the paymaster for the round sum of £1,000, leaving the remainder to the next account. I consider this payment as good luck, having never been able to obtain that remainder—of which more hereafter.

This General was, I think, a brave man, and might probably have made a figure as a good officer in some European war. But he had too much self-confidence, too high an opinion of the validity of regular troops, and too mean a one of both Americans and Indians. George Croghan, our Indian interpreter, joined him on his march with one hundred of those people, who might have been of great use to his army as guides, scouts, etc., if he had treated them kindly; but he slighted and neglected them, and they gradually left him. In conversation with him one day, he was giving me some account of his intended progress. "After taking Fort Duquesne," says he, "I am to proceed to Niagara, and having taken that, to Frontenac, if the season will allow time, and I suppose it will; for Duquesne can hardly detain me above three or four days; and then I see nothing that can obstruct my march to Niagara." Having before revolved in my mind the long line his army must make in their march by a very narrow road to be cut for them thro' the woods and bushes, and also what I had read of a former defeat of 1,500 French who invaded the Iroquois country, I had conceived some doubts and some fears for the event of the campaign. But I ventured only to say, "To be sure, sir, if you arrive well before Duquesne with these fine troops so well provided with artillery, that place, not yet completely fortified and, as we hear, with no very strong garrison, can probably make but a short resistance. The only danger I apprehend of obstruction to your march, is from the ambuscades of Indians, who by constant practice are dextrous in laying and executing them. And the slender line, near four miles long, which your army must make, may expose it to be attacked by surprize in its flanks, and to be cut like a thread into several pieces, which from their distance cannot come up in time to support each other." He smiled at my ignorance and replied, "These savages may indeed be a formidable enemy to your raw American militia; but upon the King's regular and disciplined troops, sir, it is impossible they should make any impression." I was conscious of an impropriety in my disputing with a military man in matters of his profession and said no more. The enemy, however, did not take the advantage of his army while I apprehended its long line of march exposed it to, but let it advance without interruption till within nine miles of the place; and then when more in a body (for it had just passed a river, where the front had halted till all were come over) and in a more open part of the woods than any it had passed, attacked its advance guard by a heavy fire from behind trees and bushes—which was the first intelligence the General had of an enemy's being near him. This guard being disordered, the General hurried the troops up to their assistance, which was done in great confusion thro' waggons, baggage, and cattle. And presently the fire came upon their flank; the officers, being on horseback, were more easily distinguished, picked out as marks, and fell very fast; and the soldiers were crowded together in a huddle, having or hearing no orders, and standing to be shot at till two-thirds of them were killed, and then being seized with a panic the whole fled with precipitation. The waggoners took each a horse out of his team and scampered; their example was immediately followed by others so that all the waggons, provisions, artillery, and stores were left to the enemy. The General, being wounded, was brought off with difficulty; his secretary, Mr. Shirley, was killed by his side; and out of 86 officers, 63 were killed or wounded, and 714 men killed out of 1,100. These 1,100 had been picked men from the whole army, the rest had been left behind with Col. Dunbar, who was to follow with the heavier part of the stores, provisions, and baggage. The flyers, not being pursued, arrived at Dunbar's camp, and the panic they brought with them instantly seized him and all his people. And tho' he had now about 1,000 men and the enemy who had beaten Braddock did not at most exceed 400 Indians and French together, instead of proceeding and endeavouring to recover some of the lost honour, he ordered all the stores, ammunition, etc., to be destroyed that he might have more horses to assist his flight towards the settlements and less lumber to remove. He was there met with requests from the governors of Virginia, Maryland, and Pennsylvania that he would post his troops on the frontiers so as to afford some protection to the inhabitants; but he continued his hasty march thro' all the country, not thinking himself safe till he arrived at Philadelphia, where the inhabitants could protect him. This whole transaction gave us Americans the first suspicion that our exalted ideas of the prowess of British regulars had not been well founded.

In their first march, too, from their landing till they got beyond the settlements, they had plundered and stripped the inhabitants, totally ruining some poor families, besides insulting, abusing, and confining the people if they remonstrated. This was enough to put us out of conceit of such defenders if we had really wanted any.

How different was the conduct of our French friends in 1781, who during a march thro' the most inhabited part of our country from Rhode Island to Virginia, near seven hundred miles, occasioned not the smallest complaint for the loss of a pig, a chicken, or even an apple!

Captain Orme, who was one of the General's aides-de-camp and, being grievously wounded, was brought off with him and continued with him to his death, which happened in a few days, told me that he was totally silent all the first day and at night only said, "Who would have thought it?"; that he was silent again the following day, only saying at last, "We shall better know how to deal with them another time," and died a few minutes after.

The secretary's papers with all the General's orders, instructions, and correspondence falling into the enemy's hands, they selected and translated into French a number of the articles, which they printed to prove the hostile intentions of the British court before the declaration of war. Among these I saw some letters of the General to the ministry speaking highly of the great service I had rendered the army and recommending me to their notice. David Hume, too, who was some years after secretary to Lord Hertford when Minister in France and afterwards to General Conway when Secretary of State, told me he had seen among the papers in that office letters from Braddock highly recommending me. But the expedition having been unfortunate, my service, it seems, was not thought of much value, for those recommendations were never of any use to me. As to rewards from himself, I asked only one, which was that he would give orders to his officers not to enlist any more of our bought servants and that he would discharge such as had been already enlisted. This he readily granted, and several were accordingly returned to their masters on my application. Dunbar, when the command devolved on him, was not so generous. He being at Philadelphia on his retreat, or rather flight, I applied to him for the discharge of the servants of three poor farmers of Lancaster County that he had enlisted, reminding him of the late General's orders on that head. He promised me that if the masters would come to him at Trenton, where he should be in a few days on his march to New York, he would there deliver their men to them. They accordingly were at the expence and trouble of going to Trenton, and there he refused to perform his promise, to their great loss and disappointment.

As soon as the loss of the waggons and horses was generally known, all the owners came upon me for the valuation which I had given bond to pay. Their demands gave me a great deal of trouble. I acquainted them that the money was ready in the paymaster's hands, but that orders for paying it must first be obtained from General Shirley, and that I had applied for it; but he being at a distance, an answer could not soon be received, and they must have patience. All this was not sufficient to satisfy, and some began to sue me. General Shirley at length relieved me from this terrible situation by appointing commissioners to examine the claims and ordering payment. They amounted to near £20,000, which to pay would have ruined me.

Before we had the news of this defeat, the two Doctors Bond came to me with a subscription paper for raising money to defray the expence of a grand firework, which it was intended to exhibit at a rejoicing on receipt of the news of our taking Fort Duquesne. I looked grave and said it would, I thought, be time enough to prepare for the rejoicing when we knew we should have occasion to rejoice. They seemed surprised that I did not immediately comply with their proposal. "Why, the d——l," says one of them, "you surely don't suppose that the fort will not be taken?" "I don't know that it will not be taken; but I know that the events of war are subject to great uncertainty." I gave them the reasons of my doubting. The subscription was dropped and the projectors thereby missed the mortification they would have undergone if the firework had been prepared. Dr. Bond on some other occasions afterwards said that he did not like Franklin's forebodings.

Governor Morris, who had continually worried the Assembly with message after message before the defeat of Braddock to beat them into the making of acts to raise money for the defence of the province without taxing, among others, the proprietary estates, and had rejected all their bills for not having such an exempting clause, now redoubled his attacks, with more hope of success, the danger and necessity being greater. The Assembly, however, continued firm, believing they had justice on their side and that it would be giving up an essential right if they suffered the Governor to amend their money bills. In one of the last, indeed, which was for granting £50,000, his proposed amendment was only of a single word: the bill expressed that all estates real and personal were to be taxed, those of the Proprietaries *not* excepted. His amendment was, for "not" read "only"—a small but very material alteration! However, when the news of this disaster reached England, our friends there whom we had taken care to furnish with all the Assembly's answers to the Governor's messages, raised a clamour against the Proprietaries for their meanness and injustice in giving their Governor such instructions, some going so far as to say that by obstructing the defence of their province, they forfeited their right to it. They were intimidated by this, and sent orders to their receiver-general to add £5,000 of their money to whatever sum might be given by the Assembly for such purpose. This, being notified to the House, was accepted in lieu of their share of a general tax, and a new bill was formed with an exempting clause which passed accordingly. By this act I was appointed one of the commissioners for disposing of the money, £60,000. I had been active in modelling it and procuring its passage, and had at the same time drawn a bill for establishing and disciplining a voluntary militia, which I carried thro' the House without much difficulty, as care was taken in it to leave the Quakers at their liberty. To promote the association necessary to form the militia, I wrote a dialogue* stating and answering all the objections I could think of to such a militia, which was printed and had, as I thought, great effect. While the several companies in the city and country were forming and learning their exercise, the Governor prevailed with me to take charge of our northwestern frontier, which was infested by the enemy, and provide for the defence of the inhabitants by raising troops, and building a line of forts.

*This dialogue and the Militia Act, are in the *Gentleman's Magazine* for February and March 1756.

I undertook this military business, tho' I did not conceive myself well-qualified for it. He gave me a commission with full powers and a parcel of blank commissions for officers, to be given to whom I thought fit. I had but little difficulty in raising men, having soon 560 under my command. My son, who had in the preceding war been an officer in the army raised against Canada, was my aide-de-camp, and of great use to me. The Indians had burned Gnadenhut,* a village settled by the Moravians, and massacred the inhabitants, but the place was thought a good situation for one of the forts. In order to march thither, I assembled the companies at Bethlehem, the chief establishment of those people. I was surprized to find it in so good a posture of defence. The destruction of Gnadenhut had made them apprehend danger. The principal buildings were defended by a stockade. They had purchased a quantity of arms and ammunition from New York, and had even placed quantities of small paving stones between the windows of their high stone houses, for their women to throw down upon the heads of any Indians that should attempt to force into them. The armed brethren, too, kept watch, and relieved as methodically as in any garrison town. In conversation with Bishop Spangenberg, I mentioned my surprize; for knowing they had obtained an act of Parliament exempting them from military duties in the Colonies, I had supposed they were conscientiously scrupulous of bearing arms. He answered me that it was not one of their established principles, but that at the time of their obtaining that act it was thought to be a principle with many of their people. On this occasion, however, they to their surprize found it adopted by but a few. It seems they were either deceived in themselves or deceived the Parliament. But common sense, aided by present danger, will sometimes be too strong for whimsical opinions.

It was the beginning of January when we set out upon this business of building forts. I sent one detachment

---

*Franklin refers to the town now called "Gnadenhutten." It is described as follows in *Lippincott's Gazetteer of the World* (Philadelphia and London, 1922 ed.), p. 730: "Gnadenhutten, a post-village of Tuscarawas co., Ohio. . . . Gnadenhutten ('tents of grace') was once a village of Christian Indians under Moravian instruction."

towards the Minisinks, with instructions to erect one for the security of that upper part of the country; and another to the lower part, with similar instructions. And I concluded to go myself with the rest of my force to Gnadenhut, where a fort was thought more immediately necessary. The Moravians procured me five waggons for our tools, stores, baggage, etc. Just before we left Bethlehem, eleven farmers who had been driven from their plantations by the Indians, came to me requesting a supply of firearms, that they might go back and fetch off their cattle. I gave them each a gun with suitable ammunition. We had not marched many miles before it began to rain, and it continued raining all day. There were no habitations on the road to shelter us till we arrived near night at the house of a German, where, and in his barn, we were all huddled together as wet as water could make us. It was well we were not attacked in our march, for our arms were of the most ordinary sort and our men could not keep their gunlocks dry. The Indians are dextrous in contrivances for that purpose, which we had not. They met that day the eleven poor farmers above-mentioned and killed ten of them. The one who escaped informed us that his and his companions' guns would not go off, the priming being wet with the rain. The next day being fair, we continued our march and arrived at the desolated Gnadenhut. There was a sawmill near, round which were left several piles of boards, with which we soon hutted ourselves—an operation the more necessary at that inclement season as we had no tents. Our first work was to bury more effectually the dead we found there, who had been half interred by the country people. The next morning our fort was planned and marked out, the circumference measuring 455 feet, which would require as many palisades to be made of trees, one with another of a foot diameter each. Our axes, of which we had seventy, were immediately set to work to cut down trees; and our men being dextrous in the use of them, great dispatch was made. Seeing the trees fall so fast, I had the curiosity to look at my watch when two men began to cut at a pine. In six minutes they had it upon the ground, and I found it of fourteen inches diameter. Each pine made three palisades of eighteen feet long, pointed at one end. While these were preparing, our other men dug a trench all round of three feet deep in which the palisades were to be planted, and the bodies being taken off our waggons and the fore and hind wheels separated by taking out the pin which united the two parts of the perch, we had ten carriages with two horses each, to bring the palisades from the woods to the spot. When they were set up, our carpenters built a stage of boards all round within, about six feet high, for the men to stand on when to fire thro' the loopholes. We had one swivel gun which we mounted on one of the angles and fired it as soon as fixed, to let the Indians know, if any were within hearing, that we had such pieces; and thus our fort (if such a magnificent name may be given to so miserable a stockade) was finished in a week, tho' it rained so hard every other day that the men could not work.

This gave me occasion to observe that when men are employed they are best contented. For on the days they worked they were good-natured and cheerful, and with the consciousness of having done a good day's work they spent the evenings jollily; but on the idle days they were mutinous and quarrelsome, finding fault with their pork, the bread, etc., and in continual ill-humour—which put me in mind of a sea captain whose rule it was to keep his men constantly at work; and when his mate once told him that they had done everything and there was nothing further to employ them about, "Oh," says he, "make them scour the anchor."

This kind of fort, however contemptible, is a sufficient defence against Indians who have no cannon. Finding ourselves now posted securely and having a place to retreat to on occasion, we ventured out in parties to scour the adjacent country. We met with no Indians, but we found the places on the neighbouring hills where they had lain to watch our proceedings. There was an art in their contrivance of those places that seems worth mention. It being winter, a fire was necessary for them. But a common fire on the surface of the ground would by its light have discovered their position at a distance. They had therefore dug holes in the ground about three feet diameter and somewhat deeper. We saw where they had with their hatchets cut off the charcoal from the sides of burnt logs lying in the woods. With these coals they had made small fires in the bottom of the holes, and we observed among the weeds and grass the prints of their bodies made by their laying all round with their legs hanging down in the holes to keep their feet warm, which with them is an essential point. This kind of fire, so managed, could not discover them either by its light, flame, sparks, or even smoke. It appeared that their number was not great, and it seems they saw we were too many to be attacked by them with prospect of advantage.

We had for our chaplain a zealous Presbyterian minister, Mr. Beatty, who complained to me that the men did not generally attend his prayers and exhortations. When they enlisted, they were promised, besides pay and provisions, a gill of rum a day, which was punctually served out to them half in the morning and the other half in the evening, and I observed they were as punctual in attending to receive it. Upon which I said to Mr. Beatty, "It is perhaps below the dignity of your profession to act as steward of the rum. But if you were to deal it out, and only just after prayers, you would have them all about you." He liked the thought, undertook the office, and with the help of a few hands to measure out the liquor executed it to satisfaction; and never were prayers more generally and more punctually attended—so that I thought this method preferable to the punishments inflicted by some military laws for non-attendance on divine service.

I had hardly finished this business and got my fort well stored with provisions when I received a letter from the Governor, acquainting me that he had called the Assembly and wished my attendance there, if the posture of affairs on the frontiers was such that my remaining there was no longer necessary. My friends, too, of the Assembly pressing me by their letters to be, if possible, at the meeting, and my three intended forts being now completed, and the inhabitants contented to remain on their farms under that protection, I resolved to return—the more willingly as a New England officer, Col. Clapham, experienced in Indian war, being on a visit to our establishment, consented to accept the command. I gave him a commission, and, parading the garrison, had it read before them, and introduced him to them as an officer who from his skill in military affairs was much more fit to command them than myself, and giving them a little exhortation, took my leave. I was escorted as far as Bethlehem, where I rested a few days to recover from the fatigue I had undergone. The first night being in a good bed, I could hardly sleep, it was so different from my hard lodging on the floor of our hut at Gnaden, wrapped only in a blanket or two.

While at Bethlehem, I enquired a little into the practices of the Moravians. Some of them had accompanied me, and all were very kind to me. I found they worked for a common stock, eat at common tables, and slept in common dormitories, great numbers together. In the dormitories I observed loopholes at certain distances all along just under the ceiling, which I thought judiciously placed for change of air. I was at their church, where I was entertained with good music, the organ being accompanied with violins, hautboys, flutes, clarinets, etc. I understand that their sermons were not usually preached to mixed congregations of men, women, and children, as is our common practice; but that they assembled sometimes the married men, at other times their wives, then the young men, the young women, and the little children, each division by itself. The sermon I heard was to the latter, who came in and were placed in rows on benches, the boys under the conduct of a young man their tutor, and the girls conducted by a young woman. The discourse seemed well adapted to their capacities and was delivered in a pleasing, familiar manner, coaxing them, as it were, to be good. They behaved very orderly, but looked pale and unhealthy, which made me suspect they were kept too much within-doors or not allowed sufficient exercise. I enquired concerning the Moravian marriages, whether the report was true that they were by lot. I was told that lots were used only in particular cases; that generally when a young man found himself disposed to marry, he informed the elders of his class, who consulted the elder ladies that governed the young women. As these elders of the different sexes were well acquainted with the tempers and dispositions of their respective pupils, they could best judge what matches were suitable, and their judgments were generally acquiesced in. But if, for example, it should happen that two or three young women were found to be equally proper for the young man, the lot was then recurred to. I objected, "If the matches are not made by the mutual choice of the parties, some of them may chance to be very unhappy." "And so they may," answered my informer, "if you let the parties choose for themselves"—which, indeed, I could not deny.

Being returned to Philadelphia, I found the association went on swimmingly, the inhabitants that were not Quakers having pretty generally come into it, formed themselves into companies, and [had] chosen their captains, lieutenants, and ensigns according to the new law. Dr. Bond visited me, and gave me an account of the pains he had taken to spread a general good liking to the law, and ascribed much to those endeavours. I had had the vanity to ascribe all to my dialogue; however, not knowing but that he might be in the right, I let him enjoy his opinion, which I take to be generally the best way in such cases. The officers' meeting chose me to be colonel of the regiment, which I this time accepted. I forget how many companies we had, but we paraded about 1,200 well-looking men, with a company of artillery who had been furnished with six brass field pieces, which they had become so expert in the use of as to fire twelve times in a minute. The first time I reviewed my regiment, they accompanied me to my house and would salute me with some rounds fired before my door, which shook down and broke several glasses of my electrical apparatus. And my new honour proved not much less brittle, for all our commissions were soon after broke by a repeal of the law in England.

During the short time of my colonelship, being about to set out on a journey to Virginia, the officers of my regiment took it into their heads that it would be proper for them to escort me out of town as far as the lower ferry. Just as I was getting on horseback, they came to my door, between thirty and forty, mounted, and all in their uniforms. I had not been previously acquainted with the project or I should have prevented it, being naturally averse to the assuming of state on any occasion, and I was a good deal chagrined at their appearance as I could

not avoid their accompanying me. What made it worse
was that as soon as we began to move, they drew their
swords and rode with them naked all the way. Somebody
wrote an account of this to the Proprietor, and it gave
him great offence. No such honour had been paid him
when in the province, nor to any of his governors; and
he said it was only proper to princes of the blood royal—
which may be true for aught I know, who was, and still
am, ignorant of the etiquette in such cases. This silly
affair, however, greatly increased his rancour against me
which was before not a little on account of my conduct
in the Assembly respecting the exemption of his estate
from taxation, which I had always opposed very warmly,
and not without severe reflections on his meanness and
injustice in contending for it. He accused me to the ministry as being the great obstacle to the King's service,
preventing by my influence in the House the proper form
of the bills for raising money; and he instanced this pa-
rade with my officers as a proof of my having an intention
to take the government of the province out of his hands
by force. He also applied to Sir Everard Fauckener, the
Postmaster-General, to deprive me of my office. But it
had no other effect than to procure from Sir Everard a
gentle admonition.

Notwithstanding the continual wrangle between the
Governor and the House, in which I as a member had
so large a share, there still subsisted a civil intercourse
between that gentleman and myself, and we never had
any personal difference. I have sometimes since thought
that his little or no resentment against me for the answers
it was known I drew up to his messages, might be the
effect of professional habit, and that, being bred a lawyer, he might consider us both as merely advocates for
contending clients in a suit, he for the Proprietaries and
I for the Assembly. He would therefore sometimes call
in a friendly way to advise with me on difficult points
and sometimes, tho' not often, take my advice. We acted
in concert to supply Braddock's army with provisions,
and when the shocking news arrived of his defeat, the
Governor sent in haste for me to consult with him on
measures for preventing the desertion of the back counties. I forget now the advice I gave, but I think it was

that Dunbar should be written to and prevailed with, if possible, to post his troops on the frontiers for their protection, till by reinforcements from the Colonies he might be able to proceed on the expedition. And after my return from the frontier, he would have had me undertake the conduct of such an expedition with provincial troops for the reduction of Fort Duquesne, Dunbar and his men being otherwise employed; and he proposed to commission me as general. I had not so good an opinion of my military abilities as he professed to have, and I believe his professions must have exceeded his real sentiments. But probably he might think that my popularity would facilitate the raising of the men and my influence in Assembly the grant of money to pay them, and that, perhaps, without taxing the proprietary estate. Finding me not so forward to engage as he expected, the project was dropped; and he soon after left the government, being superseded by Capt. Denny.

Before I proceed in relating the part I had in public affairs under this new Governor's administration, it may not be amiss here to give some account of the rise and progress of my philosophical reputation.

In 1746 being at Boston, I met there with a Dr. Spence, who was lately arrived from Scotland, and showed me some electric experiments. They were imperfectly performed, as he was not very expert; but being on a subject quite new to me, they equally surprized and pleased me. Soon after my return to Philadelphia, our library company received from Mr. Peter Collinson, F.R.S., of London, a present of a glass tube, with some account of the use of it in making such experiments. I eagerly seized the opportunity of repeating what I had seen at Boston, and by much practice acquired great readiness in performing those also which we had an account of from England, adding a number of new ones. I say much practice, for my house was continually full for some time with people who came to see these new wonders. To divide a little this incumbrance among my friends, I caused a number of similar tubes to be blown at our glass house, with which they furnished themselves, so that we had at length several performers. Among these the principal was Mr. Kinnersley, an ingenious neighbour, who, being out of business, I encouraged to undertake showing the experiments for money, and drew up for him two lectures in which the experiments were ranged in such order and accompanied with explanations, in such method as that the foregoing should assist in comprehending the following. He procured an elegant apparatus for the purpose, in which all the little machines that I had roughly made for myself were nicely formed by instrument makers. His lectures were well attended and gave great satisfaction, and after some time he went thro' the Colonies exhibiting them in every capital town and picked up some money. In the West India Islands, indeed, it was with difficulty the experiments could be made, from the general moisture of the air.

Obliged as we were to Mr. Colinson for his present of the tube, etc., I thought it right he should be informed of our success in using it and wrote him several letters containing accounts of our experiments. He got them read in the Royal Society, where they were not at first thought worth so much notice as to be printed in their transactions. One paper which I wrote for Mr. Kinnersley, on the sameness of lightning with electricity, I sent to Dr. Mitchel, an acquaintance of mine and one of the members also of that Society, who wrote me word that it had been read but was laughed at by the connoisseurs. The papers, however, being shown to Dr. Fothergill, he thought them of too much value to be stifled and advised the printing of them. Mr. Colinson then gave them to Cave for publication in his *Gentleman's Magazine;* but he chose to print them separately in a pamphlet, and Dr. Fothergill wrote the preface. Cave, it seems, judged rightly for his profit; for by the additions that arrived afterwards, they swelled to a quarto volume, which has had five editions and cost him nothing for copy-money.

It was, however, some time before those papers were much taken notice of in England. A copy of them happening to fall into the hands of the Count De Buffon, a philosopher deservedly of great reputation in France and indeed all over Europe, he prevailed with Mr. Dalibard to translate them into French, and they were printed at Paris. The publication offended the Abbé Nollet, preceptor in natural philosophy to the royal family, and an able experimenter who had formed and published a theory of electricity which then had the general vogue. He could not at first believe that such a work came from America and said it must have been fabricated by his enemies at Paris to decry his system. Afterwards having been assured that there really existed such a person as Franklin of Philadelphia, which he had doubted, he wrote and published a volume of letters, chiefly addressed to me, defend.ng his theory and denying the verity of my experiments and of the positions deduced from them. I once purposed answering the Abbé and actually began the answer. But on consideration that my writings contained only a description of experiments which anyone might repeat and verify, and, if not to be verified, could not be defended; or of observations offered as conjectures and not delivered dogmatically, therefore not laying me under any obligation to defend them; and reflecting that a dispute between two persons writing in different languages might be lengthened greatly by mistranslations, and thence misconceptions, of one another's meaning—much of one of the Abbé's letter being founded on an error in the translation; I concluded to let my papers shift for themselves, believing it was better to spend what time I could spare from public business in making new experiments than in disputing about those already made. I therefore never answered M. Nollet, and the event gave me no cause to repent my silence, for my friend M. le Roy of the Royal Academy of Sciences took up my cause and refuted him; my book was translated into the Italian, German, and Latin languages; and the doctrine it contained was by degrees universally adopted by the philosophers of Europe in preference to that of the Abbé, so that he lived to see himself the last of his sect—except Mr. B.——, his *élève* and immediate disciple.

What gave my book the more sudden and general celebrity was the success of one of its proposed experiments made by Messrs. Dalibard and Delor at Marly for drawing lightning from the clouds. This engaged the public attention everywhere. M. Delor, who had an apparatus for experimental philosophy and lectured in that branch of science, undertook to repeat what he called the "Philadelphia Experiments," and after they were performed before the King and court, all the curious of Paris flocked to see them. I will not swell this narrative with an account of that capital experiment, nor of the infinite pleasure I received in the success of a similar one I made soon after with a kite at Philadelphia, as both are to be found in the histories of electricity. Dr. Wright, an English physician then at Paris, wrote to a friend who was of the Royal Society an account of the high esteem my experiments were in among the learned abroad, and of their wonder that my writings had been so little noticed in England. The Society on this resumed the consideration of the letters that had been read to them, and the celebrated Dr. Watson drew up a summary account of them and of all I had afterwards sent to England on the subject, which he accompanied with some praise of the writer. This summary was then printed in their transactions. And some members of the Society in London, particularly the very ingenious Mr. Canton, having verified the experiment of procuring lightning from the clouds by a pointed rod and acquainting them with the success, they soon made me more than amends for the slight with which they had before treated me. Without my having made any application for that honour, they chose me a member and voted that I should be excused the customary payments, which would have amounted to twenty-five guineas, and ever since have given me their transactions gratis. They also presented me with the gold medal of Sir Godfrey Copley for the year 1753, the delivery of which was accompanied by a very handsome speech of the president, Lord Macclesfield, wherein I was highly honoured.

Our new Governor, Capt. Denny, brought over for me the before-mentioned medal from the Royal Society, which he presented to me at an entertainment given him by the city. He accompanied it with very polite expressions of his esteem for me, having, as he said, been long acquainted with my character. After dinner, when the company, as was customary at that time, were engaged in drinking, he took me aside into another room and acquainted me that he had been advised by his friends in England to cultivate a friendship with me, as one who was capable of giving him the best advice and of contributing most effectually to the making his administration easy, that he therefore desired of all things to have a good understanding with me; and he begged me to be assured of his readiness on all occasions to render me every service that might be in his power. He said much to me also of the Proprietor's good dispositions towards the province and of the advantage it might be to us all, and to me in particular, if the opposition that had been so long continued to his measures were dropped and harmony restored between him and the people, in effecting which it was thought no one could be more serviceable than myself, and I might depend on adequate acknowledgments and recompenses, etc., etc. The drinkers, finding we did not return immediately to the table, sent us a decanter of Madeira, which the Governor made liberal use of, and in proportion became more profuse of his solicitations and promises. My answers were to this purpose: that my circumstances, thanks to God, were such as to make proprietary favours unnecessary to me; and that being a member of the Assembly, I could not possibly accept of any; that, however, I had no personal enmity to the Proprietary; and that whenever the public measures he proposed should appear to be for the good of the people, no one should espouse and forward them more zealously than myself, my past opposition having been founded on this—that the measures which had been urged were evidently intended to serve the proprietary interest with great prejudice to that of the people; that I was much obliged to him (the Governor) for his professions of regard to me, and that he might rely on everything in my power to make his administration as easy to him as possible, hoping at the same time that he had not brought with him the same unfortunate instructions his predecessor had been hampered with. On this he did not then explain himself. But when he afterwards came to do business with the Assembly, they appeared again; the disputes were renewed; and I was as active as ever in the opposition, being the penman first of the request to have a communication of the instructions and then of the remarks upon them, which may be found in the votes of the time and in the historical review I afterwards published. But between us personally no enmity arose; we were often together; he was a man of letters, had seen much of the world, and was very entertaining and pleasing in conversation. He gave me the first information that my old friend Jas. Ralph was still alive, that he was esteemed one of the best political writers in England, had been employed in the dispute between Prince Frederick and the King, and had obtained a pension of three hundred a year; that his reputation was indeed small as a poet, Pope having damned his poetry in the *Dunciad,* but his prose was thought as good as any man's.

The Assembly finally, finding the Proprietaries obstinately persisted in manacling their deputies with instructions inconsistent not only with the privileges of the people but with the service of the Crown, resolved to petition the King against them, and appointed me their agent to go over to England to present and support the petition. The House had sent up a bill to the Governor granting a sum of £60,000 for the King's use (£10,000 of which was subjected to the orders of the then General, Lord Loudon), which the Governor absolutely refused to pass in compliance with his instructions. I had agreed with Captain Morris of the packet at New York for my passage, and my stores were put on board, when Lord Loudon arrived at Philadelphia, expressly, as he told me, to endeavour an accommodation between the Governor and Assembly, that His Majesty's service might not be obstructed by their dissensions. Accordingly, he desired the Governor and myself to meet him, that he might hear what was to be said on both sides. We met and discussed the business. In behalf of the Assembly I urged all the arguments that may be found in the public papers of that time, which were of my writing and are printed with the minutes of the Assembly; and the Governor pleaded his instructions, the bond he had given to observe them, and his ruin if he disobeyed, yet seemed not unwilling to hazard himself if Lord Loudon would advise it. This His Lordship did not choose to do, tho' I once thought I had nearly prevailed with him to do it; but finally he rather chose to urge the compliance of the Assembly; and he entreated me to use my endeavours with them for that purpose, declaring he could spare none of the King's troops for the defence of our frontiers, and that if we did not continue to provide for that defence ourselves, they must remain exposed to the enemy. I acquainted the House with what had passed; and presenting them with a set of resolutions I had drawn up, declaring our rights and that we did not relinquish our claim to those rights but only suspended the exercise of them on this occasion thro' *force,* against which we protested; they at length agreed to drop that bill and frame another conformable to the proprietary instructions. This of course the Governor passed, and I was then at liberty to proceed on my voyage. But in the meantime the packet had sailed with my sea stores, which was some loss to me, and my only recompense was His Lordship's thanks for my service, all the credit of obtaining the accommodation falling to his share.

He set out for New York before me; and as the time for dispatching the packet boats was in his disposition and there were two then remaining there, one of which he said was to sail very soon, I requested to know the precise time that I might not miss her by any delay of mine. His answer was, "I have given out that she is to sail on Saturday next, but I may let you know, *entre nous,* that if you are there by Monday morning you will be in time, but do not delay longer." By some accidental hindrance at a ferry, it was Monday noon before I arrived, and I was much afraid she might have sailed as the wind was fair, but I was soon made easy by the information that she was still in the harbour and would not move till the next day.

One would imagine that I was now on the very point of departing for Europe. I thought so; but I was not then so well acquainted with His Lordship's character, of which *indecision* was one of the strongest features. I shall give some instances. It was about the beginning of April that I came to New York, and I think it was near the end of June before we sailed. There were then two of the packet boats which had been long in port but were detained for the General's letters, which were always to be ready tomorrow. Another packet arrived, and she too was detained, and before we sailed a fourth was expected. Ours was the first to be dispatched, as having been there longest. Passengers were engaged in all, and some extremely impatient to be gone, and the merchants uneasy about their letters, and the orders they had given for insurance (it being wartime), and for fall goods. But their anxiety availed nothing; His Lordship's letters were not ready. And yet whoever waited on him found him always at his desk, pen in hand, and concluded he must needs write abundantly. Going myself one morning to pay my respects, I found in his antichamber one Innis, a messenger of Philadelphia, who had come from thence express with a packet from Governor Denny for the General. He delivered to me some letters from my friends there, which occasioned my enquiring when he was to return and where he lodged, that I might send some letters by him. He told me he was ordered to call tomorrow at nine for the General's answer to the Governor and should set off immediately. I put my letters into his hands the same day. A fortnight after I met him again in the same place.

"So you are soon returned, Innis!"

"Returned! No, I am not gone yet."

"How so?"

"I have called here by order every morning these two weeks past for His Lordship's letter, and it is not yet ready."

"Is it possible, when he is so great a writer, for I see him constantly at his scritoire."

"Yes," says Innis, "but he is like St. George on the signs, *always on horseback, and never rides on.*"

This observation of the messenger was, it seems, well founded; for when in England, I understood that Mr. Pitt give it as one reason for removing this General and sending Amherst and Wolf, that "the ministers never heard from him, and could not know what he was doing."

This daily expectation of sailing, and all the three packets going down to Sandy Hook to join the fleet there, the passengers thought it best to be on board, lest by a sudden order the ships should sail and they be left behind. There, if I remember right, we were about six weeks, consuming our sea stores and obliged to procure more. At length the fleet sailed, the General and all his army on board, bound to Louisburg with intent to besiege and take that fortress; all the packet boats in company, ordered to attend the General's ship, ready to receive his dispatches when they should be ready. We were out five days before we got a letter with leave to part, and then our ship quitted the fleet and steered for England. The other two packets he still detained, carried them with him to Halifax, where he stayed some time to exercise the men in sham attacks upon sham forts, then altered his mind as to besieging Louisburg and returned to New York with all his troops, together with the two packets above-mentioned and all their passengers. During his absence the French and savages had taken Fort George on the frontier of that province, and the savages had massacred many of the garrison after capitulation. I saw afterwards in London Capt. Bonnell, who commanded one of those packets. He told me that when he had been detained a month, he acquainted His Lordship that his ship was grown foul to a degree that must necessarily hinder her fast sailing—a point of consequence for a packet boat—and requested an allowance of time to heave her down and clean her bottom. He was asked how long time that would require. He answered three days. The General replied, "If you can do it in one day, I give leave; otherwise not, for you must certainly sail the day after tomorrow." So he never obtained leave, tho' detained afterwards from day to day during full three months. I saw also in London one of Bonnell's passengers who was so enraged against His Lordship for deceiving and detaining him so long at New York and then carrying him to Halifax and back again, that he swore he would sue him for damages. Whether he did or not, I never heard; but as he represented the injury to his affairs, it was very considerable. On the whole I then wondered much how such a man came to be entrusted with so important a business as the conduct of a great army; but having since seen more of the great world, and the means of obtaining and motives for giving places, my wonder is diminished. General Shirley, on whom the command of the army devolved upon the death of Braddock, would in my opinion, if continued in place, have made a much better campaign than that of Loudon in 1757, which was frivolous, expensive, and disgraceful to our nation beyond conception. For tho' Shirley was not a bred soldier, he was sensible and sagacious in himself, and attentive to good advice from others, capable of forming judicious plans, and quick and active in carrying them into execution. Loudon, instead of defending the Colonies with his great army, left them totally exposed while he paraded it idly at Halifax, by which means Fort George was lost; besides he deranged all our mercantile operations and distressed our trade by a long embargo on the exportation of provisions, on pretence of keeping supplies from being obtained by the enemy, but in reality for beating down their price in favour of the contractors, in whose profits, it was said—perhaps from suspicion only—he had a share. And when at length the embargo was taken off, by neglecting to send notice of it to Charlestown, the Carolina fleet was detained near three months longer, whereby their bottoms were so much damaged by the worm that a great part of them foundered in the passage home. Shirley was, I believe, sincerely glad of being relieved from so burthensome a charge as the conduct of an army must be to a man unacquainted with military business. I was at the entertainment given by the City of New York, to Lord Loudon on his taking upon him the command. Shirley, tho' thereby superseded, was present also. There was a great company of officers, citizens, and strangers, and some chairs having been borrowed in the neighbourhood, there was one among them very low which fell to the lot of Mr. Shirley. Perceiving it as I sat by him, I said, "They have given you, sir, too low a seat." "No matter," says he, "Mr. Franklin, I find *a low seat the easiest!*"

While I was, as aforementioned, detained at New York, I received all the accounts of the provisions, etc., that I had furnished to Braddock, some of which accounts could not sooner be obtained from the different persons I had employed to assist in the business. I presented them to Lord Loudon, desiring to be paid the balance. He caused them to be regularly examined by the proper officer, who, after comparing every article with its voucher, certified them to be right and the balance due, for which His Lordship promised to give me an order on the paymaster. This, however, was put off from time to time, and tho' I called often for it by appointment, I did not get it. At length, just before my departure, he told me he had on better consideration concluded not to mix his accounts with those of his predecessors. "And you," says he, "when in England, have only to exhibit your accounts at the Treasury, and you will be paid immediately." I mentioned, but without effect, the great and unexpected expence I had been put to by being detained so long at New York, as a reason for my desiring to be presently paid; and on my observing that it was not right I should be put to any further trouble or delay in obtaining the money I had advanced, as I charged no commissions for my service, "O, sir," says he, "you must not think of persuading us that you are no gainer. We understand better those affairs and know that everyone concerned in supplying the army finds means in the doing it to fill his own pockets." I assured him that was not my case and that I had not pocketed a farthing. But he appeared clearly not to believe me, and indeed I have since learned that immense fortunes are often made in such employments. As to my balance, I am not paid it to this day, of which more hereafter.

Our captain of the packet had boasted much before we sailed of the swiftness of his ship. Unfortunately, when we came to sea, she proved the dullest of ninety-six sail, to his no small mortification. After many conjectures respecting the cause, when we were near another ship almost as dull as ours (which, however, gained upon us), the captain ordered all hands to come aft and stand as near the ensign staff as possible. We were, passengers included, about forty persons. While we stood there, the ship mended her pace and soon left her neighbour far behind, which proved clearly what our captain suspected, that she was loaded too much by the head. The casks of water, it seems, had been all placed forward. These he therefore ordered to be removed farther aft, on which the ship recovered her character and proved the best sailer in the fleet. The captain said she had once gone at the rate of thirteen knots, which is accounted thirteen miles per hour. We had on board as a passenger Captain Kennedy of the Royal Navy, who contended that it was impossible, that no ship ever sailed so fast, and that there must have been some error in the division of the log line or some mistake in heaving the log. A wager ensued between the two captains, to be decided when there should be sufficient wind. Kennedy thereupon examined rigorously the log line, and being satisfied with that, he determined to throw the log himself. Accordingly, some days after when the wind blew very fair and fresh and the captain of the packet (*Lutwidge*) said he believed she then went at the rate of thirteen knots, Kennedy made the experiment and owned his wager lost. The above fact I give for the sake of the following observation. It has been remarked as an imperfection in the art of shipbuilding that it can never be known 'till she is tried whether a new ship will or will not be a good sailer, for that the model of a good sailing ship has been exactly followed in a new one, which has proved, on the contrary, remarkably dull. I apprehend this may be partly occasioned by the different opinions of seamen respecting the modes of lading, rigging, and sailing of a ship. Each has his system. And the same vessel laden by the judgment and orders of one captain shall sail better or worse than when by the orders of another. Besides, it scarce ever happens that a ship is formed, fitted for the sea, and sailed by the same person. One man builds the hull, another rigs her, a third lades and sails her. No one of these has the advantage of knowing all the ideas and experience of the others, and therefore cannot draw just conclusions from a combination of the whole. Even in the simple operation of sailing when at sea, I have often observed different judgments in the officers who commanded the successive watches, the wind being the same. One would have the sails trimmed sharper or flatter than another, so that they seemed to have no certain rule to govern by. Yet I think a set of experiments might be instituted: first, to determine the most proper form of the hull for swift sailing; next, the best dimensions and properest place for the masts; then, the form and quantity of sails, and their position as the winds may be; and lastly, the disposition of the lading. This is the age of experiments, and such a set accurately made and combined would be of great use. I am therefore persuaded that ere long some ingenious philosopher will undertake it—to whom I wish success.

We were several times chased in our passage, but outsailed everything and in thirty days had soundings. We had a good observation, and the captain judged himself so near our port (Falmouth) that if we made a good run in the night, we might be off the mouth of the harbour in the morning, and by running in the night might escape the notice of the enemy's privateers, who often cruised near the entrance of the Channel. Accordingly, all the sail was set that we could possibly make, and the wind being very fresh and fair, we went right before it and made great way. The captain after his observation, shaped his course—as he thought—so as to pass wide of the Scilly Isles; but it seems there is sometimes a strong indraught setting up St. George's Channel which deceives seamen and caused the loss of Sir Cloudsley Shovel's squadron. This indraught was probably the cause of what happened to us. We had a watchman placed in the bow to whom they often called, "Look well out before, there"; and he as often answered, "Aye, aye!" But perhaps had his eyes shut and was half asleep at the time, they sometimes answering, as is said, mechanically. For he did not see a light just before us which had been hid by the studding sails from the man at helm and from the rest of the watch, but by an accidental yaw of the ship was discovered and occasioned a great alarm—we being very near it, the light appearing to me as big as a cart wheel. It was midnight, and our captain fast asleep. But Capt. Kennedy jumping upon deck and seeing the danger, ordered the ship to wear round, all sails standing—an operation dangerous to the masts, but it carried us clear, and we escaped shipwreck, for we were running right upon the rocks on which the lighthouse was erected. This deliverance impressed me strongly with the utility of lighthouses and made me resolve to encourage the building more of them in America, if I should live to return there.

In the morning it was found by the soundings, etc., that we were near our port, but a thick fog hid the land from our sight. About nine o'clock the fog began to rise and seemed to be lifted up from the water like the curtain at a playhouse, discovering underneath the town of Falmouth, the vessels in its harbour, and the fields that surrounded it. A most pleasing spectacle to those who had been so long without any other prospects than the uniform view of a vacant ocean! And it gave us the more pleasure, as we were now freed from the anxieties which the state of war occasioned.

I set out immediately with my son for London, and we only stopped a little by the way to view Stonehenge on Salisbury Plain, and Lord Pembroke's house and gardens, with his very curious antiquities, at Wilton.

We arrived in London the 27th of July, 1757. As soon as I was settled in a lodging Mr. Charles had provided for me, I went to visit Dr. Fothergill, to whom I was strongly recommended and whose counsel respecting my proceedings I was advised to obtain. He was against an immediate complaint to government and thought the Proprietaries should first be personally applied to, who might possibly be induced by the interposition and persuasion of some private friends to accommodate matters amicably. I then waited on my old friend and correspondent, Mr. Peter Collinson, who told me that John Hanbury, the great Virginia merchant, had requested to be informed when I should arrive that he might carry me to Lord Granville's, who was then President of the Council, and wished to see me as soon as possible. I agreed to go with him the next morning. Accordingly, Mr. Hanbury called for me and took me in his carriage to that nobleman's, who received me with great civility; and after some questions respecting the present state of affairs in America, and discourse thereupon, he said to me, "You Americans have wrong ideas of the nature of your constitution; you contend that the King's instructions to his governors are not laws and think yourselves at liberty to regard or disregard them at your own discretion. But those instructions are not like the pocket instructions given to a minister going abroad for regulating his conduct in some trifling point of ceremony. They are first drawn up by judges learned in the laws; they are then considered, debated, and perhaps amended in Council, after which they are signed by the King. They are then so far as relates to you, the *law of the land;* for THE KING IS THE LEGISLATOR OF THE COLONIES." I told His Lordship this was new doctrine to me. I had always understood from our charters that our laws were to be made by our Assemblies, to be presented, indeed, to the King for his royal assent, but that being once given, the King could not repeal or alter them. And as the Assemblies could not make permanent laws without his assent, so neither could he make a law for them without theirs. He assured me I was totally mistaken. I did not think so, however. And His Lordship's conversation having a little alarmed me as to what might be the sentiments of the court concerning us, I wrote it down as soon as I returned to my lodgings. I recollected that about twenty years before a clause in a bill brought into Parliament by the ministry had proposed to make the King's instructions laws in the Colonies; but the clause was thrown out by the Commons, for which we adored them as our friends and friends of liberty, till by their conduct towards us in 1765, it seemed that they had refused that point of sovereignty to the King only that they might reserve it for themselves.

After some days, Dr. Fothergill having spoken to the Proprietaries, they agreed to a meeting with me at Mr. T. Penn's house in Spring Garden. The conversation at first consisted of mutual declarations of disposition to reasonable accommodation, but I suppose each party had its own ideas of what should be meant by *reasonable*. We then went into consideration of our several points of complaint which I enumerated. The Proprietaries justified their conduct as well as they could, and I the Assembly's. We now appeared very wide, and so far from each other in our opinions as to discourage all hope of agreement. However, it was concluded that I should give them the heads of our complaints in writing, and they promised then to consider them. I did so soon after; but they put the paper into the hands of their solicitor, Ferdinando John Paris, who managed for them all their law business in their great suit with the neighbouring Proprietary of Maryland, Lord Baltimore, which had subsisted seventy years, and wrote for them all their papers and messages in their dispute with the Assembly. He was a proud, angry man; and as I had occasionally in the answers of the Assembly treated his papers with some severity, they being really weak in point of argument, and haughty in expression, he had conceived a mortal enmity to me, which discovering itself whenever we met, I declined the Proprietary's proposal that he and I should discuss the heads of complaint between our two selves and refused treating with any one but them. They then by his advice put the paper into the hands of the Attorney- and Solicitor-General for their opinion and counsel upon it, where it lay unanswered a year wanting eight days, during which time I made frequent demands of an answer from the Proprietaries but without obtaining any other than that they had not yet received the opinion of the Attorney- and Solicitor-General. What it was when they did receive it, I never learned, for they did not communicate it to me, but sent a long message to the Assembly drawn and signed by Paris reciting my paper, complaining of its want of formality as a rudeness on my part, and giving a flimsy justification of their conduct, adding that they should be willing to accommodate matters if the Assembly would send over "some person of candour" to treat with them for that purpose, intimating thereby that I was not such.

The want of formality or rudeness was probably my not having addressed the paper to them with their assumed titles of true and absolute Proprietaries of the Province of Pennsylvania, which I omitted as not thinking it necessary in a paper, the intention of which was only to reduce to a certainty by writing what in conversation I had delivered *viva voce*. But during this delay, the Assembly having prevailed with Governor Denny to pass an act taxing the proprietary estate in common with the estates of the people, which was the grand point in dispute, they omitted answering the message.

When this act, however, came over, the Proprietaries counselled by Paris determined to oppose its receiving the royal assent. Accordingly, they petitioned the King in Council, and a hearing was appointed, in which two lawyers were employed by them against the act and two by me in support of it. They alleged that the act was intended to load the proprietary estate in order to spare those of the people, and that if it were suffered to continue in force and the Proprietaries, who were in odium with the people, left to their mercy in proportioning the taxes, they would inevitably be ruined. We replied that the act had no such intention and would have no such effect, that the assessors were honest and discreet men, under an oath to assess fairly and equitably, and that any advantage each of them might expect in lessening his own tax by augmenting that of the Proprietaries was too trifling to induce them to perjure themselves. This is the purport of what I remember as urged by both sides, except that we insisted strongly on the mischievous consequences that must attend a repeal; for that the money (£100,000) being printed and given to the King's use, expended in his service, and now spread among the people, the repeal would strike it dead in their hands to the ruin of many and the total discouragement of future grants; and the selfishness of the Proprietors in soliciting such a general catastrophe, merely from a groundless fear of their estate being taxed too highly, was insisted on in the stronger terms. On this Lord Mansfield, one of the Council, rose, and beckoning to me, took me into the clerks' chamber, while the lawyers were pleading, and asked me if I was really of opinion that no injury would be done the proprietary estate in the execution of the act. I said, "Certainly." "Then," says he, "you can have little objection to enter into an engagement to assure that point." I answered, "None at all." He then called in Paris, and after some discourse His Lordship's proposition was accepted on both sides; a paper to the purpose was drawn up by the clerk of the Council, which I signed with Mr. Charles, who was also an agent of the province for their ordinary affairs, when Lord Mansfield returned to the council chamber, where finally the law was allowed to pass. Some changes were, however, recommended, and we also engaged they should be made by a subsequent law; but the Assembly did not think them necessary. For one year's tax having been levied by the act before the order of Council arrived, they appointed a committee to examine the proceedings of the assessors, and on this committee they put several particular friends of the Proprietaries. After a full enquiry they unanimously signed a report that they found the tax had been assessed with perfect equity. The Assembly looked on my entering into the first part of the engagement as an essential service to the province, since it secured the credit of the paper money then spread over all the country; and they gave me their thanks in form when I returned. But the Proprietaries were enraged at Governor

Denny for having passed the act and turned him out, with threats of suing him for breach of instructions which he had given bond to observe. He, however, having done it at the instance of the General and for His Majesty's service, and having some powerful interest at court, despised the threats, and they were never put in execution.

PART TWO

Selected Writings

I

THE WAY TO WEALTH

For many people, "Poor Richard" is the first association which comes to mind in connection with Benjamin Franklin. While Franklin was merely the "ghost writer" for Richard Saunders—they are too often seen as indistinguishable—he did believe in the usefulness of Poor Richard's advice. When he was away and could not advise his daughter, Sally, directly, he instructed her to "Study Poor Richard a little. . . ."

In Richard Saunders's Almanack, *and in Franklin's other writings, readers found ample suggestions for achieving the good life. Would the reader be healthy, wealthy, and wise? Franklin would show him how. Health, wealth, and wisdom—still, today, a fair definition of the good life—needed no redefinition to the society of the eighteenth century. People were interested in the means of achieving these ideals, and Franklin furnished the answers.*

In this, the first of six chapters, we see one of Franklin's many sides; here is the well-known public figure of prudent advice and helpful maxims. His writings in this area brought success to Franklin, and to others, success which often brought leisure for productive and socially useful activity.

Plan for Future Conduct

Franklin kept a journal on his return voyage from En-gland in 1726. "Perhaps the most important Part of that Journal," he wrote in his Memoirs, *was the plan for regulating his future conduct.*

[1726]

Those who write of the art of poetry teach us that if we would write what may be worth the reading, we ought always, before we begin, to form a regular plan and de-sign of our piece: otherwise, we shall be in danger of incongruity. I am apt to think it is the same as to life. I have never fixed a regular design in life; by which means its has been a confused variety of different scenes. I am now entering upon a new one: let me, therefore, make some resolutions, and form some scheme of action, that, henceforth, I may live in all respects like a rational crea-ture.

1. It is necessary for me to be extremely frugal for some time, till I have paid what I owe.

2. To endeavour to speak truth in every instance; to give nobody expectations that are not likely to be an-swered, but aim at sincerity in every word and action—the most amiable excellence in a rational being.

3. To apply myself industriously to whatever business I take in hand, and not divert my mind from my business by any foolish project of growing suddenly rich; for in-dustry and patience are the surest means of plenty.

4. I resolve to speak ill of no man whatever, not even in a matter of truth; but rather by some means excuse the faults I hear charged upon others, and upon proper oc-casions speak all the good I know of every body.

[1]*

*Numbered references refer to the notes on sources, pp. 337–339.

Advice to a Young Girl

On his twenty-first birthday Franklin wrote, in the role of a big brother, to his fourteen-year-old sister. Their correspondence would continue for sixty-three years, Franklin writing more letters to her than to any other one person.

TO JANE FRANKLIN

January 6, 1727

Dear Sister,

I am highly pleased with the account captain Freeman gives me of you. I always judged by your behaviour when a child that you would make a good, agreeable woman, and you know you were ever my peculiar favorite. I have been thinking what would be a suitable present for me to make, and for you to receive, as I hear you are grown a celebrated beauty. I had almost determined on a tea table, but when I considered that the character of a good housewife was far preferable to that of being only a pretty gentlewoman, I concluded to send you a *spinning wheel,* which I hope you will accept as a small token of my sincere love and affection.

Sister, farewell, and remember that modesty, as it makes the most homely virgin amiable and charming, so the want of it infallibly renders the most perfect beauty disagreeable and odious. But when the brightest of female virtues shines among other perfections of body and mind in the same person, it makes the woman more lovely than an angel. Excuse this freedom, and use the same with me. I am, dear Jenny, your loving brother,

B. Franklin

[2]

The Art of Conversation

Before the first Poor Richard's Almanack appeared late in 1732, the Pennsylvania Gazette was Franklin's public voice. In its columns he published essays advising his readers "On Conversation" and "On Ill Natured Speaking." Such advice, boiled down to pithy maxims, would later fill the Almanack. Franklin's thought on the art of conversation is succinctly stated in a passage in his Commonplace Book.

[1732]

The great Secret of succeeding in Conversation, is, To admire little, to hear much: allways to distrust our own Reason, and sometimes that of our Friends; never to pretend to Wit, but to make that of others appear as much as possibly we can: to hearken to what is said, and to answer to the purpose. . . . **[3]**

Advice to a Young Tradesman

In 1748 Franklin published an American edition of The Instructor; or Young Man's Best Companion, an English manual containing diverse information for the young tradesman. In adapting The Instructor to the American environment Franklin omitted some items and added others, including the following:

TO MY FRIEND, A.B.

July 21, 1748

As you have desired it of me, I write the following Hints, which have been of Service to me, and may, if observed, be so to you.

Remember that TIME is Money. He that can earn Ten Shillings a Day by his Labour, and goes abroad, or sits idle one half of that Day, tho' he spends but Sixpence during his Diversion or Idleness, ought not to reckon That the only Expence; he has really spent or rather thrown away Five Shillings besides.

Remember that CREDIT is Money. If a Man lets his Money lie in my Hands after it is due, he gives me the Interest, or so much as I can make of it during that Time. This amounts to a considerable Sum where a Man has good and large Credit, and makes good Use of it.

Remember that Money is of a prolific generating Nature. Money can beget Money, and its Offspring can beget more, and so on. Five Shillings turn'd, is *Six:* Turn'd again, 'tis Seven and Three Pence; and so on 'til it becomes an Hundred Pound. The more there is of it, the more it produces every Turning, so that the Profits rise quicker and quicker. He that kills a breeding Sow, destroys all her Offspring to the thousandth Generation. He that murders a Crown, destroys all it might have produc'd, even Scores of Pounds.

Remember that Six Pounds a Year is but a Groat a Day. For this little Sum (which may be daily wasted either in Time or Expence unperceiv'd) a Man of Credit may on his own Security have the constant Possession and Use of an Hundred Pounds. So much in Stock briskly turn'd by an industrious Man, produces great Advantage.

Remember this Saying, *That the good Paymaster is Lord of another Man's Purse.* He that is known to pay punctually and exactly to the Time he promises, may at any Time, and on any Occasion, raise all the Money his Friends can spare. This is sometimes of great Use: Therefore never keep borrow'd Money an Hour beyond the Time you promis'd, lest a Disappointment shuts up your Friends Purse forever.

The most trifling Actions that affect a Man's Credit, are to be regarded. The Sound of your Hammer at Five in the Morning or Nine at Night, heard by a Creditor, makes him easy Six Months longer. But if he sees you at a Billiard Table, or hears your Voice in a Tavern, when you should be at Work, he sends for his Money the next Day. Finer Cloaths than he or his Wife wears, or greater

Expence in any particular than he affords himself, shocks his Pride, and he duns you to humble you. Creditors are a kind of People, that have the sharpest Eyes and Ears, as well as the best Memories of any in the World.

Good-natur'd Creditors (and such one would always chuse to deal with if one could) feel Pain when they are oblig'd to ask for Money. Spare 'em that Pain, and they will love you. When you receive a Sum of Money, divide it among 'em in Proportion to your Debts. Don't be asham'd of paying a small Sum because you owe a greater. Money, more or less, is always welcome; and your Creditor had rather be at the Trouble of receiving Ten Pounds voluntarily brought him, tho' at ten different Times of Payments, than be oblig'd to go ten Times to demand it before he can receive it in a Lump. It shews, besides, that you are mindful of what you owe; it makes you appear a careful as well as an honest Man; and that still encreases your Credit.

Beware of thinking all your own that you possess, and of living accordingly. 'Tis a Mistake that many People who have Credit fall into. To prevent this, keep an exact Account for some Time of both your Expences and your Incomes. If you take the Pains at first to mention Particulars, it will have this good Effect; you will discover how wonderfully small trifling Expences mount up to large Sums, and will discern what might have been, and may for the future be saved, without occasioning any great Inconvenience.

In short, the Way to Wealth, if you desire it, is as plain as the Way to Market. It depends chiefly on two Words, INDUSTRY and FRUGALITY: i.e. Waste neither Time nor Money, but make the best Use of both. He that gets all he can honestly, and saves all he gets (necessary Expences excepted) will certainly become RICH: If that Being who governs the World, to whom all should look for a Blessing on their honest Endeavors, doth not in his wise Providence otherwise determine.

[4]

"The Way to Wealth"

One of Franklin's better-known pieces, "The Way to Wealth," properly closes this section as it marks the conclusion of his career as rising tradesman and the beginning of his career as diplomat. Sailing to London in the summer of 1757, he used his leisure for a retrospective look over twenty-five years of Poor Richard's advice. He took some of the better maxims, trimmed and polished them, and strung them together in one continuous narrative which he published as an extended preface to the Almanack *for 1758. Reprinted in hundreds of editions under diverse auspices and translated into French, German, Italian, and more than a half-dozen other languages (including Russian and Chinese), "The Way to Wealth" epitomizes the American popular image of Franklin and, to a large extent, the non-American image of America.*

July 7, 1757

COURTEOUS READER,

I have heard that nothing gives an Author so great Pleasure, as to find his Works respectfully quoted by other learned Authors. This Pleasure I have seldom enjoyed; for tho' I have been, if I may say it without Vanity, an *eminent Author* of Almanacks annually now a full Quarter of a Century, my Brother Authors in the same Way, for what Reason I know not, have ever been very sparing in their Applauses; and no other Author has taken the least Notice of me, so that did not my Writings produce me some solid *Pudding,* the great Deficiency of *Praise* would have quite discouraged me.

I concluded at length, that the People were the best Judges of my Merit; for they buy my Works; and besides, in my Rambles, where I am not personally known, I have frequently heard one or other of my Adages repeated, with, *as Poor Richard says,* at the End on't; this gave me some Satisfaction, as it showed not only that my Instructions were regarded, but discovered likewise some Respect for my Authority; and I own, that to encourage the Practice of remembering and repeating those wise Sentences, I have sometimes *quoted myself* with great Gravity.

Judge then how much I must have been gratified by an Incident I am going to relate to you. I stopt my Horse lately where a great Number of People were collected at a Vendue of Merchant Goods. The Hour of Sale not being come, they were conversing on the Badness of the Times, and one of the Company call'd to a plain clean old Man, with white Locks, *Pray, Father* Abraham, *what think you of the Times? Won't these heavy Taxes quite ruin the Country? How shall we ever be able to pay them? What would you advise us to?*——Father *Abraham* stood up, and reply'd, If you'd have my Advice, I'll give it you in short, for a *Word to the Wise is enough,* and *many Words won't fill a Bushel,* as *Poor Richard* says. They join'd in desiring him to speak his Mind, and gathering round him, he proceeded as follows:

Friends, says he, and Neighbours, the Taxes are indeed very heavy, and if those laid on by the Government were the only Ones we had to pay, we might more easily discharge them; but we have many others, and much more grievous to some of us. We are taxed twice as much by our *Idleness,* three times as much by our *Pride,* and four times as much by our *Folly,* and from these Taxes the Commissioners cannot ease or deliver us by allowing an Abatement. However let us hearken to good Advice, and something may be done for us; *God helps them that help themselves,* as *Poor Richard* says, in his Almanack of 1733.

It would be thought a hard Government that should tax its People one tenth Part of their *Time,* to be employed in its Service. But *Idleness* taxes many of us much more, if we reckon all that is spent in absolute *Sloth,* or doing of nothing, with that which is spent in idle Employments or Amusements, that amount to nothing. *Sloth,* by bringing on Diseases, absolutely shortens Life. *Sloth, like Rust, consumes faster than Labour wears, while the used Key is always bright,* as *Poor Richard* says. But *dost thou love Life, then do not squander Time, for that's the Stuff Life is made of,* as *Poor Richard* says.—How much more than is necessary do we spend in Sleep! forgetting that *The sleeping Fox catches no Poultry,* and that *there will be sleeping enough in the Grave,* as *Poor Richard* says. If Time be of all Things the most precious, *wasting Time* must be, as *Poor Richard* says, *the greatest Prodigality,* since, as he elsewhere tells us, *Lost Time is never found again;* and what we call *Time-enough, always proves little enough;* Let us then up and be doing, and doing to the Purpose; so by Diligence shall we do more with less Perplexity. *Sloth makes all Things difficult, but Industry all easy,* as *Poor Richard* says; and *He that riseth late, must trot all Day, and shall scarce overtake his Business at Night.* While *Laziness travels so slowly, that Poverty soon overtakes him,* as we read in *Poor Richard,* who adds, *Drive thy Business, let not that drive thee;* and *Early to Bed, and early to rise, makes a Man healthy, wealthy and wise.*

So what signifies *wishing* and *hoping* for better Times. We may make these Times better if we bestir ourselves. *Industry need not wish,* as *Poor Richard* says, and *He that lives upon Hope will die fasting. There are no Gains, without Pains;* then *Help Hands, for I have no Lands,* or if I have, they are smartly taxed. And, as *Poor Richard* likewise observes, *He that hath a Trade hath an Estate,* and *He that hath a Calling, hath an Office of Profit and Honour;* but then the *Trade* must be worked at, and the *Calling* well followed, or neither the *Estate,* nor the *Office,* will enable us to pay our Taxes.—If we are industrious we shall never starve; for, as *Poor Richard* says, *At the working Man's House* Hunger *looks in, but dares not enter.* Nor will the Bailiff or the Constable enter, for *Industry pays Debts, while Despair encreaseth them,* says *Poor Richard.*—What though you have found no Treasure, nor has any rich Relation left you a Legacy, *Diligence is the Mother of Good luck,* as *Poor Richard* says, and *God gives all Things to Industry.* Then *plough deep, while Sluggards sleep, and you shall have Corn to sell and to keep,* says *Poor Dick.* Work while it is called To-day, for you know not how much you may be hindered To-morrow, which makes *Poor Richard* say, *One To-day is worth two To-morrows;* and farther, *Have you somewhat to do To-morrow, do it To-day.* If you were a Servant, would you not be ashamed that a good Master should catch you idle? Are you then your own Master, *be ashamed to catch yourself idle,* as *Poor Dick* says. When there is so much to be done for yourself, your Family, your Country, and your gracious King, be up by Peep of Day; *Let not the Sun look down and say, Inglorious here he lies.* Handle your Tools without Mittens; remember that *the Cat in Gloves catches no Mice,* as *Poor Richard* says. 'Tis true there is much to be done, and perhaps you are weak handed, but stick to it steadily, and you will see great Effects, for *constant Dropping wears away Stones,* and by *Diligence and Patience the Mouse ate in two the Cable;* and *little Strokes fell great Oaks,* as *Poor Richard* says in his Almanack, the Year I cannot just now remember.

Methinks I hear some of you say, *Must a Man afford himself no Leisure?*—I will tell thee, my Friend, what *Poor Richard* says, *Employ thy Time well if thou meanest to gain Leisure;* and *since thou art not sure of a Minute, throw not away an Hour.* Leisure, is Time for doing something useful; this Leisure the diligent Man will obtain, but the lazy Man never; so that, as *Poor Richard* says, a *Life of Leisure and a Life of Laziness are two Things.* Do you imagine that Sloth will afford you more Comfort than Labour? No, for as *Poor Richard* says, *Trouble springs from Idleness, and grievous Toil from needless Ease. Many without Labour, would live by their* WITS *only, but they break for want of Stock.* Whereas Industry gives Comfort, and Plenty, and Respect: *Fly Pleasures, and they'll follow you. The diligent Spinner has a large Shift;* and *now I have a Sheep and a Cow, every Body bids me Good morrow;* all which is well said by *Poor Richard.*

But with our Industry, we must likewise be *steady, settled* and *careful,* and oversee our own Affairs *with our own Eyes,* and not trust too much to others; for, as *Poor Richard* says,

> *I never saw an oft removed Tree,*
> *Nor yet an oft removed Family,*
> *That throve so well as those that settled be.*

And again, *Three Removes is as bad as a Fire;* and again, *Keep thy Shop, and thy Shop will keep thee;* and again, *If you would have your Business done, go; If not, send.* And again,

> *He that by the Plough would thrive,*
> *Himself must either hold or drive.*

And again, *The Eye of a Master will do more Work than both his Hands;* and again, *Want of Care does us more Damage than Want of Knowledge;* and again, *Not to oversee Workmen, is to leave them your Purse open.* Trusting too much to others Care is the Ruin of many; for, as the *Almanack* says, *In the Affairs of this World, Men are saved, not by Faith, but by the Want of it;* but a Man's own Care is profitable; for, saith *Poor Dick, Learning is to the Studious,* and *Riches to the Careful,* as well as *Power to the Bold,* and *Heaven to the Virtuous.* And farther, *If you would have a faithful Servant, and one that you like, serve yourself.* And again, he adviseth to Circumspection and Care, even in the smallest Matters, because sometimes *a little Neglect may breed great Mischief;* adding, *For want of a Nail the Shoe was lost; for want of a Shoe the Horse was lost; and for want of a Horse the Rider was lost,* being overtaken and slain by the Enemy, all for want of Care about a Horse shoe Nail.

So much for Industry, my Friends, and Attention to one's own Business; but to these we must add *Frugality,* if we would make our *Industry* more certainly successful. A Man may, if he knows not how to save as he gets, *keep his Nose all his Life to the Grindstone,* and die not worth a *Groat* at last. *A fat Kitchen makes a lean Will,* as *Poor Richard* says; and,

> *Many Estates are spent in the Getting,*
> *Since Women for Tea forsook Spinning and Knitting,*
> *And Men for Punch forsook Hewing and Splitting.*

If you would be wealthy, says he, in another *Almanack, think of Saving as well as of Getting: The* Indies *have not made* Spain *rich, because her* Outgoes *are greater than her* Incomes. Away then with your expensive Follies, and you will not have so much Cause to complain of hard Times, heavy Taxes, and chargeable Families; for, as *Poor Dick* says,

> *Women and Wine, Game and Deceit,*
> *Make the Wealth small, and the Wants great.*

And farther, *What maintains one Vice, would bring up two Children.* You may think perhaps, That a *little* Tea, or a *little* Punch now and then, Diet a *little* more costly, Clothes a *little* finer, and a *little* Entertainment now and then, can be no *great* Matter; but remember what *Poor Richard* says, *Many* a Little *makes a Mickle;* and farther, *Beware of* little *Expences; a small Leak will sink a great Ship;* and again, *Who Dainties love, shall Beggars prove;* and moreover, *Fools make Feasts, and wise Men eat them.*

Here you are all got together at this Vendue of *Fineries* and *Knicknacks.* You call them *Goods,* but if you do not take Care, they will prove *Evils* to some of you. You expect they will be sold *cheap,* and perhaps they may for less than they cost; but if you have no Occasion for them, they must be *dear* to you. Remember what *Poor Richard* says, *Buy what thou hast no Need of, and ere long thou shalt sell thy Necessaries.* And again, *At a great Pennyworth pause a while:* He means, that perhaps the Cheapness is *apparent* only, and not *real;* or the Bargain, by straitning thee in thy Business, may do thee more Harm than Good. For in another Place he says, *Many have been ruined by buying good Pennyworths.* Again, *Poor Richard* says, *'Tis foolish to lay out Money in a Purchase of Repentance;* and yet this Folly is practised every Day at Vendues, for want of minding the *Almanack. Wise Men,* as *Poor Dick* says, *learn by others Harms, Fools scarcely by their own;* but *Felix quem faciunt aliena Pericula cautum.* Many a one, for the Sake of Finery on the Back, have gone with a hungry Belly, and half starved their Families; *Silks and Sattins, Scarlet and Velvets,* as *Poor Richard* says, *put out the Kitchen Fire.* These are not the *Necessaries* of Life; they can scarcely be called the *Conveniencies,* and yet only because they look pretty, how many *want to have* them. The *artificial* Wants of Mankind thus become more numerous than the *natural;* and, as *Poor Dick* says, *For one* poor *Person, there are an* hundred *indigent.* By these, and other Extravagancies, the Genteel are reduced to Poverty, and forced to borrow of those whom they formerly despised, but who through *Industry* and *Frugality* have maintained their Standing; in which Case it appears plainly, that a *Ploughman on his Legs is higher than a Gentleman on his Knees,* as *Poor Richard* says. Perhaps they have had a small Estate left them which they knew not the Getting of; they think *'tis Day, and will never be Night;* that a little to be spent out of *so much,* is not worth minding; (*a Child and a Fool,* as Poor Richard says, *imagine* Twenty Shillings *and* Twenty Years *can never be spent*) but, *always taking out of, the Meal-tub, and never putting in, soon comes to the Bottom;* then, as *Poor Dick* says, *When the Well's dry, they know the Worth of Water.* But this they might have known before, if they had taken his Advice; *If you would know the Value of Money, go and try to borrow some;* for, *he that goes a borrowing goes a sorrowing;* and indeed so does he that lends to such People, when he goes to get it in again.—*Poor Dick* farther advises, and says,

> *Fond* Pride of Dress *is sure a very Curse;*
> *E'er* Fancy *you consult, consult your Purse.*

And again, *Pride is as loud a Beggar as Want, and a great deal more saucy.* When you have bought one fine Thing you must buy ten more, that your Appearance may be all of a Piece; but *Poor Dick* says, *'Tis easier to sup-press the first Desire, than to* satisfy *all that follow it.* And 'tis as truly Folly for the Poor to ape the Rich, as for the Frog to swell, in order to equal the Ox.

> *Great Estates may venture more,*
> *But little Boats should keep near Shore.*

'Tis however a Folly soon punished; for *Pride that dines on Vanity sups on Contempt,* as *Poor Richard* says. And in another Place, *Pride breakfasted with Plenty, dined with Poverty, and supped with Infamy.* And after all, of what Use is this *Pride of Appearance,* for which so much is risked, so much is suffered? It cannot promote Health, or ease Pain; it makes no Increase of Merit in the Person, it creates Envy, it hastens Misfortune.

> *What is a Butterfly? At best*
> *He's but a Caterpillar drest.*
> *The gaudy Fop's his Picture just,*

as *Poor Richard* says.

But what Madness must it be to *run in Debt* for these Superfluities! We are offered, by the Terms of this Vendue, *Six Months Credit;* and that perhaps has induced some of us to attend it, because we cannot spare the ready Money, and hope now to be fine without it. But, ah, think what you do when you run in Debt; *You give to another, Power over your Liberty.* If you cannot pay at the Time, you will be ashamed to see your Creditor; you will be in Fear when you speak to him; you will make poor pitiful sneaking Excuses, and by Degrees come to lose your Veracity, and sink into base downright lying; for, as *Poor Richard* says, *The second Vice is Lying, the first is running in Debt.* And again, to the same Purpose, *Lying rides upon Debt's Back.* Whereas a freeborn *Englishman* ought not to be ashamed or afraid to see or speak to any Man living. But Poverty often deprives a Man of all Spirit and Virtue: *'Tis hard for an empty Bag to stand upright,* as *Poor Richard* truly says. What would you think of that Prince, or that Government, who should issue an Edict forbidding you to dress like a Gentleman or a Gentlewoman, on Pain of Imprisonment or Servitude? Would you not say, that you are free, have a Right to dress as you please, and that such an Edict would be a Breach of your Privileges, and such a Government tyrannical? And yet you are about to put yourself under that Tyranny when you run in Debt for such Dress! Your Creditor has Authority at his Pleasure to deprive you of your Liberty, by confining you in Goal [*sic*] for Life, or to sell you for a Servant, if you should not be able to pay him! When you have got your Bargain, you may, perhaps, think little of Payment; but *Creditors, Poor Richard* tells us, *have better Memories than Debtors;* and in another Place says, *Creditors are a superstitious Sect, great Ob-*

servers of set Days and Times. The Day comes round before you are aware, and the Demand is made before you are prepared to satisfy it. Or if you bear your Debt in Mind, the Term which at first seemed so long, will, as it lessens, appear extreamly short. *Time* will seem to have added Wings to his Heels as well as Shoulders. *Those have a short Lent,* saith *Poor Richard, who owe Money to be paid at Easter.* Then since, as he says, *The Borrower is a Slave to the Lender, and the Debtor to the Creditor,* disdain the Chain, preserve your Freedom; and maintain your Independency: Be *industrious* and *free;* be *frugal* and *free.* At present, perhaps, you may think yourself in thriving Circumstances, and that you can bear a little Extravangance [*sic*] without Injury; but,

> *For Age and Want, save while you may;*
> *No Morning Sun lasts a whole Day,*

as *Poor Richard* says—Gain may be temporary and uncertain, but ever while you live, Expence is constant and certain; and *'tis easier to build two Chimnies than to keep one in Fuel,* as Poor Richard says. *So rather go to Bed supperless than rise in Debt.*

> *Get what you can, and what you get hold;*
> *'Tis the Stone that will turn all your Lead into Gold,*

as *Poor Richard* says. And when you have got the Philosopher's Stone, sure you will no longer complain of bad Times, or the Difficulty of paying Taxes.

This Doctrine, my Friends, is *Reason* and *Wisdom;* but after all, do not depend too much upon your own *Industry,* and *Frugality,* and *Prudence,* though excellent Things, for they may all be blasted without the Blessing of Heaven; and therefore ask that Blessing humbly, and be not uncharitable to those that at present seem to want it, but comfort and help them. Remember *Job* suffered, and was afterwards prosperous.

And now to conclude, *Experience keeps a dear School, but Fools will learn in no other, and scarce in that;* for it is true, *we may give Advice, but we cannot give Conduct,* as *Poor Richard* says: However, remember this,

They that won't be counselled, can't be helped, as *Poor Richard* says: And farther, That *if you will not hear Reason, she'll surely rap your Knuckles.*

Thus the old Gentleman ended his Harangue. The People heard it, and approved the Doctrine and immediately practised the contrary, just as if it had been a common Sermon; for the Vendue opened, and they began to buy extravagantly, notwithstanding all his Cautions, and their own Fear of Taxes.—I found the good Man had thoroughly studied my Almanacks, and digested all I had dropt on those Topicks during the Course of Five-and-twenty Years. The frequent Mention he made of me must have tired any one else, but my Vanity was wonderfully delighted with it, though I was conscious that not a tenth Part of the Wisdom was my own which he ascribed to me, but rather the *Gleanings* I had made of the Sense of all Ages and Nations. However, I resolved to be the better for the Echo of it; and though I had at first determined to buy Stuff for a new Coat, I went away resolved to wear my old One a little longer. *Reader,* if thou wilt do the same, thy Profit will be as great as mine.

I am, as ever,

Thine to serve thee,

RICHARD SAUNDERS.

[5]

II

ESSAYS TO DO GOOD

"When I was a boy," wrote Benjamin Franklin to Cotton Mather's son, *"I met with a book, entitled* Essays to do Good, *which I think was written by your father. It had been so little regarded by a former possessor, that several leaves of it were torn out; but the remainder gave me such a turn of thinking, as to have an influence on my conduct through life; for I have always set a greater value on the character of a* doer of good, *than on any other kind of reputation; and if I have been, as you seem to*

think, a useful citizen, the public owes the advantage of it to that book.''

The beneficent persona—the image Franklin held of himself—counterbalanced the materialistic one: active beneficence was the obverse of the coin of active acquisitiveness. Doing good had its social uses, too, and the projects of Franklin's Philadelphia years are both ingredient and reflection of his own extraordinary social rise.

A primary instrument of that ascent was the Junto, an association of aggressive young "leather-apron men" not old enough or respected enough for membership in one of the town's gentlemen's clubs. Mather's "Young Men Associated" and Defoe's "Friendly-Societies" served as models, and Franklin perhaps also drew on early observations of the workings of the New England town meeting. The lesson of all three models was clear: men associated could do more to help society and, not incidentally, themselves, than could men isolated. The great individualist saw the uses of collectivism.

Standing Queries for the Junto

In the autumn of 1727 the Junto began its Friday evening meetings. Franklin's "standing Queries" illustrate the young tradesmen's interest both in getting ahead and in doing good, and the entanglement of the two goals.

1732

Previous question, to be answered at every meeting:

Have you read over these queries this morning, in order to consider what you might have to offer the Junto [touching] any one of them? viz.

1. Have you met with any thing in the author you last read, remarkable, or suitable to be communicated to the Junto? particularly in history, morality, poetry, physic, travels, mechanic arts, or other parts of knowledge.

2. What new story have you lately heard agreeable for telling in conversation?

3. Hath any citizen in your knowledge failed in his business lately, and what have you heard of the cause?

4. Have you lately heard of any citizen's thriving well, and by what means?

5. Have you lately heard how any present rich man, here or elsewhere, got his estate?

6. Do you know of any fellow citizen, who has lately done a worthy action, deserving praise and imitation? or who has committed an error proper for us to be warned against and avoid?

7. What unhappy effects of intemperance have you lately observed or heard? of imprudence? of passion? or of any other vice or folly?

8. What happy effects of temperance? of prudence? of moderation? or of any other virtue?

9. Have you or any of your acquaintances been lately sick or wounded? If so, what remedies were used, and what were their effects?

10. Whom do you know that are shortly going voyages or journies, if one should have occasion to send by them?

11. Do you think of any thing at present, in which the Junto may be serviceable to *mankind?* to their country, to their friends, or to themselves?

12. Hath any deserving stranger arrived in town since last meeting, that you heard of? and what have you heard or observed of his character or merits? and whether think you, it lies in the power of the Junto to oblige him, or encourage him as he deserves?

13. Do you know of any deserving young beginner lately set up, whom it lies in the power of the Junto any way to encourage?

14. Have you lately observed any defect in the laws of your *country*, [of] which it would be proper to move the legislature for an amendment? Or do you know of any beneficial law that is wanting?

15. Have you lately observed any encroachment on the just liberties of the people?

16. Hath any body attacked your reputation lately? And what can the Junto do towards securing it?

17. Is there any man whose friendship you want, and which the Junto or any of them, can procure for you?

18. Have you lately heard any member's character attacked, and how have you defended it?

19. Hath any man injured you, from whom it is in the power of the Junto to procure redress?

20. In what manner can the Junto, or any of them, assist you in any of your honourable designs?

21. Have you any weighty affairs in hand, in which you think the advice of the Junto may be of service?

22. What benefits have you lately received from any man not present?

23. Is there any difficulty in matters of opinion, of justice, and injustice, which you would gladly have discussed at this time?

24. Do you see any thing amiss in the present customs or proceedings of the Junto, which might be amended?

Any person to be qualified, to stand up, and lay his hand on his breast, and be asked these questions; viz.

1. Have you any particular disrespect to any present members? *Answer.* I have not.

2. Do you sincerely declare, that you love mankind in general; of what profession or religion soever? *Answer.* I do.

3. Do you think any person ought to be harmed in his body, name or goods, for mere speculative opinions, or his external way of worship? *Answer.* No.

4. Do you love truth for truth's sake, and will you endeavour impartially to find and receive it yourself, and communicate it to others? *Answer.* Yes.

[1]

"A Short Account of the Library"

The "Leather-Apron Club," as the Junto was called in its early days, furnished the personnel and organization for many of Franklin's later civic projects. The first of these projects, the establishment of a subscription library in Philadelphia, helped to raise the quasi-secret society to a position of respectability. Franklin wrote a brief history of the Library Company to fill a blank page in a catalogue which he printed ten years after the institution's founding.

[1741]

The Library-Company was form'd in 1731, by Constitutions or Articles entred into by 50 Persons, each obliging himself to pay 40 *s. per annum* to defray Charges and encrease the Library.

Ten Directors or Managers of the Library, and a Treasurer, are chosen yearly by Vote, at a General Meeting of the Company.

The Number of Members are now encreased to upwards of 70. Persons enclining to be admitted, apply to any one of the Directors, who nominates them at the next monthly Meeting of Directors; and being allowed, and paying to the Treasurer the Value of a Share at the Time, and signing the Articles, they become Members.

Any Member may borrow a Book for 2, 3, or 4 Weeks, leaving his Note for double Value, and paying a small Penalty if 'tis not return'd at the Time agreed; which Penalties are applied to defraying Charges, or purchasing more Books.

Every Member has an absolute Property in his Share; may devise it in his Will, or dispose of it when he pleases to any Person the Directors approve. And Shares so sold have always hitherto yielded as much as they had cost. As Shares encrease yearly in Value 10 *s.* so much being yearly added by each Subscriber to the Stock of Books, a Share which at first was worth but 40 *s.* is now valued at 6£. 10 *s.* But for this small Sum, which, laid out in Books, would go but a little Way, every Member has the Use of a Library now worth upwards of 500 £. whereby *Knowledge* is in this City render'd more cheap and easy to be come at, to the great Pleasure and Advantage of the studious Part of the Inhabitants.

Those who are not Subscribers may notwithstanding borrow Books, leaving in the Hands of the Librarian, as a Pledge, a Sum of Money proportion'd to the value of the Book borrow'd, and paying a small Acknowledgment for the Reading, which is apply'd to the Use of the Library.

The Library is open and Attendance given every Saturday Afternoon from 4 a clock 'til 8.

Besides the Books in this Catalogue given to the Library, the Company have been favour'd with several generous Donations; as, a curious Air-Pump, with its Apparatus, a large double Microscope, and other valuable Instruments, from the Hon. John Penn, Esq; a handsome Lot of Ground whereon to build a House for the Library, from the Hon. Thomas Penn, Esq; Proprietaries of the Province; and the Sum of 34 £ *Sterl.* (to be laid out in Books) from Dr. *Sydserfe,* late of *Antigua.*

At present the Books are deposited in the West Wing of the State-House, by Favour of the General Assembly.

It is now Ten Years since the Company was first established; and we have the Pleasure of observing, That tho' 'tis composed of so many Persons of different Sects, Parties and Ways of Thinking, yet no Differences relating to the Affairs of the Library, have arisen among us; but every Thing has been conducted with great Harmony, and to general Satisfaction. Which happy Circumstance will, we hope, always continue. Note, *A Copy of the Articles or Constitutions is left in the Library, for the Perusal of all that desire to be more fully informed.*

[2]

Fire-Fighting

Franklin tried out his ideas in the Junto before presenting them to the public. Many of his urban projects— fire prevention, the city watch, the paving, cleaning and lighting of the streets—are described in his Memoirs. *Supplementing the autobiography's account of the genesis of the Union Fire Company, and incidentally illustrating Franklin's organizational technique, is a paper which he first read in the Junto and then published in the form of a letter to himself in the* Pennsylvania Gazette.

Mr. Franklin,   February 4, 1735

Being old and lame of my Hands, and thereby uncapable of assisting my Fellow Citizens, when their Houses are on Fire; I must beg them to take in good Part the following Hints on the Subject of Fires.

In the first Place, as *an Ounce of Prevention is worth a Pound of Cure,* I would advise 'em to take Care how they suffer living Brandsends, or Coals in a full Shovel, to be carried out of one Room into another, or up or down Stairs, unless in a warmingpan shut; for Scraps of Fire may fall into Chinks, and make no Appearance till Midnight; when your Stairs being in Flames, you may be forced, (as I once was) to leap out of your Windows, and hazard your Necks to avoid being over-roasted.

And now we talk of Prevention, where would be the Damage, if, to the Act for preventing Fires, by regulating Bakehouses and Coopers Shops, a Clause were added to regulate all other Houses in the particulars of too shallow Hearths, and the detestable Practice of putting Wooden Mouldings on each side the Fire Place, which being commonly of Heart-of-Pine and full of Turpentine, stand ready to flame as soon as a Coal or a small Brande shall roul against them.

Once more; If Chimneys were more frequently and more carefully clean'd, some Fires might thereby be prevented. I have known foul Chimneys burn most furiously a few Days after they were swept: People in Confidence that they are clean, making large Fires. Every Body among us is allow'd to sweep Chimneys, that please to undertake that Business; and if a Chimney fires thro' fault of the Sweeper, the Owner pays the Fine, and the Sweeper goes free. This Thing is not right. Those who undertake sweeping of Chimneys, and employ Servants for that Purpose, ought to be licensed by the Mayor; and if any Chimney fires and flames out 15 Days after Sweeping, the Fine should be paid by the Sweeper; for it is his Fault.

We have at present got Engines enough in the Town, but I question, whether in many Parts of the Town, Water enough can be had to keep them going for half an Hour together. It seems to me some Publick Pumps are wanting; but that I submit to better Judgments.

As to our Conduct in the Affair of Extinguishing Fires, tho' we do not want Hands or Good-Will, yet we seem to want Order and Method, and therefore I believe I cannot do better than to offer for our Imitation, the Example of a City in a Neighbouring Province. There is, as I am well inform'd, a Club or Society of active Men belonging to each Fire Engine; whose Business is to attend all Fires with it whenever they happen; and to work it once a Quarter, and see it kept in order: Some of these are to handle the Fire-hooks, and others the Axes, which are always kept with the Engine; and for this Service they are consider'd in an Abatement or Exemption in the Taxes. In Time of Fire, they are commanded by Officers appointed by Law, called *Fire-wards*, who are distinguish'd by a Red Staff of five Feet long, headed with a Brass Flame of 6 Inches; And being Men of Prudence and Authority, they direct the opening and stripping of Roofs by the Ax-Men, the pulling down burning Timbers by the Hookmen, and the playing of the Engines, and command the making of Lanes, &c. and they are impowered to require Assistance for the Removing of Goods out of Houses on fire or in Danger of Fire and to appoint Guards for securing such Goods; and Disobedience, to these Officers in any, at such Times, is punished by a Fine of 40 *s.* or Ten Days Imprisonment. These Officers, with the Men belonging to the Engine, at their Quarterly Meetings, discourse of Fires, of the Faults committed at some, the good Management in some Cases at others, and thus communicating their Thoughts and Experiences they grow wise in the Thing, and know how to command and to execute in the best manner upon every Emergency. Since the Establishment of this Regulation, it seems there has been no extraordinary Fire in that Place; and I wish there never may be any here. But they suffer'd before they made such a Regulation, and so must we; for *Englishmen* feel but cannot see; as the *Italian* says of us. And it has pleased God, that in the Fires we have hitherto had, all the bad Circumstances have never happened together, such as dry Season, high Wind, narrow Street, and little or low Water: which perhaps tends to make us secure in our own Minds; but if a Fire with those Circumstances, which God forbid, should happen, we should afterwards be careful enough.

Let me say one thing more, and I will be silent. I could wish, that either Tiles would come in Use for a Covering to Buildings; or else that those who build, would make their Roofs more safe to walk upon, by carrying the Wall above the Eves, in the Manner of the new Buildings in

London, and as Mr. *Turners* House in *Front Street*, or Mr. *Nichols's* in *Chestnut Street*, are built; which I conceive would tend considerably to their Preservation.

Let others communicate their Thoughts as freely as I have done mine, and perhaps something useful may be drawn from the Whole.

I am yours, &c.

A.A.

[3]

The American Philosophical Society

The oldest American learned society, which still exists today, was founded by Franklin as a kind of expanded Junto on a continental scale. David Rittenhouse and Thomas Jefferson were among those who followed Franklin as President of the group. The American Philosophical Society still interests itself in fields of knowledge as diverse as those which interested its founder: Physics, medicine, anthropology, history, and literature are well represented in the pages of its publications, the Transactions *and the* Proceedings. *The following proposal was printed and circulated by Franklin himself.*

A PROPOSAL FOR PROMOTING USEFUL KNOWLEDGE AMONG THE BRITISH PLANTATIONS IN AMERICA

Philadelphia, May 14, 1743

The English are possessed of a long tract of continent, from Nova Scotia to Georgia, extending north and south through different climates, having different soils, producing different plants, mines, and minerals, and capable of different improvements, manufactures, &c.

The first drudgery of settling new colonies, which confines the attention of people to mere necessaries, is now pretty well over; and there are many in every province in circumstances that set them at ease, and afford leisure to cultivate the finer arts and improve the common stock of knowledge. To such of these who are men of speculation, many hints must from time to time arise, many observations occur, which if well examined, pursued, and improved, might produce discoveries to the advantage of some or all of the British plantations, or to the benefit of mankind in general.

But as from the extent of the country such persons are widely separated, and seldom can see and converse or be acquainted with each other, so that many useful particulars remain uncommunicated, die with the discoverers, and are lost to mankind; it is, to remedy this inconvenience for the future, proposed,

That one society be formed of *virtuosi* or ingenious men, residing in the several colonies, to be called *The American Philosophical Society*, who are to maintain a constant correspondence.

That Philadelphia, being the city nearest the centre of the continent colonies, communicating with all of them northward and southward by post, and with all the islands by sea, and having the advantage of a good growing library, be the centre of the Society.

That at Philadelphia there be always at least seven members, viz. a physician, a botanist, a mathematician, a chemist, a mechanician, a geographer, and a general natural philosopher, besides a president, treasurer, and secretary.

That these members meet once a month, or oftener, at their own expense, to communicate to each other their observations and experiments, to receive, read, and consider such letters, communications, or queries as shall be sent from distant members; to direct the dispersing of copies of such communications as are valuable, to other distant members, in order to procure their sentiments thereupon.

That the subjects of the correspondence be: all new-discovered plants, herbs, trees, roots, their virtues, uses, &c.; methods of propagating them, and making such as are useful, but particular to some plantations, more general; improvements of vegetable juices, as ciders, wines, &c.; new methods of curing or preventing diseases; all new-discovered fossils in different countries, as mines, minerals, and quarries; new and useful improvements in any branch of mathematics; new discoveries in chemistry, such as improvements in distillation, brewing, and assaying of ores; new mechanical inventions for saving labour, as mills and carriages, and for raising and conveying of water, draining of meadows, &c., all new arts, trades, and manufactures, that may be proposed or thought of; surveys, maps, and charts of particular parts of the sea-coasts or inland countries; course and junction of rivers and great roads, situation of lakes and mountains, nature of the soil and productions; new methods of improving the breed of useful animals; introducing other sorts from foreign countries; new improvements in planting, gardening, and clearing land; and all philosophical experiments that let light into the nature of things, tend to increase the power of man over matter, and multiply the conveniences or pleasures of life.

That a correspondence, already begun by some intended members, shall be kept up by this Society with the ROYAL SOCIETY of London, and with the DUBLIN SOCIETY.

That every member shall have abstracts sent him quarterly, of every thing valuable communicated to the Society's Secretary at Philadelphia; free of all charge except the yearly payment hereafter mentioned.

That, by permission of the postmaster-general, such communications pass between the Secretary of the Society and the members, postage-free.

That, for defraying the expense of such experiments as the Society shall judge proper to cause to be made, and other contingent charges for the common good, every member send a piece of eight per annum to the treasurer, at Philadelphia, to form a common stock, to be disbursed by order of the President with the consent of the majority of the members that can conveniently be consulted thereupon, to such persons and places where and by whom the experiments are to be made, and otherwise as there shall be occasion; of which disbursements an exact account shall be kept, and communicated yearly to every member.

That, at the first meetings of the members at Philadelphia, such rules be formed for regulating their meetings and transactions for the general benefit, as shall be convenient and necessary; to be afterwards changed and improved as there shall be occasion, wherein due regard is to be had to the advice of distant members.

That, at the end of every year, collections be made and printed, of such experiments, discoveries, and improvements, as may be thought of public advantage; and that every member have a copy sent him.

That the business and duty of the Secretary be to receive all letters intended for the Society, and lay them before the President and members at their meetings; to abstract, correct, and methodize such papers as require it, and as he shall be directed to do by the President, after they have been considered, debated, and digested in the Society; to enter copies thereof in the Society's books, and make out copies for distant members; to answer their letters by direction of the President, and keep records of all material transactions of the Society.

Benjamin Franklin, the writer of this Proposal, offers himself to serve the Society as their secretary, till they shall be provided with one more capable.

[4]

The Pennsylvania Academy

The Junto's discussions of Franklin's proposals for the establishment of a college in Pennsylvania led him to write and publish a pamphlet on the subject. Soon after publication of the paper in 1749, the Pennsylvania Academy was established, with Franklin as its president. The University of Pennsylvania traces its origins to Franklin's academy.

PROPOSALS RELATING TO THE
EDUCATION OF YOUTH IN PENNSYLVANIA

ADVERTISEMENT TO THE READER

It has long been regretted as a Misfortune to the Youth of this Province, that we have no ACADEMY, in which they might receive the Accomplishments of a regular Education. The following Paper of Hints towards forming a

Plan for that Purpose, is so far approv'd by some publick-spirited Gentlemen, to whom it has been privately communicated, that they have directed a Number of Copies to be made by the Press, and properly distributed, in order to obtain the Sentiments and Advice of Men of Learning, Understanding, and Experience in these Matters; and have determined to use their Interest and best Endeavours, to have the Scheme, when compleated, carried gradually into Execution; in which they have Reason to believe they shall have the hearty Concurrence and Assistance of many who are Wellwishers to their Country. Those who incline to favour the Design with their Advice, either as to the Parts of Learning to be taught, the Order of Study, the Method of Teaching, the Œconomy of the School, or any other Matter of Importance to the Success of the Undertaking, are desired to communicate their Sentiments as soon as may be, by Letter directed to B. FRANKLIN, *Printer*, in PHILADELPHIA.

PROPOSALS

The good Education of Youth has been esteemed by wise Men in all Ages, as the surest Foundation of the Happiness both of private Families and of Commonwealths. Almost all Governments have therefore made it a principal Object of their Attention, to establish and endow with proper Revenues, such Seminaries of Learning, as might supply the succeeding Age with Men qualified to serve the Publick with Honour to themselves, and to their Country.

Many of the first Settlers of these Provinces were Men who had received a good Education in *Europe,* and to their Wisdom and good Management we owe much of our present Prosperity. But their hands were full, and they could not do all Things. The present Race are not thought to be generally of equal Ability: For though the *American* Youth are allow'd not to want Capacity; yet the best Capacities require Cultivation, it being truly with them, as with the best Ground, which unless well tilled and sowed with profitable Seed, produces only ranker Weeds.

That we may obtain the Advantages arising from an

Increase of Knowledge, and prevent as much as may be the mischievous Consequences that would attend a general Ignorance among us, the following *Hints* are offered towards forming a Plan for the Education of the Youth of *Pennsylvania,* viz.

It is propos'd,

That some Persons of Leisure and publick Spirit apply for a CHARTER, by which they may be incorporated, with Power to erect an ACADEMY for the Education of Youth, to govern the same, provide Masters, make Rules, receive Donations, purchase Lands, etc., and to add to their Number, from Time to Time such other Persons as they shall judge suitable.

That the Members of the Corporation make it their Pleasure, and in some Degree their Business, to visit the Academy often, encourage and countenance the Youth, countenance and assist the Masters, and by all Means in their Power advance the Usefulness and Reputation of the Design; that they look on the Students as in some Sort their Children, treat them with Familiarity and Affection, and, when they have behav'd well, and gone through their Studies, and are to enter the World, zealously unite, and make all the Interest that can be made to establish them, whether in Business, Offices, Marriages, or any other Thing for their Advantage, preferably to all other Persons whatsoever even of equal Merit.

And if Men may, and frequently do, catch such a Taste for cultivating Flowers, for Planting, Grafting, Inoculating, and the like, as to despise all other Amusements for their Sake, why may not we expect they should acquire a Relish for that *more useful* Culture of young Minds. *Thompson* says,

> " 'Tis Joy to see the human Blossoms blow,
> When infant Reason grows apace, and calls
> For the kind Hand of an assiduous Care.
> Delightful Task! to rear the tender Thought,
> To teach the young Idea how to shoot;
> To pour the fresh Instruction o'er the Mind,
> To breathe th' enliv'ning Spirit, and to fix
> The generous Purpose in the glowing Breast."

That a House be provided for the ACADEMY, if not in the Town, not many Miles from it; the Situation high and dry, and if it may be, not far from a River, having a Garden, Orchard, Meadow, and a Field or two.

That the House be furnished with a Library (if in the Country, if in the Town, the Town Libraries may serve) with Maps of all Countries, Globes, some mathematical Instruments, an Apparatus for Experiments in Natural Philosophy, and for Mechanics; Prints, of all Kinds, Prospects, Buildings, Machines, &c.

That the Rector be a Man of good Understanding, good Morals, diligent and patient, learn'd in the Languages and Sciences, and a correct pure Speaker and Writer of the *English* Tongue; to have such Tutors under him as shall be necessary.

That the boarding Scholars diet together, plainly, temperately, and frugally.

That, to keep them in Health, and to strengthen and render active their Bodies, they be frequently exercis'd in Running, Leaping, Wrestling, and Swimming, &c.

That they have peculiar Habits to distinguish them from other Youth, if the Academy be in or near the Town; for this, among other Reasons, that their Behaviour may be the better observed.

As to their STUDIES, it would be well if they could be taught *every Thing* that is useful, and *every Thing* that is ornamental: But Art is long, and their Time is short. It is therefore propos'd that they learn those Things that are likely to be *most useful* and *most ornamental.* Regard being had to the several Professions for which they are intended.

All should be taught to write a *fair Hand,* and swift, as that is useful for All. And with it may be learnt something of *Drawing,* by Imitation of Prints, and some of the first Principles of Perspective.

Arithmetick, Accounts, and some of the first Principles of *Geometry* and *Astronomy.*

The *English* Language might be taught by Grammar; in which some of our best Writers, as *Tillotson, Addison, Pope, Algernoon Sidney, Cato's Letters,* &c., should be Classicks: the *Stiles* principally to be cultivated, being the *clear* and the *concise.* Reading should also be taught, and pronouncing, properly, distinctly, emphatically; not with an even Tone, which *under-does,* nor a theatrical, which *over-does* Nature.

To form their Stile they should bé put on Writing Letters to each other, making Abstracts of what they read; or writing the same Things in their own Words; telling or writing Stories lately read, in their own Expressions. All to be revis'd and corrected by the Tutor, who should give his Reasons, and explain the Force and Import of Words, &c.

To form their Pronunciation, they may be put on making Declamations, repeating Speeches, delivering Orations, &c.; The Tutor assisting at the Rehearsals, teaching, advising, correcting their Accent, &c.

But if History be made a constant Part of their Reading, such as the Translations of the *Greek* and *Roman* Historians, and the modern Histories of ancient *Greece* and *Rome,* &c. may not almost all Kinds of useful Knowledge be that Way introduc'd to Advantage, and with Pleasure to the Student? As

GEOGRAPHY, by reading with Maps, and being required to point out the Places *where* the greatest Actions were done, to give their old and new Names, with the Bounds, Situation, Extent of the Countries concern'd, &c.

CHRONOLOGY, by the Help of *Helvicus* or some other Writer of the Kind, who will enable them to tell *when* those Events happened; what Princes were Cotemporaries, what States or famous Men flourish'd about that Time, &c. The several principal Epochas to be first well fix'd in their Memories.

ANTIENT CUSTOMS, religious and civil, being frequently mentioned in History, will give Occasion for explaining them; in which the Prints of Medals, Basso-Relievos, and antient Monuments will greatly assist.

MORALITY, by descanting and making continual Observations on the Causes of the Rise or Fall of any Man's Character, Fortune, Power &c. mention'd in History; the Advantages of Temperance, Order, Frugality, Industry, Perseverance &c. &c. Indeed the general natural Tendency of Reading good History must be, to fix in the Minds of Youth deep Impressions of the Beauty and Usefulness of Virtue of all Kinds, Publick Spirit, Fortitude, &c.

History will show the wonderful Effects of ORATORY, in governing, turning and leading great Bodies of Mankind, Armies, Cities, Nations. When the Minds of Youth are struck with Admiration at this, then is the Time to give them the Principles of that Art, which they will study with Taste and Application. Then they may be made acquainted with the best Models among the antients, their Beauties being particularly pointed out to them. Modern Political Oratory being chiefly performed by the Pen and Press, its Advantages over the Antient in some Respects are to be shown; as that its Effects are more extensive, more lasting, &c.

History will also afford frequent Opportunities of showing the Necessity of a *Publick Religion,* from its Usefulness to the Publick; the Advantage of a Religious Character among private Persons; the Mischiefs of Superstition, &c. and the Excellency of the CHRISTIAN RELIGION above all others antient or modern.

History will also give Occasion to expatiate on the Advantage of Civil Orders and Constitutions; how Men and their Properties are protected by joining in Societies and establishing Government; their Industry encouraged and rewarded, Arts invented, and Life made more comfortable: The Advantages of *Liberty,* Mischiefs of *Licentiousness,* Benefits arising from good Laws and a due Execution of Justice, &c. Thus may the first Principles of sound *Politicks* be fix'd in the Minds of Youth.

On *Historical* Occasions, Questions of Right and Wrong, Justice and Injustice, will naturally arise, and may be put to Youth, which they may debate in Conversation and in Writing. When they ardently desire Victory, for the Sake of the Praise attending it, they will begin to feel the Want, and be sensible of the Use of *Logic,* or the Art of Reasoning to *discover* Truth, and of Arguing to *defend* it, and *convince* Adversaries. This would be the Time to acquaint them with the Principles of that Art. Grotius, Puffendorff, and some other Writers of the same Kind, may be used on these Occasions to decide their Disputes. Publick Disputes warm the Imagination, whet the Industry, and strengthen the natural Abilities.

When Youth are told, that the Great Men whose Lives and Actions they read in History, spoke two of the best Languages that ever were, the most expressive, copious, beautiful; and that the finest Writings, the most correct Compositions, the most perfect Productions of human Wit and Wisdom, are in those Languages, which have endured Ages, and will endure while there are Men; that no Translation can do them Justice, or give the Pleasure found in Reading the Originals; that those Languages contain all Science; that one of them is become almost universal, being the Language of Learned Men in all Countries; that to understand them is a distinguishing Ornament, &c. they may be thereby made desirous of learning those Languages, and their Industry sharpen'd in the Acquisition of them. All intended for Divinity, should be taught the *Latin* and *Greek;* for Physick, the *Latin, Greek,* and *French;* for Law, the *Latin* and *French;* Merchants, the *French, German,* and *Spanish:* And though all should not be compell'd to learn *Latin, Greek,* or the modern foreign Languages; yet none that have an ardent Desire to learn them should be refused; their *English,* Arithmetick and other Studies absolutely necessary, being at the same Time not neglected.

If the new *Universal History* were also read, it would give a *connected* Idea of human Affairs, so far as it goes, which should be follow'd by the best modern Histories, particularly of our Mother Country; then of these Colonies; which should be accompanied with Observations on their Rise, Encrease, Use to *Great Britain,* Encouragements, Discouragements, etc. the Means to make them flourish, secure their Liberties, &c.

With the History of Men, Times, and Nations, should be read at proper Hours or Days, some of the best *Histories of Nature,* which would not only be delightful to Youth, and furnish them with Matter for their Letters, &c. as well as other History; but afterwards of great Use to them, whether they are Merchants, Handicrafts, or Divines; enabling the first the better to understand many Commodities, Drugs, &c; the second to improve his Trade or Handicraft by new Mixtures, Materials, &c., and the last to adorn his Discourses by beautiful Comparisons, and strengthen them by new Proofs of Divine

Providence. The Conversation of all will be improved by it, as Occasions frequently occur of making Natural Observations, which are instructive, agreeable, and entertaining in almost all Companies. *Natural History* will also afford Opportunities of introducing many Observations, relating to the Preservation of Health, which may be afterwards of great Use. *Arbuthnot* on Air and *Aliment, Sanctorius* on Perspiration, *Lemery* on Foods, and some others, may now be read, and a very little Explanation will make them sufficiently intelligible to Youth.

While they are reading Natural History, might not a little *Gardening, Planting, Grafting, Inoculating,* etc., be taught and practised; and now and then Excursions made to the neighbouring Plantations of the best Farmers, their Methods observ'd and reason'd upon for the Information of Youth? The Improvement of Agriculture being useful to all, and Skill in it no Disparagement to any.

The History of *Commerce,* of the Invention of Arts, Rise of Manufactures, Progress of Trade, Change of its Seats, with the Reasons, Causes, &c., may also be made entertaining to Youth, and will be useful to all. And this, with the Accounts in other History of the prodigious Force and Effect of Engines and Machines used in War, will naturally introduce a Desire to be instructed in *Mechanicks,* and to be inform'd of the Principles of that Art by which weak Men perform such Wonders, Labour is sav'd, Manufactures expedited, &c. This will be the Time to show them Prints of antient and modern Machines, to explain them, to let them be copied, and to give Lectures in Mechanical Philosophy.

With the whole should be constantly inculcated and cultivated, that *Benignity of Mind,* which shows itself in *searching for* and *seizing* every Opportunity *to serve* and *to oblige;* and is the Foundation of what is called Good Breeding; highly useful to the Possessor, and most agreeable to all.

The Idea of what is *true Merit* should also be often presented to Youth, explain'd and impress'd on their Minds, as consisting in an *Inclination* join'd with an *Ability* to serve Mankind, one's Country, Friends and Family; which *Ability* is (with the Blessing of God) to be acquir'd

or greatly encreas'd by *true Learning;* and should indeed
be the great *Aim* and *End* of all Learning.

[5]

III

THE NEW PROMETHEUS, I:
FRANKLIN THE SCIENTIST

*In 1778 the French Statesman Turgot wrote an epigram
for inscription on a bust of Franklin: "He snatched the
lightning from the sky and the sceptre from tyrants."*
Turgot thus likened Franklin to Prometheus, who stole
fire from Olympus and gave it to man. In this chapter we
examine one aspect of the American Prometheus. Franklin, the scientist, enlisted the forces of nature in the service of mankind.*

*Franklin signed an agreement with his partner in the
printing business on January 1, 1748, whereby Franklin
in effect retired from active participation in the firm—at
the age of forty-two. For eighteen years thereafter he received nearly 500 pounds annually as his share of the
profits. He moved to the outskirts of the city and exchanged the pewter of the tradesman for the silver service
of the gentleman. He managed to get his son into the first
Philadelphia Assembly in the winter of 1748.*

*Thus industry, frugality, and immense social skill, cou-
pled with an extraordinary intelligence, had brought the
expected reward: Benjamin Franklin had become a man
of leisure.*

*The life he expected to lead in his retirement is de-
scribed in a letter to a member of the American Philosophical Society. Cadwallader Colden, who shared a long
and rich correspondence with Franklin was a scientist,
historian, philosopher, and lieutenant governor of New
York during part of the turbulent sixties and seventies.*

Sixteen years later, when politics had begun to make

---

*Or, in Turgot's original Latin, Eripuit coelo fulmen sceptrumque
tyrannis.

his own retirement a faded dream, he somewhat wistfully wrote to John Fothergill, a Scottish doctor, about the latter's plans for a life of leisure.

TO CADWALLADER COLDEN

September 29, 1748

I received your favour of the 12th instant, which gave me the greater pleasure, as it was so long since I had heard from you. I congratulate you on your return to your beloved retirement. I, too, am taking the proper measures for obtaining leisure to enjoy life and my friends, more than heretofore, having put my printing house under the care of my partner, David Hall, absolutely left off bookselling, and removed to a more quiet part of the town, where I am settling my old accounts, and hope soon to be quite master of my own time, and no longer, as the song has it, *at every one's call but my own.* If health continue, I hope to be able in another year to visit the most distant friend I have, without inconvenience.

With the same views I have refused engaging further in public affairs. The share I had in the late Association, &c., having given me a little present run of popularity, there was a pretty general intention of choosing me a representative of the city at the next election of Assembly men; but I have desired all my friends, who spoke to me about it, to discourage it, declaring that I would not serve, if chosen. Thus you see I am in a fair way of having no other tasks, than such as I shall like to give myself, and of enjoying what I look upon as a great happiness, leisure to read, study, make experiments, and converse at large with such ingenious and worthy men, as are pleased to honour me with their friendship or acquaintance, on such points as may produce something for the common benefit of mankind, uninterrupted by the little cares and fatigues of business. Among other pleasures I promise myself, that of corresponding more frequently and fully with Dr. Colden is none of the least. I shall only wish that what must be so agreeable to me may not prove troublesome to you. . . .

I am, with great esteem and respect, dear Sir, &c.

[1]

TO JOHN FOTHERGILL

March 14, 1764

. . . By the way, when do you intend to live—*i.e.*, to enjoy life . . . will you retire to your villa, give yourself repose, delight in viewing the operations of nature in the vegetable creation, assist her in her works, get your ingenious friends at times about you, make them happy with your conversation, and enjoy theirs: or, if alone, amuse yourself with your books and elegant collections. . . .

[2]

The Young Naturalist

One retired to find leisure, and leisure meant two things: the "sweet society" of one's friends and the pursuit of knowledge. To science Franklin brought an experimental inquisitiveness and strong deductive powers. Both were already evident in the Journal which the twenty-year-old scientist had kept on his return voyage from England in 1726.

Sunday, August 21

This morning we lost sight of the Yorker, having a brisk gale of wind at East. Towards night a poor little bird came on board us, being almost tired to death, and suffered itself to be taken by the hand. We reckon ourselves near two hundred leagues from land, so that no doubt a little rest was very acceptable to the unfortunate wanderer, who 'tis like was blown off the coast in thick weather, and could not find its way back again. We receive it hospitably and tender it victuals and drink; but he refuses both, and I suppose will not live long. There was one came on board some days ago in the same circumstances with this, which I think the cat destroyed.

Monday, August 22

This morning I saw several flying-fish, but they were small. A favourable wind all day.

Tuesday, August 23

Fair winds, nothing remarkable . . .

Wednesday,——24

Friday, September 2

This morning the wind changed, a little fair. We caught a couple of dolphins, and fried them for dinner. They tasted tolerably well. These fish make a glorious appearance in the water: their bodies are of a bright green, mixed with a silver colour, and their tails of a shining golden yellow; but all this vanishes presently after they are taken out of their element, and they change all over to a light grey. I observed that cutting off pieces of a just-caught living dolphin for baits, those pieces did not lose their lustre and fine colours when the dolphin died, but retained them perfectly. Every one takes notice of that vulgar error of the painters, who always represent this fish monstrously crooked and deformed, when it is in reality as beautiful and well shaped a fish as any that swims. I cannot think what should be the original of this chimera of theirs, (since there is not a creature in nature that in the least resembles their dolphin) unless it proceeded at first from a false imitation of a fish in the posture of leaping, which they have since improved into a crooked monster with a head and eyes like a bull, a hog's snout, and a tail like a blown tulip. But the sailors give me another reason, though a whimsical one, viz. that as this most beautiful fish is only to be caught at sea, and that very far to the Southward, they say the painters wilfully deform it in their representations, lest pregnant women should long for what it is impossible to procure for them. . . .

Wednesday, September 21

This morning our Steward was brought to the geers and whipped, for making an extravagent use of flour in the puddings, and for several other misdemeanors. It has been perfectly calm all this day, and very hot. I was determined to wash myself in the sea today, and should have done so had not the appearance of a shark, that mortal enemy to swimmers, deterred me: he seemed to be about five feet long, moves round the ship at some distance in a slow majestic manner, attended by near a dozen of those they call pilot-fish, of different sizes; the largest of them is not so big as a small mackerel, and the smallest not bigger than my little finger. Two of these diminutive pilots keep just before his nose, and he seems to govern himself in his motions by their direction; while the rest surround him on every side indifferently. A shark is never seen without a retinue of these, who are his purveyors, discovering and distinguishing his prey for him; while he in return gratefully protects them from the ravenous hungry dolphin. They are commonly counted a very greedy fish; yet this refuses to meddle with the bait we have thrown out for him. 'Tis likely he has lately made a full meal. . . .

Wednesday, September 28

We had very variable winds and weather last night, accompanied with abundance of rain; and now the wind is come about westerly again, but we must bear it with patience. This afternoon we took up several branches of gulf weed (with which the sea is spread all over from the Western Isles to the coast of America); but one of these branches had something peculiar in it. In common with the rest it had a leaf about three quarters of an inch long, indented like a saw, and a small yellow berry filled with nothing but wind; besides which it bore a fruit of the animal kind, very surprising to see. It was a small shellfish like a heart, the stalk by which it proceeded from the branch being partly of a gristly kind. Upon this one branch of the weed there were near forty of these vegetable animals; the smallest of them near the end contained a substance somewhat like an oyster, but the larger were visibly animated, opening their shells every moment, and thrusting out a set of unformed claws, not unlike those of a crab; but the inner part was still a kind of soft jelly. Observing the weed more narrowly, I spied a very small crab crawling among it, about as big as the head of a ten-penny nail, and of a yellowish colour, like the weed itself. This gave me some reason to think that he was a native of the branch, that he had not long since been in the same condition with the rest of those little embrios that appeared in the shells, this being the method of their generation; and that consequently all the rest of this odd kind of fruit might be crabs in due time. To strengthen my conjecture, I have resolved to keep the weed in salt water, renewing it every day till we come on shore, by this experiment to see whether any more crabs will be produced or not in this manner. I remember that the last calm we had, we took notice of a large crab upon the surface of the sea, swimming from one branch of weed to another, which he seemed to prey upon; and I likewise recollect that at Boston, in New England, I have often seen small crabs with a shell like a snail's upon their backs, crawling about in the salt water; and likewise at Portsmouth in England. It is likely nature has provided this hard shell to secure them till their own proper shell has acquired a sufficient hardness, which once perfected, they quit their old habitation and venture abroad safe in their own strength. The various changes that silk-worms, butterflies, and several other insects go through, make such alterations and metamorphoses not improbable. This day the captain of the snow* with one his passengers came on board us; but the wind beginning to blow, they did not stay dinner, but returned to their own vessel.

Thursday, September 29

Upon shifting the water in which I had put the weed yesterday, I found another crab, much smaller than the former, who seemed to have newly left his habitation. But the weed begins to wither, and the rest of the embrios are dead. This new comer fully convinces me, that at least this sort of crabs are generated in this manner. The snow's Captain dined on board us this day. Little or no wind.

*A square-rigged type of vessel, this one from Dublin, which over-took the vessel on which Frankin was traveling.

Friday, September 30

I sat up last night to observe an eclipse of the moon, which the calendar calculated for London informed us would happen at five o'clock in the morning, September 30. It began with us about eleven last night, and continued till near two this morning, darkening her body about six digits, or one half; the middle of it being about half an hour after twelve, by which we may discover that we are in a meridian of about four hours and half from London, or 67½ degrees of longitude, and consequently have not much above one hundred leagues to run. This is the second eclipse we have had within these fifteen days. We lost our consort in the night, but saw him again this morning near two leagues to windward. This afternoon we spoke with him again. We have had abundance of dolphins about us these three or four days; but we have not taken any more than one, they being shy of the bait. I took in some more gulf-weed to-day with the boat-hook, with shells upon it like that before mentioned, and three living perfect crabs, each less than the nail of my little finger. One of them had something particularly observable, to wit, a thin piece of the white shell which I before noticed as their covering while they remained in the condition of embrios, sticking close to his natural shell upon his back. This sufficiently confirms me in my opinion of the manner of their generation. I have put this remarkable crab with a piece of the gulf-weed, shell, &c. into a glass phial filled with salt water, (for want of spirits of wine) in hopes to preserve the curiosity till I come on shore. The wind is South-West. . . .

Tuesday, October 11

This morning we weighed anchor with a gentle breeze, and passed by Newcastle, whence they hailed us and bade us welcome. 'Tis extreme fine weather. The sun enlivens our stiff limbs with his glorious rays of warmth and brightness. The sky looks gay, with here and there a silver cloud. The fresh breezes from the woods refresh us, the immediate prospect of liberty after so long and irksome confinement ravishes us. In short all things conspire to make this the most joyful day I ever knew. As we passed by Chester some of the company went on shore, impatient once more to tread on *terra firma*, and designing for Philadelphia by land. Four of us remained on board, not caring for the fatigue of travel when we knew the voyage had much weakened us. About eight at night, the wind failing us, we cast anchor at Redbank, six miles from Philadelphia, and thought we must be obliged to lie on board that night: but some young Philadelphians happening to be out upon their pleasure in a boat, they came on board, and offered to take us up with them: we accepted of their kind proposal, and about ten o'clock landed at Philadelphia, heartily congratulating each other upon our having happily completed so tedious and dangerous a voyage. Thank God!

[3]

The Meteorologist

The same curiosity and logicality continued to develop in the mature Franklin. We share the excitement of discovery in two accounts of his meteorological observations written to two of his most constant correspondents. Jared Eliot, a Connecticut clergyman, was interested, like Franklin, in many scientific subjects, but especially agriculture. Peter Collinson was a London clothing merchant, botanist, and Fellow of the Royal Society whose wide correspondence did much to establish communication between colonial scientists and those in England.

TO JARED ELIOT

February 13, 1750

Dear Sir

You desire to know my thoughts about the north-east storms beginning to leeward. Some years since, there was an eclipse of the moon at nine o'clock in the evening, which I intended to observe; but before night a storm blew up at north-east, and continued violent all night and all the next day; the sky thick-clouded, dark, and rainy, so that neither moon nor stars could be seen.

The storm did a great deal of damage all along the coast, for we had accounts of it in the newspapers from Boston, Newport, New York, Maryland, and Virginia; but what surprised me was to find in the Boston newspapers an account of an observation of the eclipse made there; for I thought, as the storm came from the north-east, it must have been sooner at Boston than with us, and consequently have prevented such observation. I wrote to my brother about it, and he informed me that the eclipse was over there an hour before the storm began. Since which I have made inquiries from time to time of travellers, and of my correspondents north-eastward and south-westward, and observed the accounts in the newspapers from New England, New York, Maryland, Virginia, and South Carolina; and I find it to be a constant fact that north-east storms begin to go leeward and are often more violent there than farther to windward. Thus the last October storm, which with you was on the 8th, began on the 7th in Virginia and North Carolina, and was most violent there.

As to the reason of this, I can only give you my conjectures. Suppose a great tract of country, land and sea, to wit, Florida and the Bay of Mexico, to have clear weather for several days, and to be heated by the sun, and its air thereby exceedingly rarefied. Suppose the country north-eastward, as Pennsylvania, New England, Nova Scotia, and Newfoundland, to be at the same time covered with clouds, and its air chilled and condensed. The rarefied air being lighter must rise, and the denser air next to it will press into its place; that will be followed by the next denser air, that by the next, and so on. Thus, when I have a fire in my chimney, there is a current of air constantly flowing from the door to the chimney; but the beginning of the motion was at the chimney, where the air being rarefied by the fire rising, its place was supplied by the cooler air that was next to it, and the place of that by the next, and so on to the door. So the water in a long sluice or millrace, being stopped by a gate, is at rest like the air in a calm; but as soon as you open the gate at one end to let it out, the water next the gate begins first to move, that which is next to it follows; and so, though the water proceeds forward to the gate, the motion which began there runs backwards, if one may so speak, to the upper end of the race, where the water is last in motion. We have on this continent a long ridge of mountains running from north-east to south-west, and the coast runs the same course. These may, perhaps, contribute towards the direction of the winds, or at least influence them in some degree. If these conjectures do not satisfy you, I wish to have yours on the subject. . . .

I am sir, your obliged humble servant. . . .

[4]

TO PETER COLLINSON

DEAR SIR,— Philadelphia, Aug. 25, 1755.

As you have my former papers on Whirlwinds, &c., I now send you an account of one which I had lately an opportunity of seeing and examining myself.

Being in *Maryland,* riding with Colonel *Tasker,* and some other gentlemen to his country-seat, where I and my son were entertained by that amiable and worthy man with great hospitality and kindness, we saw in the vale below us, a small whirlwind beginning in the road, and shewing itself by the dust it raised and contained. It appeared in the form of a sugar-loaf, spinning on its point, moving up the hill towards us, and enlarging as it came forward. When it passed by us, its smaller part near the ground, appeared no bigger than a common barrel, but widening upwards, it seemed, at 40 or 50 feet high, to be 20 or 30 feet in diameter. The rest of the company stood looking after it, but my curiosity being stronger, I followed it, riding close by its side, and observed its licking up, in its progress, all the dust that was under its smaller part. As it is a common opinion that a shot, fired through a water-spout, will break it, I tried to break this little whirlwind, by striking my whip frequently through it, but without any effect. Soon after, it quitted the road and took into the woods, growing every moment larger and stronger, raising, instead of dust, the old dry leaves with which the ground was thick covered, and making a great noise with them and the branches of the trees, bending some tall trees round in a circle swiftly and very surprizingly, though the progressive motion of the whirl was not so swift but that a man on foot might have kept pace with it; but the circular motion was amazingly rapid. By the leaves it was now filled with, I could plainly perceive that the current of air they were driven by, moved upwards in a spiral line; and when I saw the trunks and bodies of large trees invelop'd in the passing whirl, which continued intire after it had left them I no longer wondered that my whip had no effect on it in its smaller state. I accompanied it about three quarters of a mile, till some limbs of dead trees, broken off by the whirl, flying about and falling near me, made me more apprehensive of danger; and then I stopped, looking at the top of it as it went on, which was visible, by means of the leaves contained in it, for a very great height above the trees. Many of the leaves, as they got loose from the upper and widest part, were scattered in the wind; but so great was their height in the air, that they appeared no bigger than flies. My son, who was by this time come up with me, followed the whirlwind till it left the woods, and crossed an old tobacco-field, where, finding neither dust nor leaves to take up, it gradually became invisible below as it went away over that field. The course of the general wind then blowing was along with us as we travelled, and the progressive motion of the whirlwind was in a direction nearly opposite, though it did not keep a strait line, nor was its progressive motion uniform, it making little sallies on either hand as it went, proceeding sometimes faster and sometimes slower, and seeming sometimes for a few seconds almost stationary, then starting forward pretty fast again. When we rejoined the company, they were admiring the vast height of the leaves now brought by the common wind, over our heads. These leaves accompanied us as we travelled, some falling now and then round about us, and some not reaching the ground till we had gone near three miles from the place where we first saw the whirlwind begin. Upon my asking Colonel *Tasker* if such whirlwinds were common in *Maryland,* he answered pleasantly, "No, not at all common; but we got this on purpose to treat Mr. Franklin." And a very high treat it was, to

Dear Sir,

Your affectionate friend and humble servant. . . .

[5]

Experimenter in Electricity

We remember Franklin the scientist primarily for his inventions: the lightning rod, bifocals, the Franklin stove. But the inventor delighted in science for its own sake, and as an end in itself, and had a special devotion to electricity.

What good, Franklin asked, was a new invention? What good, he answered, was a newborn baby? His two most lasting innovations—his conception of electricity as a single fluid and his application of the terms positive and negative—are in pure science rather than applied technology.

TO PETER COLLINSON

March 28, 1747

Sir,

Your kind present of an electric tube, with directions for using it, has put several of us on making electrical experiments, in which we have observed some particular phaenomena, that we look upon to be new. I shall therefore communicate them to you in my next, though possibly they may not be new to you, as among the numbers daily employed in those experiments on your side the water, 'tis probable some one or other has hit on the same observations. For my own part, I never was before engaged in any study that so totally engrossed my attention and my time as this has lately done; for what with making experiments when I can be alone, and repeating them to my Friends and Acquaintance, who, from the novelty of the thing, come continually in crouds to see them, I have, during some months past, had little leisure for any thing else. . . .

[6]

July 11, 1747

Sir,

In my last I informed you that, in pursuing our electrical enquiries, we had observed some particular phaenomena, which we looked upon to be new, and of which I promised to give you some account, though I apprehended they might possibly not be new to you, as so many hands are daily employed in electrical experiments on your side the water, some or other of which would probably hit on the same observations.

The first is the wonderful effect of pointed bodies, both in *drawing off* and *throwing off* the electrical fire. For example,

Place an iron shot of three or four inches diameter on the mouth of a clean dry glass bottle. By a fine silken thread from the ceiling, right over the mouth of the bottle, suspend a small cork ball, about the bigness of a marble; the thread of such a length, as that the cork ball may rest against the side of the shot. Electrify the shot, and the ball will be repelled to the distance of four or five inches, more or less, according to the quantity of Electricity. When in this state, if you present to the shot the point of a long slender sharp bodkin, at six or eight inches distance, the repellency is instantly destroy'd, and the cork flies to the shot. A blunt body must be brought within an inch, and draw a spark, to produce the same effect. To prove that the electrical fire is *drawn off* by the point, if you take the blade of the bodkin out of the wooden handle, and fix it in a stick of sealing-wax, and then present it at the distance aforesaid, or if you bring it very near, no such effect follows; but sliding the finger along the wax till you touch the blade, and the ball flies to the shot immediately. If you present the point in the dark, you will see, sometimes at a foot distance, and more, a light gather upon it, like that of a fire-fly, or glow-worm; the less sharp the point, the nearer you must bring it to observe the light; and, at whatever distance you see the light, you may draw off the electrical fire, and destroy the repellency. If a cork ball so suspended be repelled by the tube, and a point be presented quick to it, tho' at a considerable distance, 'tis surprizing to see how suddenly it flies back to the tube. Points of wood will do near as well as those of iron, provided the wood is not dry; for perfectly dry wood will no more conduct Electricity than sealing-wax.

To shew that points will *throw off* as well as *draw off* the electrical fire; lay a long sharp needle upon the shot, and you cannot electrise the shot so as to make it repel the rock ball. Or fix a needle to the end of a suspended gun-barrel, or iron rod, so as to point beyond it like a little bayonet; and while it remains there, the gun-barrel, or rod, cannot by applying the tube to the other end be electrised so as to give a spark, the fire continually running out silently at the point. In the dark you may see it make the same appearance as it does in the case before mentioned.

The repellency between the cork ball and the shot is likewise destroyed. 1, by sifting fine sand on it; this does it gradually. 2, by breathing on it. 3, by making a smoke about it from burning wood. 4, by candle-light, even though the candle is at a foot distance: these do it suddenly. The light of a bright coal from a wood fire; and the light of red-hot iron do it likewise; but not at so great a distance. Smoke from the dry rosin dropt on hot iron, does not destroy the repellency; but is attracted by both shot and cork ball, forming proportionable atmospheres round them, making them look beautifully, somewhat like some of the figures in *Burnet's* or *Whiston's Theory of the Earth*.

N.B. This experiment should be made in a closet, where the air is very still, or it will be apt to fail.

The light of the sun thrown strongly on both cork and shot by a looking-glass for a long time together, does not impair the repellency in the least. This difference between fire-light and sun-light is another thing that seems new and extraordinary to us.

We had for some time been of opinion, that the electrical fire was not created by friction, but collected, being really an element diffus'd among, and attracted by other matter, particularly by water and metals. We had even discovered and demonstrated its afflux to the electrical sphere, as well as its efflux, by means of little light windmill-wheels made of stiff paper vanes, fixed obliquely and turning freely on fine wire axes; also by little wheels of the same matter, but formed like water-wheels. Of the disposition and application of which wheels, and the various phaenomena resulting, I could, if I had time, fill you a sheet. The impossibility of electrising one's self (through standing on wax) by rubbing the tube, and drawing the fire from it; and the manner of doing it, by passing the tube near a person or thing standing on the floor, &c., had also occurred to us some months before Mr. *Watson's* ingenious *Sequel* came to hand, and these were some of the new things I intended to have communicated to you. But now I need only mention some particulars not hinted in that piece, with our reasonings thereupon; though perhaps the latter might well enough be spared.

1. A person standing on wax, and rubbing the tube, and another person on wax drawing the fire, they will both of them (provided they do not stand so as to touch one another) appear to be electrised, to a person standing on the floor; that is, he will receive a spark on approaching each of them with his knuckle.

2. But, if the persons on wax touch one another during the exciting of the tube, neither of them will appear to be electrised.

3. If they touch one another after exciting the tube, and drawing the fire as aforesaid, there will be a stronger spark between them, than was between either of them and the person on the floor.

4. After such strong spark, neither of them discover any electricity.

These appearances we attempt to account for thus: We suppose, as aforesaid, that electrical fire is a common element, of which every one of the three persons above mentioned has his equal share, before any operation is begun with the tube. *A,* who stands on wax and rubs the tube, collects the electrical fire from himself into the glass; and his communication with the common stock being cut off by the wax, his body is not again immediately supply'd. *B*, (who stands on wax likewise) passing his knuckle along near the tube, receives the fire which was collected by the glass from *A;* and his communication with the common stock being likewise cut off, he retains the additional quantity received. To *C*, standing on the floor, both appear to be electrised: for he having only the middle quantity of electrical fire, receives a spark upon approaching *B*, who has an over quantity; but gives one to *A*, who has an under quantity. If *A* and *B* approach to touch each other, the spark is stronger, because the difference between them is greater: after such touch there is no spark between either of them and *C*, because the electrical fire in all is reduced to the original equality. If they touch while electrising, the equality is never destroy'd, the fire only circulating. Hence have arisen some new terms among us: we say *B*, (and bodies like circumstanced) is electrised *positively; A, negatively*. Or rather, *B* is electrised *plus; A, minus*. And we daily in our experiments electrise bodies *plus* or *minus*, as we think proper. To electrise *plus* or *minus*, no more needs to be known than this, that the parts of the tube or sphere that are rubbed, do, in the instant of the friction, attract the electrical fire, and therefore take it from the thing rubbing: the same parts immediately, as the friction upon them ceases, are disposed to give the fire they have received, to any body that has less. Thus you may circulate it, as Mr. *Watson* has shewn; you may also accumulate or subtract it upon, or from any body, as you connect that body with the rubber or with the receiver, the communication with the common stock being cut off. We think that ingenious gentleman was deceived when he imagined (in his *Sequel*) that the electrical fire came down the wire from the ceiling to the gunbarrel, thence to the sphere, and so electrised the machine and the man turning the wheel, &c. We suppose it was *driven off,* and not brought on through that wire; and that the machine and man, &c., were electrised *minus, i.e.* had less electrical fire in them than things in common.

As the vessel is just upon sailing, I cannot give you so large an account of *American* electricity as I intended: I shall only mention a few particulars more. We find granulated lead better to fill the phial with, than water, being easily warmed, and keeping warm and dry in damp air. We fire spirits with the wire of the phial. We light candles, just blown out, by drawing a spark among the smoke, between the wire and snuffers. We represent lightning, by passing the wire in the dark, over a China plate, that has gilt flowers, or applying it to gilt frames of looking-glasses, &c. We electrise a person twenty or more times running, with a touch of the finger on the wire, thus; He stands on wax. Give him the electrised bottle in his hand. Touch the wire with your finger, and then touch his hand or face; there are sparks every time. We increase the force of the electrical kiss vastly, thus: Let A and B stand on wax; or A on wax, and B on the floor; give one of them the electrised phial in hand; let the other take hold of the wire; there will be a small spark; but when their lips approach, they will be struck and shock'd. The same if another gentleman and lady, C and D, standing also on wax, and joining hands with A and B, salute or shake hands. We suspend by fine silk thread a counterfeit spider, made of a small piece of burnt cork, with legs of linnen thread, and a grain or two of lead stuck in him, to give him more weight. Upon the table, over which he hangs, we stick a wire upright, as high as the phial and wire, two or three inches from the spider: then we animate him by setting the electrified phial at the same distance on the other side of him; he will immediately fly to the wire of the phial, bend his legs in touching it; then spring off, and fly to the wire on the table; thence again to the wire of the phial, playing with his legs against both, in a very entertaining manner, appearing perfectly alive to persons unacquainted. He will continue this motion an hour or more in dry weather. We electrify, upon wax in the dark, a book that has a double line of gold round upon the covers, and then apply a knuckle to the gilding; the fire appears everywhere upon the gold like a flash of lightning: not upon the leather, nor, if you touch the leather instead of the gold. We rub our tubes with buckskin, and observe always to keep the same side to the tube, and never to sully the tube by

handling; thus they work readily and easily, without the
least fatigue, especially if kept in tight pasteboard cases,
lined with flannel, and sitting close to the tube. This I
mention, because the *European* papers on Electricity,
frequently speak of rubbing the tube, as a fatiguing exercise. Our spheres are fixed on iron axes, which pass
through them. At one end of the axis there is a small
handle, with which you turn the sphere like a common
grindstone. This we find very commodious, as the machine takes up but little room, is portable, and may be
enclosed in a tight box, when not in use. 'Tis true, the
sphere does not turn so swift as when the great wheel is
used: but swiftness we think of little importance, since
a few turns will charge the phial, &c., sufficiently. . . .

[7]

Franklin's Kite

*Franklin's new principles led to the famous kite exper-
iment, best described by the English chemist Joseph
Priestley in a later account written under Franklin's
guidance.*

[1767]

As every circumstance relating to so capital a discovery
(the greatest, perhaps, since the time of Sir Isaac Newton) cannot but give pleasure to all my readers, I shall
endeavour to gratify them with the communication of a
few particulars which I have from the best authority.

The Doctor, having published his method of verifying
his hypothesis concerning the sameness of electricity with
the matter of lightning, was waiting for the erection of a
spire in Philadelphia to carry his views into execution,
not imagining that a pointed rod of a moderate height
could answer the purpose, when it occurred to him that
by means of a common kite he could have better access
to the regions of thunder than by any spire whatever.
Preparing, therefore, a large silk handkerchief and two
cross-sticks of a proper length on which to extend it, he
took the opportunity of the first approaching thunder-

storm to take a walk in the fields, in which there was a shed convenient for his purpose. But, dreading the ridicule which too commonly attends unsuccessful attempts in science, he communicated his intended experiment to nobody but his son who assisted him in raising the kite.

The kite being raised, a considerable time elapsed before there was any appearance of its being electrified. One very promising cloud had passed over it without any effect, when, at length, just as he was beginning to despair of his contrivance, he observed some loose threads of the hempen string to stand erect and to avoid one another, just as if they had been suspended on a common conductor. Struck with this promising appearance, he immediately presented his knuckle to the key, and (let the reader judge of the exquisite pleasure he must have felt at that moment) the discovery was complete. He perceived a very evident electric spark. Others succeeded, even before the string was wet, so as to put the matter past all dispute, and when the rain had wet the string he collected electric fire very copiously. This happened in June 1752, a month after the electricians in France had verified the same theory, but before he heard of anything they had done.

[8]

The Lightning Rod

If Franklin found pleasure in pure science, he nonetheless saw to it that the new-born baby grew up to be a useful citizen. At about the same time that he was telling readers of his Gazette *about the kite experiment he was giving the public, in* Poor Richard *for 1753, his first instructions on ''How to Secure Houses from Lightning.''*

It has pleased God in his Goodness to Mankind, at length to discover to them the Means of securing their Habitations and other Buildings from Mischief by Thunder and Lightning. The Method is this: Provide a small Iron Rod (it may be made of the Rod-iron used by the Nailers) but of such a Length, that one End being three or four Feet in the moist Ground, the other may be six or eight Feet above the highest Part of the Building. To the upper End of the Rod fasten about a Foot of Brass Wire, the Size of a common Knitting-needle sharpened to a fine Point; the Rod may be secured to the House by a few small Staples. If the House or Barn be long, there may be a Rod and Point at each End, and a middling Wire along the Ridge from one to the other. A House thus furnished will not be damaged by Lightning, it being attracted by the Points, and passing thro' the Metal into the Ground without hurting any Thing. Vessels also, having a sharp pointed Rod fix'd on the Top of their Masts, with a Wire from the Foot of the Rod reaching down, round one of the Shrouds, to the Water, will not be hurt by Lightning.

[9]

Humane Slaughtering

Franklin, Immanuel Kant said, was a new Prometheus who had stolen fire from heaven. Having stolen the fire, Franklin took over its promotion; refusing patents, he propagandized for his inventions. The quality of his humanitarianism and the depth of his dilettantism—and dilettante was an honorific term in the eighteenth century—are illustrated in some of his inventions and discoveries and in what he said about them.

The men to whom the following communication is addressed, Dubourg and Dalibard, were both French scientists. They corresponded with Franklin a great deal and translated many of his works into French.

TO BARBEU DUBOURG AND THOMAS FRANCOIS DALIBARD

[1773]

My Dear Friends,

My answer to your questions concerning the mode of rendering meat tender by electricity, can only be founded upon conjecture; for I have not experiments enough to warrant the facts. All that I can say at present is, that I think electricity might be employed for this purpose, and I shall state what follows as the observations or reasons which make me presume so.

It has been observed that lightning, by rarefying and reducing into vapour the moisture contained in solid wood, in an oak, for instance, has forcibly separated its fibres, and broken it into small splinters; that, by penetrating intimately the hardest metals, as iron, it has separated the parts in an instant, so as to convert a perfect solid into a state of fluidity; it is not then improbable, that the same subtile matter, passing through the bodies of animals with rapidity, should possess sufficient force to produce an effect nearly similar.

The flesh of animals, fresh killed in the usual manner, is firm, hard, and not in a very eatable state, because the particles adhere too forcibly to each other. At a certain period, the cohesion is weakened, and, in its progress towards putrefaction, which tends to produce a total separation, the flesh becomes what we call tender, or is in that state most proper to be used as our food.

It has frequently been remarked, that animals killed by lightning putrefy immediately. This cannot be invariably the case, since a quantity of lightning, sufficient to kill, may not be sufficient to tear and divide the fibres and particles of flesh, and reduce them to that tender state, which is the prelude to putrefaction. Hence it is, that some animals killed in this manner will keep longer than others. But the putrefaction sometimes proceeds with surprising celerity. A respectable person assured me that he once knew a remarkable instance of this. A whole flock of sheep in Scotland, being closely assembled under a tree, were killed by a flash of lightning; and, it being rather late in the evening, the proprietor, desirous of saving something, sent persons early the next morning to flay them; but the putrefaction was such, and the stench so abominable, that they had not the courage to execute their orders, and the bodies were accordingly buried in their skins. It is not unreasonable to presume, that, between the period of their death and that of their putrefaction, a time intervened in which the flesh might be only tender, and only sufficiently so to be served at table. Add to this that persons, who have eaten of fowls killed by our feeble imitation of lightning (electricity), and dressed immediately, have asserted, that the flesh was remarkably tender.

The little utility of this practice has perhaps prevented its being much adopted. For, though it sometimes happens, that a company unexpectedly arriving at a country-house, or an unusual conflux of travellers to an inn, may render it necessary to kill a number of animals for immediate use; yet, as travellers have commonly a good appetite, little attention has been paid to the trifling inconvenience of having their meat a little tough. As this kind of death is nevertheless more sudden, and consequently less severe, than any other, if this should operate as a motive with compassionate persons to employ it for animals sacrificed for their use, they may conduct the process thus.

Having prepared a battery of six large glass jars (each from twenty to twenty-four pints) as for the Leyden experiment, and having established a communication, as usual, from the interior surface of each with the prime conductor, and having given them a full charge (which, with a good machine, may be executed in a few minutes, and may be estimated by an electrometer), a chain which communicates with the exterior of the jars must be wrapped round the thighs of the fowl; after which the operator, holding it by the wings, turned back and made to touch behind, must raise it so high that the head may receive the first shock from the prime conductor. The animal dies instantly. Let the head be immediately cut off to make it bleed, when it may be plucked and dressed immediately. This quantity of electricity is supposed sufficient for a turkey of ten pounds weight, and perhaps for a lamb. Experience alone will inform us of the requisite proportions for animals of different forms and ages. Probably not less will be required to render a small bird, which is very old, tender, than for a larger one, which is young. It is easy to furnish the requisite quantity of electricity, by employing a greater or less number of jars. As six jars, however, discharged at once, are capable of giving a very violent shock, the operator must be very circumspect, lest he should happen to make the experiment on his own flesh, instead of that of the fowl. . . .*

[10]

The Franklin Stove

Franklin invented the Pennsylvania fireplace in 1739 or 1740. The stoves were manufactured by his friend Robert Grace, and were sold at first at the Philadelphia Post Office. The inventor was offered a patent, but refused on the ground that, since we enjoy the benefits of the inventions of others, we ought to be generous with our own inventions. He wrote the following pamphlet to promote sales.

AN ACCOUNT OF THE NEW-INVENTED
PENNSYLVANIAN FIRE-PLACES

1744

In these Northern Colonies the Inhabitants keep Fires to sit by, generally *Seven Months* in the Year; that is, from the Beginning of *October* to the End of *April;* and in some Winters near *Eight Months,* by taking in part of *September* and *May.*

Wood, our common Fewel, which within these 100 Years might be had at every Man's Door, must now be fetch'd near 100 Miles to some Towns, and makes a very considerable Article in the Expence of Families.

As therefore so much of the Comfort and Conveniency of our Lives, for so great a Part of the Year, depends on the Article of *Fire;* since Fuel is become so expensive, and (as the Country is more clear'd and settled) will of course grow scarcer and dearer; any new Proposal for Saving the Wood, and for lessening the Charge and aug-

---

*Twenty years before, Franklin had inadvertently given himself a tremendous shock while preparing to electrocute a Christmas turkey. He likened his blunder to that of the man "who, being about to steal powder, made a hole in the cask with a hot iron."

menting the Benefit of Fire, by some particular Method of Making and Managing it, may at least be thought worth Consideration.

The New Fire-Places are a late Invention to that purpose, (experienced now three Winters by a great Number of Families in *Pennsylvania*) of which this Paper is intended to give a particular Account.

That the Reader may better judge whether this Method of Managing Fire has any Advantage over those heretofore in Use, it may be proper to consider both the old and new Methods, separately and particularly, and afterwards make the Comparison.

In order to this 'tis necessary to understand well some few of the Properties of Air and Fire, *viz*.

1. Air is rarified by *Heat*, and condens'd by *Cold, i.e.* the same Quantity of Air takes up more Space when warm than when cold. This may be shown by several very easy Experiments. Take any clear Glass Bottle (a *Florence* Flask stript of the Straw is best), place it before the Fire, and, as the Air within is warm'd and rarified, part of it will be driven out of the Bottle; turn it up, place its Mouth in a Vessel of Water, and remove it from the Fire; then, as the Air within cools and contracts, you will see the Water rise in the Neck of the Bottle, supplying the Place of just so much Air as was driven out. Hold a large hot Coal near the Side of the Bottle, and as the Air within feels the Heat, it will again distend and force out the Water. Or, Fill a Bladder half-full of Air, tie the Neck tight, and lay it before a Fire as near as may be without scorching the Bladder; as the Air within heats, you will perceive it to swell and fill the Bladder, till it becomes tight, as if full blown: Remove it to a cool Place, and you will see it fall gradually, till it becomes as lank as at first.

2. Air rarified and distended by Heat is specifically lighter than it was before, and will rise in other Air of greater Density. As Wood, Oil, or any other Matter specifically lighter than Water, if plac'd at the Bottom of a Vessel of Water, will rise till it comes to the Top; so rarified Air will rise in common Air, till it either comes to Air of equal Weight, or is by Cold reduc'd to its former Density.

* * *

A Fire then being made in any Chimney, the Air over the Fire is rarified by the Heat, becomes lighter and therefore immediately rises in the Funnel, and goes out; the other Air in the Room (flowing towards the Chimney) supplies its Place, is rarified in its turn, and rises likewise; the Place of the Air thus carried out of the Room is supplied by fresh Air coming in thro' Doors and Windows, or, if they be shut, thro' every Crevice with Violence, as may be seen by holding a Candle to a Key-hole: If the Room be so tight as that all the Crevices together will not supply so much Air as is continually carried off, then in a little time the Current up the Funnel must flag, and the Smoke, being no longer driven up must come into the Room.

1. Fire (*i.e.* Common Fire) throws out Light, Heat, and Smoke (or Fume). The two first move in right Lines, and with great Swiftness; the latter is but just separated from the Fuel, and then moves only as it is carried by the Stream of rarified Air. And without a continual Accession and Recession of Air, to carry off the smoaky Fumes, they would remain crouded about the Fire, and stifle it.

2. Heat may be separated from the Smoke as well as from the Light, by means of a Plate of Iron, which will suffer Heat to pass through it without the others.

3. Fire sends out its Rays of Heat, as well as Rays of Light, equally every way: But the greatest sensible Heat is over the Fire, where there is, besides the Rays of Heat shot upwards, a continual rising Stream of hot Air, heated by the Rays shot round on every Side. . . .

The Advantages of this Fire-Place

Its Advantages above the common Fire-Places are,

1. That your whole Room is equally warmed; so that People need not croud so close round the Fire, but may sit near the Window, and have the Benefit of the Light for Reading, Writing, Needlework, &c. They may sit with Comfort in any Part of the Room, which is a very considerable Advantage in a large Family, where there must

often be two Fires kept, because all cannot conveniently come at one.

2. If you sit near the Fire, you have not that cold Draught of uncomfortable Air nipping your Back and Heels, as when before common Fires, by which many catch Cold, being scorcht before, and, as it were, froze behind.

3. If you sit against a Crevice, there is not that sharp Draught of cold Air playing on you, as in Rooms where there are Fires in the common way; by which many catch Cold, whence proceed Coughs, Catarrhs, Tooth-achs, Fever, Pleurisies, and many other Diseases.

4. In Case of Sickness, they make most excellent Nursing-Rooms; as they constantly supply a Sufficiency of fresh Air, so warmed at the same time as to be no way inconvenient or dangerous. A small One does well in a Chamber; and, the Chimneys being fitted for it, it may be remov'd from one Room to another, as Occasion requires, and fix'd in half an Hour. The equal Temper, too, and Warmth, of the Air of the Room, is thought to be particularly advantageous in some Distempers: For 'twas observ'd in the Winters of 1730 and 1736, when the Small-Pox spread in *Pennsylvania,* that very few of the Children of the *Germans* died of that Distemper in Proportion to those of the *English;* which was ascrib'd by some to the Warmth and equal Temper of Air in their Stove-Rooms; which made the Disease as favourable as it commonly is in *West Indies*. But this Conjecture we submit to the judgment of Physicians.

5. In common Chimneys, the strongest Heat from the Fire, which is upwards, goes directly up the Chimney, and is lost; and there is such a strong Draught into the Chimney, that not only the upright Heat, but also the back, sides, and downward Heats are carried up the Chimney by that Draught of Air; and the Warmth given before the Fire, by the Rays that strike out towards the Room, is continually driven back, crouded into the Chimney and carried up, by the same Draught of Air. But here the upright heat strikes and heats the Top Plate, which warms the Air above it, and that comes into the Room. The Heat likewise, which the Fire communicates to the Sides, Back Bottom and Air-box, is all brought

into the Room; for you will find a constant Current of warm Air coming out of the Chimney-Corner into the Room. Hold a Candle just under the Mantle-Piece, or Breast of your Chimney, and you will see the Flame bent outwards: By laying a Piece of Smoaking Paper on the Hearth, on either Side, you may see how the Current of Air moves, and where it tends, for it will turn and carry the Smoke with it.

6. Thus, as very little of the Heat is lost, when this Fire-Place is us'd, *much less Wood* will serve you, which is a considerable Advantage where Wood is dear.

7. When you burn Candles near this Fire-Place, you will find that the Flame burns quite upright, and does not blare and run the Tallow down, by drawing towards the Chimney, as against common Fires.

8. This Fire-Place cures most smoaky Chimneys, and thereby preserves both the Eyes and Furniture.

9. It prevents the Fouling of Chimneys; much of the Lint and Dust that contributes to foul a Chimney, being by the low Arch oblig'd to pass thro' the Flame, where 'tis consum'd. Then, less Wood being burnt, there is less Smoke made. Again, the Shutter, or Trap-Bellows, soon blowing the Wood into a Flame, the same Wood does not yield so much Smoke as if burnt in a common Chimney: For as soon as Flame begins, Smoke, in proportion, ceases.

10. And, if a Chimney should be foul, 'tis much less likely to take Fire. If it should take Fire, 'tis easily stifled and extinguished.

11. A Fire may be very speedily made in this Fire-Place, by the Help of the Shutter, or Trap-Bellows, as aforesaid.

12. A Fire may soon be extinguished by closing it with the Shutter before, and turning the Register behind, which will stifle it, and the Brands will remain ready to rekindle.

13. The Room being once warm, the Warmth may be retain'd in it all Night.

14. And lastly, the Fire is so secur'd at Night, that not one Spark can fly out into the Room to do Damage.

With all these Conveniencies, you do not lose the pleasing Sight nor Use of the Fire, as in the Dutch Stoves, but may boil the Tea-Kettle, warm the Flat-Irons, heat Heaters, keep warm a Dish of Victuals by setting it on the Top, &c. &c.

[11]

The First American Catheter

When his brother John mentioned a need for a flexible catheter, Franklin addressed himself to the problem and soon came up with a satisfactory solution. John, like his father, was a tallow-chandler. In 1754 he became post-master at Boston.

TO JOHN FRANKLIN

December 8, 1752

Dear Brother,

Reflecting yesterday on your desire to have a flexible catheter, a thought struck into my mind, how one might probably be made; and lest you should not readily conceive it by any description of mine, I went immediately to the silver-smith's and gave directions for making one (sitting by till it was finished) that it might be ready for this post. But now it is done I have some apprehensions that it may be too large to be easy; if so, a silver-smith can easily make it less by twisting or turning it on a smaller wire, and putting a smaller pipe to the end, if the pipe is really necessary. This machine may either be covered with small fine gut, first cleaned and soaked a night in a solution of alum and salt and water, then rubbed dry, which will preserve it longer from putrefaction; then wet again and drawn on and tied to the pipes at each end, where little hollows are made for the thread to bind in and the surface greased. Or perhaps it may be used without the gut, having only a little tallow rubbed over it, to smooth it and fill the joints. I think it is as flexible as would be expected in a thing of the kind, and I imagine will readily comply with the turns of the passage, yet has stiffness enough to be protruded; if not, the enclosed wire may be used to stiffen the hinder part of the pipe while the fore part is pushed forward, and as it proceeds the wire may be gradually withdrawn. The tube is of such a nature, that when you have occasion to withdraw it its diameter will lessen, whereby it will move more easily. It is a kind of screw and may be both withdrawn and introduced by turning. Experience is necessary for the right using of all new tools or instruments, and that will perhaps suggest some improvements to this instrument as well as better direct the manner of using it. . . .

I am, my dear brother, yours most affectionately. . . .

[12]

The Glass Harmonica

Benjamin Franklin perfected the glass harmonica while he was in London in 1757, and the instrument's popularity there soon spread to America and the Continent. As Carl Van Doren says, "Franklin was . . . as famous among German musicians for his harmonicas as among German electricians for his lightning rod." Beethoven and Mozart were among those who composed for the harmonica.

Franklin's musical accomplishments were not always inventions; he also wrote a string quartet, composed with particular regard to the ease with which the musicians could play it.

In the following letter, an Italian scientist who introduced many of Franklin's electrical discoveries to Italy is told of the glass harmonica.

TO GIAMBATTISTA BECCARIA

July 13, 1762

Reverend Sir,

I once promised myself the pleasure of seeing you at *Turin;* but as that is not now likely to happen, being just about returning to my native country, *America,* I sit down to take leave of you (among others of my *European* friends that I cannot see) by writing.

I thank you for the honourable mention you have so frequently made of me in your letters to Mr. *Collinson* and others, for the generous defence you undertook and executed with so much success, of my electrical opinions; and for the valuable present you have made me of your new work, from which I have received great information and pleasure. I wish I could in return entertain you with any thing new of mine on that subject; but I have not lately pursued it. Nor do I know of any one here, that is at present much engaged in it.

Perhaps, however, it may be agreeable to you, as you live in a musical country, to have an account of the new instrument lately added here to the great number that charming science was before possessed of: As it is an instrument that seems peculiarly adapted to *Italian* music, especially that of the soft and plaintive kind, I will endeavour to give you such a description of it, and of the manner of constructing it, that you, or any of your friends may be enabled to imitate it, if you incline so to do, without being at the expence and trouble of the many experiments I have made of endeavouring to bring it to its present perfection.

You have doubtless heard the sweet tone that is drawn from a drinking-glass, by passing a wet finger round its brim. One Mr. *Puckeridge,* a gentleman from *Ireland,* was the first who thought of playing tunes, formed of these tones. He collected a number of glasses of different sizes, fixed them near each other on a table, and tuned them by putting into them water, more or less, as each note required. The tones were brought out by passing his fingers round their brims. He was unfortunately burnt here, with his instrument, in a fire which consumed the house he lived in. Mr. E. *Delaval,* a most ingenious member of our Royal Society, made one in imitation of it, with a better choice and form of glasses, which was the first I saw or heard. Being charmed by the sweetness of its tones, and the music he produced from it, I wished only to see the glasses disposed in a more convenient form, and brought together in a narrower compass, so as to admit of a greater number of tunes, and all within reach of hand to a person sitting before the instrument, which I accomplished, after various intermediate trials, and less commodious forms, both of glasses and construction, in the following manner.

The glasses are blown as near as possible in the form of hemispheres, having each an open neck or socket in the middle. . . . The thickness of the glass near the brim about a tenth of an inch, or hardly quite so much, but thicker as it comes nearer the neck, which in the largest glasses is about an inch deep, and an inch and half wide within, these dimensions lessening as the glasses themselves diminish in size, except that the neck of the smallest ought not to be shorter than half an inch. The largest glass is nine inches diameter, and the smallest three inches. Between these there are twenty-three different sizes, differing from each other a quarter of an inch in diameter. To make a single instrument there should be at least six glasses blown of each size; and out of this number one may probably pick 37 glasses, (which are sufficient for three octaves with all the semitones) that will be each either the note one wants or a little sharper than that note, and all fitting so well into each other as to taper pretty regularly from the largest to the smallest. It is true that there are not 37 sizes, but it often happens that two of the same size differ a note or half note in tone, by reason of a difference in thickness, and these may be placed one in the other without sensibly hurting the regularity of the taper form.

The glasses being chosen and every one marked with a diamond the note you intend it for, they are to be tuned by diminishing the thickness of those that are too sharp. This is done by grinding them round from the neck towards the brim, the breadth of one or two inches, as may be required; often trying the glass by a well-tuned harpsichord, comparing the tone drawn from the glass by your finger, with the note you want, as sounded by that string of the harpsichord. When you come near the matter, be careful to wipe the glass clean and dry before each trial, because the tone is something flatter when the glass is wet, than it will be when dry; and grinding a very little between each trial, you will thereby tune to great exactness. The more care is necessary in this, because if you go below your required tone, there is no sharpening it again but by grinding somewhat off the brim, which will afterwards require polishing, and thus encrease the trouble.

The glasses being thus tuned, you are to be provided with a case for them and a spindle on which they are to be fixed. . . . My case is about three feet long, eleven inches every way wide within at the biggest end, and five inches at the smallest end; for it tapers all the way, to adapt it better to the conical figure of the set of glasses. This case opens in the middle of its height, and the upper part turns up by hinges fixed behind. The spindle which is of hard iron, lies horizontally from end to end of the box within, exactly in the middle, and is made to turn on brass gudgeons at each end. It is round, an inch diameter at the thickest end, and tapering to a quarter of an inch at the smallest. A square shank comes from its thickest end through the box, on which shank a wheel is fixed by a screw. This wheel serves as a fly to make the motion equable, when the spindle, with the glasses, is turned by the foot like a spinning-wheel. My wheel is of mahogany, 18 inches diameter, and pretty thick, so as to conceal near its circumference about 25 lb of lead. An ivory pin is fixed in the face of this wheel, and about 4 inches from the axis. Over the neck of this pin is put the loop of the string that comes up from the moveable step to give it motion. The case stands on a neat frame with four legs.

To fix the glasses on the spindle, a cork is first to be fitted in each neck pretty tight, and projecting a little without the neck, that the neck of one may not touch the inside of another when put together, for that would make a jarring. These corks are to be perforated with holes of different diameters, so as to suit that part of the spindle on which they are to be fixed. When a glass is put on, by holding it stiffly between both hands, while another turns the spindle, it may be gradually brought to its place. But care must be taken that the hole be not too small, lest, in forcing it up the neck should split; nor too large, lest the glass, not being firmly fixed, should turn or move on the spindle, so as to touch and jar against its neighbouring glass. The glasses thus are placed one in another, the largest on the biggest end of the spindle which is to the left hand; the neck of this glass is towards the wheel, and the next goes into it in the same position, only about an inch of its brim appearing beyond the brim of the first; thus proceeding, every glass when fixed shows about an inch of its brim (or three quarters of an inch, or half an inch, as they grow smaller) beyond the brim of the glass that contains it; and it is from these exposed parts of each glass that the tone is drawn, by laying a finger upon one of them as the spindle and glasses turn round.

My largest glass is G, a little below the reach of a common voice, and my highest G, including three compleat octaves. To distinguish the glasses the more readily to the eye, I have painted the apparent parts of the glasses within side, every semitone white, and the other notes of the octave with the seven prismatic colors, *viz*. C, red; D, orange; E, yellow; F, green; G, blue; A, indigo; B, purple; and C, red again; so that glasses of the same colour (the white excepted) are always octaves to each other.

This instrument is played upon, by sitting before the middle of the set of glasses as before the keys of a harpsichord, turning them with the foot, and wetting them now and then with a spunge and clean water. The fingers should be first a little soaked in water, and quite free from all greasiness; a little fine chalk upon them is sometimes useful, to make them catch the glass and bring out the tone more readily. Both hands are used, by which means different parts are played together. Observe, that the tones are best drawn out when the glasses turn *from* the ends of the fingers, not when they turn *to* them.

The advantages of this instrument are, that its tones are incomparably sweet beyond those of any other; that they may be swelled and softened at pleasure by stronger or weaker pressures of the finger, and continued to any length; and that the instrument, being once well tuned, never again wants tuning.

In honour of your musical language, I have borrowed from it the name of this instrument, calling it the Armonica.

With great esteem and respect, I am &c. . . .

[13]

Youthful Inventor

Dubourg, his good friend in France, was the recipient of many engaging letters from Franklin. Here the mature man looks back on his Massachusetts boyhood and recalls some of his first experiments and inventions.

TO BARBEU DUBOURG

[1773]

. . . When I was a boy, I made two oval palettes, each about ten inches long, and six broad, with a hole for the thumb, in order to retain it fast in the palm of my hand. They much resembled a painter's palettes. In swimming I pushed the edges of these forward, and I struck the water with their flat surfaces as I drew them back. I remember I swam faster by means of these pallets, but they fatigued my wrists. I also fitted to the soles of my feet a kind of sandals; but I was not satisfied with them, because I observed that the stroke is partly given by the inside of the feet and the ancles, and not entirely with the soles of the feet.

We have here waistcoats for swimming, which are made of double sail-cloth, with small pieces of cork quilted in between them.

I know nothing of the *scaphandre* of M. de la Chapelle.

I know by experience, that it is a great comfort to a swimmer, who has a considerable distance to go, to turn himself sometimes on his back, and to vary in other respects the means of procuring a progressive motion.

When he is seized with the cramp in the leg, the method of driving it away is, to give to the parts affected a sudden, vigorous, and violent shock; which he may do in the air as he swims on his back.

During the great heats of summer there is no danger in

bathing, however warm we may be, in rivers which have been thoroughly warmed by the sun. But to thro' one's self into cold spring water, when the body has been heated by exercise in the sun, is an imprudence which may prove fatal. I once knew an instance of four young men, who, having worked at harvest in the heat of day, with a view of refreshing themselves plunged into a spring of cold water; two died upon the spot, a third the next morning, and the fourth recovered with great difficulty. A copious draught of cold water, in similar circumstances, is frequently attended with the same effect in North America.

The exercise of swimming is one of the most healthy and agreeable in the world. After having swam for an hour or two in the evening, one sleeps cooly the whole night, even during the most ardent heat of summer. Perhaps, the pores being cleansed, the insensible perspiration increases and occasions this coolness. It is certain that much swimming is the means of stopping a diarrhoea, and even of producing a constipation. With respect to those who do not know how to swim, or who are affected with a diarrhoea at a season which does not permit them to use that exercise, a warm bath, by cleansing and purifying the skin, is found very salutary, and often effects a radical cure. I speak from my own experience, frequently repeated, and that of others, to whom I have recommended this.

You will not be displeased if I conclude these hasty remarks by informing you, that as the ordinary method of swimming is reduced to the act of rowing with the arms and legs, and is consequently a laborious and fatiguing operation when the space of water to be crossed is considerable; there is a method in which a swimmer may pass to great distances with much facility, by means of a sail. This discovery I fortunately made by accident, and in the following manner.

When I was a boy, I amused myself one day with flying a paper kite; and approaching the bank of a pond, which was near a mile broad, I tied the string to a stake, and the kite ascended to a very considerable height above the pond, while I was swimming. In a little time, being de-

sirous of amusing myself with my kite, and enjoying at
the same time the pleasure of swimming, I returned; and,
loosing from the stake the string with the little stick which
was fastened to it, went again into the water, where I
found, that lying on my back and holding the stick in my
hands, I was drawn along the surface of the water in a
very agreeable manner. Having then engaged another boy
to carry my clothes round the pond, to a place which I
pointed out to him on the other side, I began to cross the
pond with my kite, which carried me quite over without
the least fatigue, and with the greatest pleasure imaginable. I was only obliged occasionally to halt a little in
my course, and resist its progress, when it appeared that,
by following too quick, I lowered the kite too much; by
doing which occasionally I made it rise again. I have
never since that time practised this singular mode of
swimming, though I think it is not impossible to cross in
this manner from Dover to Calais. The packet-boat, however, is still preferable. . . .

[14]

Bifocals

*This is another of Franklin's inventions which is still
in use today. Whatley was a London economist.*

TO GEORGE WHATLEY

May 23, 1785

Dear Old Friend,

By Mr. Dollond's Saying, that my double Spectacles
can only serve particular Eyes, I doubt he has not been
rightly informed of their Construction. I imagine it will
be found pretty generally true, that the same Convexity
of Glass, through which a Man sees clearest and best at
the Distance proper for Reading, is not the best for greater
Distances. I therefore had formerly two Pair of Spectacles, which I shifted occasionally, as in travelling I some-

times read, and often wanted to regard the Prospects. Finding this Change troublesome, and not always sufficiently ready, I had the Glasses cut, and half of each kind associated in the same Circle . . .

By this means, as I wear my Spectacles constantly, I have only to move my Eyes up or down, as I want to see distinctly far or near, the proper Glasses being always ready. This I find more particularly convenient since my being in France, the Glasses that serve me best at Table to see what I eat, not being the best to see the Faces of those on the other Side of the Table who speak to me; and when one's Ears are not well accustomed to the Sounds of a Language, a Sight of the Movements in the Features of him that speaks helps to explain; so that I understand French better by the help of my Spectacles. . . .

[15]

The Long Arm

This invention has moved from the library to the grocery. (Franklin included a sketch with this letter.)

DESCRIPTION OF AN INSTRUMENT FOR TAKING DOWN BOOKS FROM HIGH SHELVES

January, 1786

Old men find it inconvenient to mount a ladder or steps for that purpose, their heads being sometimes subject to giddinesses, and their activity, with the steadiness of their joints, being abated by age; besides the trouble of removing the steps every time a book is wanted from a different part of their library.

For a remedy, I have lately made the following simple machine, which I call the *Long Arm.*

AB, the *Arm,* is a stick of pine, an inch square and 8 feet long. *C, D,* the *Thumb* and *Finger,* are two pieces of ash lath, an inch and half wide, and a quarter of an inch thick. These are fixed by wood screws on opposite sides of the end *A* of the arm *AB;* the finger *D* being longer and standing out an inch and half farther than the thumb *C*. The outside of the ends of these laths are pared off sloping and thin, that they may more easily enter between books that stand together on a shelf. Two small holes are bored through them at *i, k. EF,* the sinew, is a cord of the size of a small goosequill, with a loop at one end. When applied to the machine it passes through the two laths, and is stopped by a knot in its other end behind the longest at *k*. The hole at *i* is nearer the end of the arm than that at *k,* about an inch. A number of knots are also on the cord, distant three or four inches from each other.

To use this instrument; put one hand into the loop, and draw the sinew straight down the side of the arm; then enter the end of the finger between the book you would take down and that which is next to it. The laths being flexible, you may easily by a slight pressure sideways open them wider if the book is thick, or close them if it is thin by pulling the string, so as to enter the shorter lath or thumb between your book and that which is next to its other side, then push till the back of your book comes to touch the string. Then draw the string or sinew tight, which will cause the thumb and finger to pinch the book strongly, so that you may draw it out. As it leaves the other books, turn the instrument a *quarter* round, so that the book may lie flat and rest on its side upon the under lath or finger. The knots on the sinew will help you to keep it tight and close to the side of the arm as you take it down hand over hand, till the book comes to you; which would drop from between the thumb and finger if the sinew was let loose.

All new tools require some practice before we can become expert in the use of them. This requires very little.

Made in the proportions above given, it serves well for books in duodecimo or octavo. Quartos and folios are too heavy for it; but those are usually placed on the lower shelves within reach of hand.

The book taken down, may, when done with, be put up again into its place by the same machine.

IV

THE NEW PROMETHEUS, II:
FRANKLIN AND THE REVOLUTION

On July 5, 1775, Franklin wrote to his old friend William Strahan: "You are a Member of Parliament, and one of that Majority which has doomed my Country to Destruction.—You have begun to burn our Towns, and murder our People.—Look upon your Hands! They are stained with the Blood of your Relations!—You and I were long Friends:—You are now my Enemy,—and I am, **[1]**
Yours,
B. Franklin"

Franklin never sent this letter, but it fully expresses the rage which British policies aroused within him. So it was that a new British imperialism interrupted Franklin in his theft of lightning from the heavens; he turned with equal ardor to snatching the scepter from the hands of tyrants. Convinced that "there never was a good War, or a bad Peace," Franklin did his best to prevent war and, when it came, to palliate the sufferings of the civilian populations on both sides. When the fighting finally ended, he tried to write into the Treaty an article forbidding privateering in future wars; if wars must happen, Franklin felt, let noncombatants be protected from their ravages.

The Stamp Act

Franklin was a master propagandist, and propaganda was a major element of his diplomacy. In 1766 he first called upon his abilities as publicist in the battle against English taxation. With the aid of some M.P.'s friendly to the American cause, he staged a brilliant question-and-answer session before Commons which helped to bring about the repeal of the Stamp Act. Some excerpts from the examination illustrate the skill with which Franklin parried both friendly and unfriendly questions.

THE EXAMINATION OF DOCTOR BENJAMIN FRANKLIN . . . IN THE BRITISH HOUSE OF COMMONS, RELATIVE TO THE REPEAL OF THE AMERICAN STAMP ACT . . .

[February, 1766]

Q. What is your name, and place of abode?

A. Franklin, of Philadelphia. . . .

Q. From the thinness of the back settlements, would not the stamp act be extremely inconvenient to the inhabitants, if executed?

A. To be sure it would; as many of the inhabitants could not get stamps when they had occasion for them without taking long journeys, and spending perhaps Three or Four Pounds, that the Crown might get Six pence.

Q. Are not the Colonies, from their circumstances, very able to pay the stamp duty?

A. In my opinion there is not gold and silver enough in the Colonies to pay the stamp duty for one year.

Q. Don't you know that the money arising from the stamps was all to be laid out in America?

A. I know it is appropriated by the act to the American service; but it will be spent in the conquered Colonies, where the soldiers are, not in the Colonies that pay it.

Q. Is there not a balance of trade due from the Colonies where the troops are posted, that will bring back the money to the old colonies?

A. I think not. I believe very little would come back. I know of no trade likely to bring it back. I think it would come from the Colonies where it was spent directly to England; for I have always observed, that in every Colony the more plenty the means of remittance to England, the more goods are sent for, and the more trade with England carried on. . . .

Q. Do not you think the people of America would submit to pay the stamp duty, if it was moderated?

A. No, never, unless compelled by force of arms. . . .

Q. What was the temper of America towards Great Britain before the year 1763?

A. The best in the world. They submitted willingly to the government of the Crown, and paid, in all their courts, obedience to acts of parliament. Numerous as the people are in the several provinces, they cost you nothing in forts, citadels, garrisons, or armies, to keep them in subjection. They are governed by this country at the expence only of a little pen, ink and paper. They were led by a thread. They had not only a respect, but an affection for Great-Britain; for its laws, its customs and manners, and even a fondness for its fashions, that greatly increased the commerce. Natives of Britain were always treated with particular regard; to be an Old-England man was, of itself, a character of some respect, and gave a kind of rank among us.

Q. And what is their temper now?

A. O, very much altered.

Q. Did you ever hear the authority of parliament to make laws for America questioned till lately?

A. The authority of Parliament was allowed to be valid in all laws, except such as should lay internal taxes. It was never disputed in laying duties to regulate commerce. . . .

Q. In what light did the people of America use to consider the parliament of Great-Britain?

A. They considered the parliament as the great bulwark and security of their liberties and privileges, and always spoke of it with the utmost respect and veneration. Arbitrary ministers, they thought, might possibly, at times, attempt to oppress them; but they relied on it, that the parliament, on application, would always give redress. They remembered, with gratitude, a strong instance of this, when a bill was brought into parliament, with a clause, to make royal instructions laws in the colonies, which the House of Commons would not pass, and it was thrown out.

Q. And have they not still the same respect for parliament?

A. No, it is greatly lessened.

Q. To what causes is that owing?

A. To a concurrence of causes; the restraints lately laid on their trade, by which the bringing of foreign gold and silver into the Colonies was prevented; the prohibition of making paper money among themselves; and then demanding a new and heavy tax by stamps; taking away, at the same time, trials by juries, and refusing to receive and hear their humble petitions.

Q. Don't you think they would submit to the stamp-act, if it was modified, the obnoxious parts taken out, and the duty reduced to some particulars, of small moment?

A. No; they will never submit to it. . . .

Q. What is your opinion of a future tax, imposed on the same principle with that of the stamp-act? How would the Americans receive it?

A. Just as they do this. They would not pay it.

Q. Have not you heard of the resolutions of this House, and of the House of Lords, asserting the right of parliament relating to America, including a power to tax the people there?

A. Yes, I have heard of such resolutions.

Q. What will be the opinion of the Americans on those resolutions?

A. They will think them unconstitutional and unjust.

Q. Was it an opinion in America before 1763, that the parliament had no right to lay taxes and duties there?

A. I never heard any objection to the right of laying duties to regulate commerce; but a right to lay internal taxes was never supposed to be in parliament, as we are not represented there. . . .

Q. Can any thing less than a military force carry the stamp act into execution?

A. I do not see how a military force can be applied to the purpose.

Q. Why may it not?

A. Suppose a military force sent into America, they will find nobody in arms; what are they then to do? They cannot force a man to take stamps who chuses to do without them. They will not find a rebellion; they may indeed make one.

Q. If the act is not repealed, what do you think will be the consequences?

A. A total loss of the respect and affection the people of America bear to this country, and of all the commerce that depends on that respect and affection.

Q. How can the commerce be affected?

A. You will find, that if the act is not repealed, they will take very little of your manufactures in a short time.

Q. Is it in their power to do without them?

A. I think they may very well do without them. . . .

Q. Don't you know, that there is, in the Pennsylvania charter, an express reservation of the right of parliament to lay taxes there?

A. I know there is a clause in the charter, by which the King grants, that he will levy no taxes on the inhabitants, unless it be with the consent of the assembly, or by act of parliament.

Q. How, then, could the assembly of Pennsylvania assert, that laying a tax on them by the stamp act was an infringement of their rights?

A. They understand it thus; by the same charter, and otherwise, they are entitled to all the privileges and liberties of Englishmen; they find in the great charters, and the petition and declaration of rights, that one of the privileges of English subjects is, that they are not to be taxed but by their common consent; they have therefore relied upon it, from the first settlement of the province, that the parliament never would, nor could, by colour of that clause in the charter, assume a right of taxing them, till it had qualified itself to exercise such right, by admitting representatives from the people to be taxed, who ought to make a part of that common consent.

Q. Are there any words in the charter that justify that construction?

A. "The common rights of Englishmen," as declared by Magna Charta, and the petition of right, all justify it.

Q. Does the distinction between internal and external taxes exist in the words of the charter?

A. No, I believe not.

Q. Then, may they not, by the same interpretation, object to the parliament's right of external taxation?

A. They never have hitherto. Many arguments have been lately used here to shew them, that there is no difference, and that, if you have no right to tax them internally, you have none to tax them externally, or make any other law to bind them. At present they do not reason so; but in time they may possibly be convinced by these arguments. . . .

Q. What used to be the pride of the Americans?
A. To indulge in the fashions and manufactures of Great Britain.
A. What is now their pride?
A. To wear their old cloaths over again, till they can make new ones.

[2]

After Repeal

Although the Stamp Act was repealed, there came a declaration of Parliament's right to legislate for the Colonies "in all cases whatsoever." There were also rumors of financial retribution for American resistance. Franklin replied to the latter threat in a pseudonymous letter to a London newspaper.

[1766]

To the Printer,—

It is reported, I know not with what Foundation, that there is an Intention of obliging the Americans to pay for all the Stamps they ought to have used, between the Commencement of the Act, and the Day on which the Repeal takes Place, viz. from the first of November 1765 to the first of May 1766; and this is to make part of an Act, which is to give Validity to the Writings and Law Proceedings, that contrary to Law have been executed without Stamps, and is to be the Condition of which they are to receive that Validity. Shall we then keep up for a Trifle the Heats and Animosities that have been occasioned by the Stamp Act? and lose all the Benefit of Harmony and good Understanding between the different Parts of the Empire, which were expected from a generous total Repeal? Is this Pittance likely to be a Whit more easily collected than the whole Duty? Where are Officers to be found who will undertake to collect it? Who is to protect them while they are about it? In my Opinion, it will meet with the same Opposition, and be attended with the same Mischiefs that would have attended an Enforcement of the Act entire.

But I hear, that this is thought necessary, to raise a Fund for defraying the Expence that has been incurred by stamping so much Paper and Parchment for the Use of America, which they have refused to take and turn'd upon our Hands; and that since they are highly favour'd by the Repeal, they cannot with any Face of Decency refuse to make good the Charges we have been at on their Account. The whole Proceeding would put one in Mind of the Frenchman that used to accost English and other Strangers on the Pont-Neuf, with many Compliments, and a red hot Iron in his Hand: *Pray Monsieur Anglois*, says he, *Do me the Favour to let me have the Honour of thrusting this hot Iron into your Backside?* Zoons, what does the Fellow mean! Begone with your Iron or I'll break your Head! *Nay Monsieur*, replies he, *if you do not chuse it I do not insist upon it. But at least, you will in Justice have the Goodness to pay me something for the heating of my Iron.*

F.B. **[3]**

The Weapon of Satire

English politicians continued to look for ways to make the Americans pay for the heating of the iron. In the fall of 1773 Franklin grew tired of "smooth Words," became "saucy," and published two harsh satires: Rules by Which a Great Empire May be Reduced to a Small One *and* An Edict by the King of Prussia. *In these essays, he wrote his sister, he "held up a Looking-Glass in which some Ministers may see their ugly Faces, & the Nation its Injustice."*

AN EDICT BY THE KING OF PRUSSIA

Dantzic, Sept. 5, [1773.]

We have long wondered here at the supineness of the English nation, under the Prussian impositions upon its trade entering our port. We did not, till lately, know the claims, ancient and modern, that hang over that nation; and therefore could not suspect that it might submit to those impositions from a sense of duty or from principles of equity. The following Edict, just made publick, may, if serious, throw some light upon this matter.

"FREDERIC, by the grace of God, King of Prussia, &c. &c. &c., to all present and to come, (*à tous présens et à venir*,) Health. The peace now enjoyed throughout our dominions, having afforded us leisure to apply ourselves to the regulation of commerce, the improvement of our finances, and at the same time the easing our domestic subjects in their taxes: For these causes, and other good considerations us thereunto moving, we hereby make known, that, after having deliberated these affairs in our council, present our dear brothers, and other great officers of the state, members of the same, we, of our certain knowledge, full power, and authority royal, have made and issued this present Edict, viz.

"Whereas it is well known to all the world, that the first German settlements made in the Island of Britain, were by colonies of people, subject to our renowned ducal ancestors, and drawn from their dominions, under the conduct of Hengist, Horsa, Hella, Uff, Cerdicus, Ida, and others; and that the said colonies have flourished under the protection of our august house for ages past; have never been emancipated therefrom; and yet have hitherto yielded little profit to the same: And whereas we ourself have in the last war fought for and defended the said colonies, against the power of France, and thereby enabled them to make conquests from the said power in America, for which we have not yet received adequate compensation: And whereas it is just and expedient that a revenue should be raised from the said colonies in Britain, towards our indemnification; and that those who are descendants of our ancient subjects, and thence still owe us due obedience, should contribute to the replenishing of our royal coffers as they must have done, had their ancestors remained in the territories now to us appertaining: We do therefore hereby ordain and command, that, from and after the date of these presents, there shall be levied and paid to our officers of the *customs*, on all goods, wares, and merchandizes, and on all grain and other produce of the earth, exported from the said Island of Britain, and on all goods of whatever kind imported into the same, a duty of four and a half per cent *ad valorem,* for the use of us and our successors. And that the said duty may more effectually be collected, we do hereby ordain, that all ships or vessels bound from Great Britain to any other part of the world, or from any other part of the world to Great Britain, shall in their respective voyages touch at our port of Koningsberg, there to be unladen, searched, and charged with the said duties.

"And whereas there hath been from time to time discovered in the said island of Great Britain, by our colonists there, many mines or beds of iron-stone; and sundry subjects, of our ancient dominion, skilful in converting the said stone into metal, have in time past transported themselves thither, carrying with them and communicating that art; and the inhabitants of the said island, presuming that they had a natural right to make the best use they could of the natural productions of their country for their own benefit, have not only built furnaces for smelting the said stone into iron, but have erected plating-forges, slitting-mills, and steel-furnaces, for the more convenient manufacturing of the same; thereby endangering a diminution of the said manufacture in our ancient dominion;—we do therefore hereby farther ordain, that, from and after the date hereof, no mill or other engine for slitting or rolling of iron, or any plating-forge to work with a tilt-hammer, or any furnace for making steel, shall be erected or continued in the said island of Great Britain: And the Lord Lieutenant of every county in the said island is hereby commanded, on information of any such erection within his county, to order and by force to cause the same to be abated and destroyed; as he shall answer the neglect thereof to us at his peril. But we are nevertheless graciously pleased to permit the inhabitants of the said island to transport their iron into Prussia, there to be manufactured, and to them returned; they paying our Prussian subjects for the workmanship, with all the costs of commission, freight, and risk, coming and returning; any thing herein contained to the contrary notwithstanding.

"We do not, however, think fit to extend this our indulgence to the article of wool; but, meaning to encourage, not only the manufacturing of woollen cloth, but also the raising of wool, in our ancient dominions, and to prevent both, as much as may be, in our said island, we do hereby absolutely forbid the transportation of wool from thence, even to the mother country, Prussia; and that those islanders may be farther and more effectually restrained in making any advantage of their own wool in the way of manufacture, we command that none shall be carried out of one county into another; nor shall any worsted, bay, or woollen yarn, cloth, says, bays, kerseys, serges, frizes, druggets, cloth-serges, shalloons, or any other drapery stuffs, or woollen manufactures whatsoever, made up or mixed with wool in any of the said counties, be carried into any other county, or be waterborne even across the smallest river or creek, on penalty of forfeiture of the same, together with the boats, carriages, horses, &c., that shall be employed in removing them. Nevertheless, our loving subjects there are hereby permitted (if they think proper) to use all their wool as manure for the improvement of their lands.

"And whereas the art and mystery of making hats hath arrived at great perfection in Prussia, and the making of hats by our remoter subjects ought to be as much as possible restrained: And forasmuch as the islanders before mentioned, being in possession of wool, beaver and other furs, have presumptuously conceived they had a right to make some advantage thereof, by manufacturing the same into hats, to the prejudice of our domestic manufacture: We do therefore hereby strictly command and ordain, that no hats or felts whatsoever, dyed or undyed, finished or unfinished, shall be loaded or put into or upon any vessel, cart, carriage, or horse, to be transported or conveyed out of one county in the said island into another county, or to any other place whatsoever, by any person or persons whatsoever; on pain of forfeiting the same, with a penalty of five hundred pounds sterling for every offence. Nor shall any hat-maker, in any of the said counties, employ more than two apprentices, on penalty of five pounds sterling per month; we intending hereby, that such hatmakers, being so restrained, both in the production and sale of their commodity, may find no advantage in continuing their business. But, lest the said islanders should suffer inconveniency by the want of hats, we are farther graciously pleased to permit them to send their beaver furs to Prussia; and we also permit hats made thereof to be exported from Prussia to Britain; the people thus favoured to pay all costs and charges of manufacturing, interest, commission to our merchants, insurance and freight going and returning, as in the case of iron.

"And, lastly, being willing farther to favour our said colonies in Britain, we do hereby also ordain and command, that all the *thieves,* highway and street robbers, house-breakers, forgerers, murderes, s[o]d[omi]tes and villains of every denomination, who have forfeited their lives to the law in Prussia; but whom we, in our great clemency, do not think fit here to hang, shall be emptied out of our gaols into the said island of Great Britain, for the better peopling of that country.

"We flatter ourselves, that these our royal regulations and commands will be thought just and reasonable by our much-favoured colonists in England; the said regulations being copied from their statutes of 10 and 11 William III. c. 10, 5 Geo. II. c. 22, 23, Geo. II. c. 29, 4 Geo. I. c. 11, and from other equitable laws made by their parliaments; or from instructions given by their Princes; or from resolutions of both Houses, entered into for the good government of their *own colonies in Ireland and America*.

"And all persons in the said island are hereby cautioned not to oppose in any wise the execution of this our Edict, or any part thereof, such opposition being high treason; of which all who are suspected shall be transported in fetters from Britain to Prussia, there to be tried and executed according to the Prussian law.

"Such is our pleasure.
"Given at Potsdam, this twenty-fifth day of the month of August, one thousand seven hundred and seventy-three, and in the thirty-third year of our reign.
"By the King, in his Council.
"RECHTMAESSIG, *Sec.*"

Some take this Edict to be merely one of the King's

Jeux d'Esprit: other suppose it serious, and that he means
a quarrel with England; but all here think the assertion
it concludes with, "that these regulations are copied from
acts of the English parliament respecting their colonies,"
a very injurious one; it being impossible to believe, that
a people distinguished for their love of liberty, a nation
so wise, so liberal in its sentiments, so just and equitable
towards its neighbours, should, from mean and injudi-
cious views of petty immediate profit, treat its own children in a manner so arbitrary and tyrannical!   [4]

A Counsel of Moderation

*Given the state of English politics and the character of
English politicians, war was now inevitable. Franklin was
dismissed from his office as Postmaster-General and was
called a thief by Solicitor-General Wedderburn for his
role in procuring private letters—subsequently published
by Boston patriots—in which Governor Hutchinson of
Massachusetts urged repressive measures against the
Americans. But Franklin continued to urge peace, both
to his British friends and to the patriots back home. In
the following letter he attempts to influence the Speaker
of the Massachusetts House.*

TO THOMAS CUSHING

October 6, 1774

Sir,
    Since my last to you which went per Capt. Foulger,
the Parliament by a sudden & unexpected Resolution in
the Cabinet, has been dissolved. Various are the Conjectures as to the Motives; among which one is that some
Advices from Boston, importing the Impossibility of carrying on Government there under the late Acts of Parliament, have made it appear necessary that a new Election
should be got through before any Ferment arises here
among the Manufacturers, which if it happen'd during the

Election (as might be expected if the old Parliament had gone on to finish its Term) would probably have been a means of Outing many of the Court Candidates. As yet it does not appear that there is any Intention of Changing Measures: But all intelligent Men are of Opinion, that if the American Congress should resolve on the Non-consumption of the Manufactures of Britain this Ministry must go out, and their late Measures be all reversed. As such a resolution, firmly adher'd to would in a peaceable and justifiable Way do every thing for us that we can wish, I am griev'd to hear of Mobs & Violence, and the pulling down the Houses, which our Friends cannot justify, and which give great Advantage against us to our Enemies.

The Electors of the Cities of London & Westminster, and Borough of Southwark, the County of Middlesex, and some other Places, have exacted of their Candidates Engagements under their hands that they will among other things endeavour a Repeal of the late iniquitous Acts against America, and 'tis suppos'd the Example of the Metropolis will be follow'd in other Places, and would have been nearly general if the Election had not been thus precipitated.—The Bishop of St. Asaph's intended speech, several Copies of which I send you, and of which many Thousands have been printed and distributed here has had an extraordinary Effect, in changing the Sentiments of Multitudes with regard to America. And when the Result of the Congress arrives, and the Measures they resolve to pursue (which I confide will be wise & good, enter'd into with Unanimity, and persisted in with Firmness) come to be known and consider'd here, I am persuaded our Friends will be multiplied, and our Enemies diminished so as to bring on an Accomodation in which our undoubted Rights shall be acknowledg'd and establish'd.—This, for the common Welfare of the British Empire, I most ardently wish. But I am in perpetual Anxiety lest the mad Measure of mixing Soldiers among a People whose minds are in such a State of Irritation, may be attended with some sudden Mischief; For an accidental Quarrel, a personal Insult, an imprudent Order, an insolent Execution or even a prudent one, or 20 other things, may produce a Tumult, unforeseen, and therefore impossible to be prevented in which such a Carnage may ensue, as to make a Breach that can never afterward be healed.—

I pray God to Govern everything for the best, and am with the greatest Esteem & Respect, Sir Your (and the Committee's) most obedient and most humble Servant. . . .

[5]

America in Arms

Parliament and the King stood firm, refusing to listen to American grievances. Franklin worked at conciliation, but finally lost patience and began to question the value of the bond between the colonies and a mother country which seemed increasingly corrupt and warlike.

Then, early in 1775, Franklin received word of a death in his family and started home. While he was on the high seas, fighting began at Lexington and Concord. Back in Philadelphia he was elected a delegate to the second Continental Congress, which included Washington, Adams, and later Jefferson. In June, Washington was chosen Commander-in-Chief, and set out for the besieged town of Boston. In July, Franklin wrote an account of American affairs to his friend Jonathan Shipley, an English bishop sympathetic to the Patriot cause.

TO JONATHAN SHIPLEY

July 7, 1775

I received with great Pleasure my dear Friend's very kind Letter of April 19, as it informed me of his Welfare, and that of the amiable Family in Jermyn Street. I am much obliged by the Information of what pass'd in Parliament after my departure; in return I will endeavor to give you a short Sketch of the State of Affairs here.

I found at my arrival all America from one End of the 12 united Provinces to the other, busily employed in learning the Use of Arms. The Attack upon the Country People near Boston by the Army had rous'd every Body and exasperated the whole Continent; The Tradesmen of this City were in the Field twice a day, at 5 in the Morning, and Six in the Afternoon, disciplining with the utmost Diligence, all being Volunteers. We have now three Battalions, a Troop of Light Horse, and a Company of Artillery who have made surprizing Progress. The same Spirit appears everywhere and the Unanimity is amazing.

The day after my Arrival, I was unanimously chosen by our Assembly, then sitting, an additional Delegate to the Congress, which met the next Week. The numerous Visits of old Friends, and the publick Business has since devoured all my time: for We meet at nine in the Morning, and often sit 'till four. I am also upon a Committee of Safety appointed by the Assembly, which meets at Six, and sits 'till near nine. The Members attend closely without being bribed to it, by either Salary, Place or Pension, or the hopes of any; which I mention for your Reflection on the difference, between a new virtuous People, who have publick Spirit, and an old corrupt one, who have not so much as an Idea that such a thing exists in Nature. There has not been a dissenting Voice among us in any Resolution for Defence, and our Army which is already formed, will soon consist of above 20,000 Men.

You will have heard before this reaches you of the Defeat the Ministerial Troops met with on their first *Sortie;* the several small Advantages we have since had of them, and the more considerable Affair of the 17th when after two severe Repulses, they carry'd the unfinished Trenches of the Post we had just taken on a Hill near Charlestown. They suffered greatly however, and I believe are convinc'd by this time, that they have Men to deal with, tho' unexperienced, and not yet well arm'd. In their way to this Action, without the least Necessity, they barbourously plundered and burnt a fine, undefended Town, opposite to Boston, called Charlestown, consisting of about 400 Houses, many of them elegantly built; some sick, aged and decrepit poor Persons, who could not be carried off in time perish'd in the Flames. In all our Wars, from our first settlement in America, to the present time, we never received so much damage from the Indian *Sav-*

ages, as in this one day from these. Perhaps Ministers may think this a means of disposing us to Reconciliation. I feel and see every where the Reverse. Most of the little Property I have, consists of Houses in the Seaport Towns, which I suppose may all soon be destroyed in the same way, and yet I think I am not half so reconcileable now, as I was a Month ago.

The Congress will send one more Petition to the King, which I suppose will be treated as the former was, and therefore will probably be the last; for tho' this may afford Britain one chance more of recovering our Affections and retaining the Connection, I think she has neither Temper nor Wisdom enough to seize the Golden Opportunity. When I look forward to the Consequences, I see an End to all Commerce between us: on our Sea Coasts she may hold some fortified Places as the Spaniards do on the Coast of Africa, but can penetrate as little into the Country: a very numerous Fleet extending 1500 Miles at an immense Expence may prevent other Nations trading with us: but as we have or may have within ourselves every thing necessary to the Comfort of Life, and generally import only Luxuries and Superfluities, her preventing our doing that, will in some Respects contribute to our Prosperity. By the present Stoppage of our Trade we save between four and five Millions per Ann which will do something towards the Expence of the War. What *she* will get by it, I must leave to be computed by her own political Arithmeticians. These are some of my present Ideas which I throw out to you in the Freedom of Friendship. Perhaps I am too sanguine in my opinion of our Abilities for the Defence of our Country after we shall have given up our Seaports to Destruction, but a little time will shew.

General Gage we understand enter'd into a Treaty with the Inhabitants of Boston, whom he had confin'd by his Works, in which Treaty it was agreed that if they delivered their Arms to the Select Men, their own Magistrates, they were to be permitted to go out with their *Effects*. As soon as they had so delivered their Arms, he seiz'd them, and then cavil'd about the meaning of the word *Effects* which he said was only wearing Apparel and Household Furniture, and not Merchandize or Shop Goods, which he therefore detains; and the continual Injuries and Insults they met with from the Soldiery, made them glad to get out by relinquishing all that kind of Property. How much those People have suffered, and are now suffering rather than submit to what they think unconstitutional Acts of Parliament is really amazing. Two or three Letters I send you enclosed may give you some, tho' a faint Idea of it. Gage's Perfidy has now made him universally detested. When I consider that all this Mischief is done my Country, by Englishmen and Protestant Christians, of a Nation among whom I have so many personal Friends, I am ashamed to feel any Consolation in a prospect of Revenge; I chuse to draw it rather from a Confidence that we shall sooner or later obtain Reparation. I have proposed therefore to our People that they keep just Accounts, and never resume the Commerce or the Union, 'till Satisfaction is made. If it is refused for 20 Years, I think we shall then be able to take it with Interest.

Your excellent Advice was, that if we must have a War, let it be carried on as between Nations who had once been Friends, and wish to be so again. In this ministerial War against us, all Europe is conjur'd not to sell us Arms or Ammunition, that we may be found defenceless, and more easily murdered. The humane Sir W. Draper, who had been hospitably entertain'd in every one of our Colonies, proposes, in his Papers call'd the Traveller, to excite the Domestic Slaves, you have sold us, to cut their Master's Throats. Dr. Johnson a Court Pensioner, in his *Taxation no Tyranny* adopts and recommends that Measure, together with another of hiring the Indian Savages to assassinate our Planters in the Back-Settlements. They are the poorest and most innocent of all People, and the Indian manner is to murder and scalp Men Women and Children. This Book I heard applauded by Lord Sandwich in Parliament, and all the ministerial People recommended it. Lord Dunmore and Governor Martin, have already, we are told, taken some Steps towards carrying one part of the Project into Execution, by exciting an Insurrection among the Blacks. And Governor Carleton, we have certain Accounts, has been very industrious in engaging the Indians to begin their horrid Work. This is making War like Nations who never had been Friends, and never wish to be such while the World stands. You see I am warm: and if a Temper naturally cool and phlegmatic can, in old age, which often cools the warmest, be thus heated, you will judge by that of the general Temper here, which is now little short of Madness. We have however as yet ask'd no foreign Power to assist us, nor made any offer of our Commerce to other Nations for their Friendship. What another year's Persecution may drive us to, is yet uncertain. I drop this disagreeable Subject, and will take up one, that I know must afford you and the good Family, as my Friends, some Pleasure. It is the State of my own Family, which I found in good Health; my Children affectionately dutifull and attentive to every thing that can be agreeable to me; with three very promising Grandsons, in whom I take great Delight So that were it not for our Publick Troubles, and the being absent from so many that I love in England, my present Felicity would be as perfect, as in this World one could well expect it. I enjoy however, what there is of it while it lasts, mindfull at the same time that its Continuance is like other earthly Goods, uncertain. Adieu my dear Friend, and believe me ever, with sincere and great Esteem Yours most Affectionately

B. Franklin

My respectfull Complts. to Mrs. Shipley.
Your Health on this side the Water is every where drank by the Name of THE BISHOP.
I send for your Amusement a Parcel of our Newspapers. When you have perused them, please to give them to mr. Hartley of Golden Square.

[6]

The French Alliance

Late in 1775 Congress sent Franklin to Paris to negotiate a treaty of commerce and amity. There he played the role the French expected: bespectacled and wearing a fur cap, he was—in their eyes—the humble philosopher from the New World, Rousseau's ideal and Voltaire's, the American Socrates. Immensely popular with Frenchmen and Frenchwomen of all classes, he combined his popularity with diplomatic skill to achieve America's first great diplomatic victory, the French Allegiance.

TO THOMAS CUSHING

February 27, 1778

Sir,

I received your favour by Mr. Austin, with your most agreeable Congratulations on the Success of the American Arms in the Northern Department. In Return, give me leave to congratulate you on the Success of our negotiations here, in the completion of the two Treaties with his Most Christian Majesty; the one of Amity and Commerce, on the Plan of that projected in Congress, with some good additions; the Other of Alliance for Mutual Defence, in which the Most Christian King agrees to make a Common Cause with the United States, if England attempts to obstruct the Commerce of his Subjects with them; and guarantees to the United States their Liberties, Sovereignty, and Independance, absolute and unlimited, with the Possessions they now have, or may have, at the Conclusion of the War; and the States in return guarantees to him his Possessions in the West Indies. The great Principle in both Treaties is a perfect Equality and reciprocity; no Advantages being demanded by France, or Privileges in Commerce, which the States may not grant to any and every other Nation.

In short, the King has treated with us Generously and Magnanimously; taking no advantage of our present Difficulties, to exact Terms which we wou'd not willingly grant, when establish'd in Prosperity and Power. I may add that he has acted wisely, in wishing the Friendship contracted by these Treaties may be durable, which probably it might not be, if a contrary Conduct had been observed.

Several of our American Ships, with Stores for the Congress, are now about sailing, under the Protection of a French Squadron. English is in great Consternation, and the Minister, on the 17th Instant, confessing in a long Speech that all his Measures had been wrong, and that Peace was necessary, proposed two Bills for Quieting America; but they are full of Artifice and Deceit, and will, I am confident, be treated accordingly by our Country.

I think you must have much satisfaction in so valuable a son, whom I wish safe back to you, and am with great esteem, &c.

B. Franklin

P.S. The treaties were signed by the plenipotentiaries on both sides, February 6th, but are still for some reason kept secret, though soon to be published. It is understood that Spain will soon accede to the same. The treaties are forwarded to Congress by this conveyance.

[7]

Busy Days

The years in France would have been exhausting for a younger man, and Franklin was in his seventies. Besides his strictly ambassadorial duties, he was in effect United States consul-general, judge of admiralty, and naval attaché. His popularity in France far exceeded that of any of his colleagues, and as a result he was subjected to the constant importunities of both crackpots and patriots, zealous soldiers, and monks who wanted him to pay their gambling debts. His account of some of these annoyances, and the form letter of recommendation which he printed on his own press, follow.

December 13, 1778. A.M.

A man came to tell me he had invented a machine which would go of itself, without the help of a spring, weight, air, water, or any of the elements, or the labour of man or beast; and with force sufficient to work four machines for cutting tobacco; that he had experienced it; would show it me if I would come to his house; and would sell the secret of it for two hundred louis. I doubted it, but promised to go to him in order to see it.

A Mons. Coder came with a proposition in writing, to levy 600 men to be employed in landing on the coast of England and Scotland to burn and ransom towns and villages in order to put a stop to the English proceedings in that way in America. I thanked him and told him I would not approve it, nor had I any money at hand for such a purpose; moreover, that it would not be permitted by the government here.

A man came with a request that I would patronize and recommend to government an invention he had, whereby a hussar might so conceal his arms and habiliments, with provision for twenty-four hours, as to appear a common traveller; by which means a considerable body might be admitted into a town, one at a time, unsuspected, and afterwards assembling, surprise it. I told him I was not a military man, of course no judge of such matters, and advised him to apply to the Bureau de la Guerre. He said he had no friends and so could procure no attention.— The number of wild schemes proposed to me is so great, and they have heretofore taken so much of my time, that I begin to reject all, though possibly *some* of them may be worth notice.

Received a parcel from an unknown philosopher, who submits to my consideration a memoir on the subject of *elementary fire*, containing experiments in a dark chamber. It seems to be well written, and is in English, with a little tincture of French idiom. I wish to see the experiments, without which I cannot well judge of it.

[8]

MODEL OF A LETTER OF RECOMMENDATION

Paris, April 2, 1777

Sir:—The bearer of this, who is going to America, presses me to give him a Letter of Recommendation, tho' I know nothing of him, not even his Name. This may seem extraordinary, but I assure you it is not uncommon here. Sometimes, indeed one unknown Person brings another equally unknown, to recommend him; and sometimes they recommend one another! As to this Gentleman, I must refer you to himself for his Character and Merits, with which he is certainly better acquainted than I can possibly be. I recommend him however to those Civilities, which every Stranger, of whom one knows no Harm, has a Right to; and I request you will do him all the good Offices, and show him all the Favour that, on further Acquaintance, you shall find him to deserve. I have the Honour to be, etc.   **[9]**

"Let us Now Forgive and Forget"

Remaining in France, where his popularity continued to grow, Franklin was appointed one of the peace commissioners for the American side in June, 1781. He and his fellow commissioners, John Jay, John Adams, and later Henry Laurens, struggled to maintain harmony among themselves and to establish American independence. Jay and Adams thought Franklin too subservient to the French and favored separate negotiations with the British, while Franklin preferred to maintain close liaison with the French as allies. Franklin eventually yielded, and the treaty was finally signed on September 3, 1783.

During the final stage of the negotiations, Franklin again wrote to Bishop Shipley, extending a friendship undiminished by the war between their two countries.

TO JONATHAN SHIPLEY

March 17, 1783

I received with great pleasure my dear and respected Friend's letter of the 5th Instant, as it informed me of the Welfare of a Family I so much esteem and love.

The Clamour against the Peace in your Parliament would alarm me for its duration, if I were not of opinion with you, that the Attack is rather against the Minister. I am confident, none of the opposition would have made a better Peace for England, if they had been in his Place; at least, I am sure that Lord Stormont, who seems loudest in Railing at it, is not the Man that could have mended it. My Reasons I will give you, when I have, what I hope to have, the great happiness of seeing you once more, and conversing with you.

They talk much of there being no *Reciprocity* in our Treaty. They think nothing, then, of our passing over in silence the Atrocities committed by their Troops, and demanding no satisfaction for their wanton Burnings and Devastations of our fair Towns and Countries. They have heretofore confest the War to be unjust, and nothing is plainer in Reasoning than that the Mischiefs done in an unjust War should be repaired. Can Englishmen be so partial to themselves, as to imagine they have a right to Plunder and destroy as much as they please, and then, without satisfying for the Injuries they have done, to have Peace on equal Terms? We were favourable, and did not demand what Justice entitled us to. We shall probably be blamed for it by our Constituents; and I still think it would be the Interest of English voluntarily to offer Reparation of those Injuries, and effect it as much as may be in her power. But this is an interest she will never see.

Let us now forgive and forget. Let each Country seek its Advancement in its own internal Advantages of Arts and Agriculture, not in retarding or preventing the Prosperity of the other. America will, with God's blessing, become a great and happy Country; and England, if she has at length gained Wisdom, will have gained something more valuable, and more essential to her Prosperity, than all she has lost; and will still be a great and respectable Nation. Her great Disease at present is the number and enormous Salaries and Emoluments of Office. Avarice and Ambition are strong Passions, and, separately, act with great Force on the human Mind; but, when both are united, and may be gratified in the same Object, their violence is almost irresistible, and they hurry Men headlong into Factions and Contentions, destructive of all good government. As long, therefore, as these great Emoluments subsist, your Parliament will be a stormy Sea, and your Public Councils confounded by private Interests. But it requires much Public Spirit and Virtue to abolish them; more perhaps than can now be found in a Nation so long corrupted. . . .

[10]

"Sketch of the Services of B. Franklin to the United States of America"

With the goal of independence achieved in 1783, Franklin wanted to go home. Jefferson was forty, Adams forty-seven, and Washington fifty-one; Franklin was seventy-seven, and his health was failing. Congress did not free him from his duties until 1785, and he then returned to Philadelphia. Until his death in 1790, Franklin tried at various times to collect back salary from a strangely ungrateful Congress. He never made public notice of his complaint, but at one point wrote privately to his friend Charles Thompson, secretary of Congress.

[December 29, 1788]

In England, he combated the Stamp Act, and his writings in the papers against it, with his examination in Parliament, were thought to have contributed much to its repeal.

He opposed the Duty Act; and, though he could not prevent its passing, he obtained of Mr. Townshend an omission of several articles, particularly salt.

In the subsequent difference he wrote and published many papers, refuting the claim of Parliament to tax the colonies.

He opposed all the oppressive acts.

He had two secret negotiations with the ministers for their repeal, of which he has written a narrative. In this he offered payment for the destroyed tea, at his own risk, in case they were repealed.

He was joined with Messrs. Bollan and Lee in all the applications to government for that purpose. Printed several pamphlets at his own considerable expense against the then measures of government, whereby he rendered himself obnoxious, was disgraced before the privy council, deprived of a place in the postoffice of £300 sterling a year, and obliged to resign his agencies, viz. of Pennsylvania . . . Massachusetts . . . New Jersey . . . Georgia. . . . In the whole £1500 sterling per annum. . . .

Returning to America, he encouraged the Revolution. Was appointed chairman of the Committee of Safety, where he projected the *chevaux de frise* for securing Philadephia, then the residence of Congress.

Was sent by Congress to head-quarters near Boston with Messrs. Harrison and Lynch, in 1775, to settle some affairs with the northern governments and General Washington.

In the spring of 1776, was sent to Canada with Messrs. Chase and Carroll, passing the Lakes while they were not yet free from ice. In Canada, was, with his colleagues, instrumental in redressing sundry grievances, and thereby reconciling the people more to our cause. He there advanced to General Arnold and other servants of Congress, then in extreme necessity, £353 in gold, out of his own pocket, on the credit of Congress, which was of great service at that juncture, in procuring provisions for our army.

Being at the time he was ordered on this service upwards of seventy years of age, he suffered in his health by the hardships of this journey; lodging in the woods, &c., in so inclement a season; but, being recovered, the Congress in the same year ordered him to France. Before his departure, he put all the money he could raise, between three and four thousand pounds, into their hands; which, demonstrating his confidence, encouraged others to lend their money in support of the cause. . . .

When the Pennsylvania Assembly sent him to England in 1764 . . . they allowed him one year's advance for his passage, and in consideration of the prejudice to his private affairs that must be occasioned by his sudden departure and absence. He has had no such allowance from Congress, was badly accomodated in a miserable vessel, improper for those northern seas, (and which actually foundered in her return,) was badly fed, so that on his arrival he had scarce strength to stand.

His services to the States as commissioner, and afterwards as minister plenipotentiary are known to Congress, as may appear in his correspondence. His *extra services* may not be so well known, and therefore may be here mentioned. No secretary ever arriving, the business was in part before, and entirely when the other commissioners left him, executed by himself, with the help of his grandson. . . .

He served as *consul* entirely several years, till the arrival of Mr. Barclay, and even after, as that gentleman was obliged to be much and long absent in Holland, Flanders, and England; during which absence, what business of the kind occurred, still came to Mr. Franklin.

He served, though without any special commission for the purpose, as a *judge of admiralty;* for, the Congress having sent him a quantity of blank commissions for privateers, he granted them to cruisers fitted out in the ports of France, some of them manned by old smugglers, who knew every creek on the coast of England, and, running all round the island, distressed the British coasting trade exceedingly, and raised their general insurance. One of those privateers alone, the *Black Prince,* took in the course of a year seventy-five sail! All the papers, taken in each prize brought in, were in virtue of an order of council sent up to Mr. Franklin, who was to examine them, judge of the legality of the capture, and write to the admiralty of the port, that he found the prize good, and that the sale might be permitted. These papers, which are very voluminous, he has to produce.

He served also as *merchant,* to make purchases, and direct the shipping of stores to a very great value, for which he has charged no commission.

But the part of his service which was the most fatiguing and confining, was that of receiving and accepting, after a due and necessary examination, the bills of exchange drawn by Congress for interest money, to the amount of *two millions and a half of livres annually;* multitudes of the bills very small, each of which, the smallest, gave as much trouble in examining, as the largest. And this careful examination was found absolutely necessary, from the constant frauds attempted by presenting *seconds* and *thirds* for payment after the *firsts* had been discharged. As these bills were arriving more or less by every ship and every post, they required constant attendance. Mr. Franklin could make no journey for exercise, as had been annually his custom, and the confinement brought on a malady that is likely to afflict him while he lives.

In short, though he has always been an active man, he never went through so much business during eight years, in any part of his life, as during those of his residence in France; which however he did not decline till he saw peace happily made, and found himself in the eightieth year of his age; when, if ever, a man has some right to expect repose.

[11]

V

The Family Man

Like most men of affairs, Franklin spent a great deal of time away from his family. His diplomatic duties kept him an ocean away from his home for many years. As a result, his relations with his family were weakened.

He married only once, to his Philadelphia landlord's daughter, by whom he had three children. In his later years in England, however, he lived with the Stevenson family and became, in effect, the head of the household during the 1760s. The Revolution, of course, interfered with this relationship, and then he went to France, where he made his spiritual home in two of the great salons of the day.

With the war over and the peace negotiated, Franklin felt that he now deserved to retire into "the Bosom of his Family." Unfortunately, the family to whom he returned in Philadelphia was much changed. His wife, Deborah, was dead; his only living son, William, now lived in England; the only one left was his daughter, who had six children. With her and a few intimate friends, he formed a family circle into which he fit comfortably for the remaining years of his life.

Deborah Read

*Franklin married Deborah Read in September, 1730,
and sometime during the following year became the father of a son, William. Thirty-three years later a mud-
slinging political pamphlet claimed that William's mother
was really a household servant named Barbara, but this
allegation remains unsubstantiated.*

*Deborah herself was not an attractive woman; Franklin
affectionately likened her shape to that of a beer mug.
Turbulent, jealous, and proud, she was difficult to get
along with on occasion. Despite her plain physical appearance, and her rather ordinary intellectual interests
and attainments, she was nevertheless a hard worker en-
dowed with many of the characteristics which would make
her helpful to a rising tradesman. The qualities which
Franklin chose to idealize in a song which he wrote twelve
years after their marriage say something about Deborah
and as much about her husband's conception of her.*

[1742]

Of their Chloes and Phillisses Poets may prate
   I sing my plain Country Joan
Now twelve Years my Wife, still the Joy of my Life
   Blest Day that I made her my own,
                  My dear Friends
   Blest Day that I made her my own.

2

Not a Word of her Face, her Shape, or her Eyes,
   Of Flames or of Darts shall you hear;
Tho' I Beauty admire 'tis Virtue I prize,
   That fades not in seventy Years,
                  My dear Friends

3

In Health a Companion delightfull and dear,
   Still easy, engaging, and Free,
In Sickness no less than the faithfullest Nurse
   As tender as tender can be,
                  My dear Friends

4

In Peace and good Order, my Houshold she keeps
  Right Careful to save what I gain
Yet chearfully spends, and smiles on the Friends
  I've the Pleasures to entertain
                My dear Friends

5

She defends my good Name ever where I'm to blame,
  Friend firmer was ne'er to Man giv'n,
Her compassionate Breast, feels for all the Distrest,
  Which draws down the Blessing from Heav'n,
                My dear Friends

6

Am I laden with Care, she takes off a large Share,
  That the Burthen ne'er makes to reel,
Does good Fortune arrive, the Joy of my Wife,
  Quite doubles the Pleasures I feel,
                My dear Friends

7

In Raptures the giddy Rake talks of his Fair,
  Enjoyment shall make him Despise,
I speak my cool sence, that long Experience,
  And Enjoyment have chang'd in no wise,
                My dear Friends

8

Were the fairest young Princess, with Million in Purse
  To be had in Exchange for my Joan,
She could not be a better Wife, mought be a Worse,
  So I'd stick to my Joggy alone
                My dear Friends,
  I'd cling to my lovely ould Joan.   **[1]**

Franky Franklin's Death

In 1732, Deborah gave birth to Francis Folger Franklin, a boy who soon became his father's favorite and then, at the age of four, tragically died of smallpox. The family was deeply grieved; in fact, when Franky would have been forty, his father still remembered him with a sigh. Even in the depths of his sorrow, however, Franklin was concerned for the public welfare, and published a notice in the Gazette *correcting a rumor that his son had died from inoculation.*

December 30, 1736

Understanding 'tis a current Report, that my son *Francis*, who died lately of the Small Pox, had it by Inoculation; and being desired to satisfy the Publick in that Particular; inasmuch as some People are, by that Report (join'd with others of the like kind, and perhaps equally groundless) deter'd from having that Operation perform'd on their children, I do hereby sincerely declare, that he was not inoculated, but receiv'd the Distemper in the common Way of Infection: And I suppose the Report could only arise from its being my known Opinion, that Inoculation was a safe and beneficial Practice; and from my having said among my Acquaintance, that I intended to have my Child inoculated, as soon as he shou'd have recovered sufficient Strength from a Flux with which he had been long afflicted. [2]

Katy Ray

Nearly fifty, and on a tour of inspection of post offices, Franklin met a twenty-three-year-old girl, Catherine Ray of Rhode Island. With her he set a pattern for relationships with younger women which he would follow until well into his eighties. Emotionally starved by a marriage which was, at its best, peaceful, he energetically sought the affection of younger women. Both lover and father, and himself confused as to which role he preferred, if rebuffed as lover he could easily retreat into paternalism and cover the hurt with humor. In 1754 Franklin began his correspondence with Catherine Ray—it lasted more than thirty years, through her marriage and the death of his wife—with a reminder of her promise to send him kisses in the northeast wind: "Your favours come mixed with the snowy fleeces, which are pure as your virgin innocence, white as your lovely bosom, and—as cold."

A letter written a year and a half later illustrates the charm which the witty philosopher held for the Rhode Island Girl.

TO CATHERINE RAY

October 16, 1755

Dear Katy

Your Favour of the 28th of June came to hand but the 28th of September, just 3 Months after it was written. I had, two Weeks before, wrote you a long Chat, and sent it to the Care of your Brother Ward. I hear you are now in Boston, gay and lovely as usual. Let me give you some fatherly Advice. Kill no more Pigeons than you can eat—Be a good Girl and dont forget your Catechism.—Go constantly to Meeting—or church—till you get a good Husband,—then stay at home, & nurse the Children, and live like a Christian—Spend your spare Hours, in sober Whisk, Prayers, or learning to cypher—You must practise *addition* to your Husband's Estate, by Industry and Frugality; *subtraction* of all unnecessary Expenses; *Multiplication* (I would gladly have taught you that myself, but you thought it was time enough, & wou'dn't learn) he will soon make you a Mistress of it. As to *Division*, I say with Brother Paul, *Let there be no Division among ye.* But as your good Sister Hubbard (my love to her) is well acquainted with *The Rule of Two,* I hope you will become an expert in the *Rule of Three;* that when I have again the pleasure of seeing you, I may find you like my Grape Vine, surrounded with Clusters, plump, juicy, blushing, pretty little rogues, like their Mama. Adieu. The Bell rings, and I must go among the Grave ones, and talk Politicks.

Your affectionate Friend

B. FRANKLIN.

P.S. The Plums came safe, and were so sweet from the Cause you mentioned, that I could scarce taste the Sugar.

[3]

Franklin's London Family

In 1757 Franklin began what were perhaps the happiest five years of his life. After arriving in England as agent of the Pennsylvania Assembly, he bought himself a new wig and two pairs of silver buckles—to match his social position—and then went out to find lodgings for himself, his son, and their two servants. They settled on Craven Street, in the home of Margaret Stevenson, a widow who lived with her daughter, Polly.

He soon found with the Stevensons the domestic warmth which had not existed in Philadelphia, and he became head of the household. All told, Franklin spent fifteen years with Mrs. Stevenson, and she was as much his wife as Deborah ever was. Their friends saw it that way, and William Strahan wrote Franklin in 1777 to say how much his London friends often thought of him, "with great Esteem and affection, particularly your wife, who expects, as you are now so near, that you will soon pay her a Visit."

The Craven Street Gazette is illustrative of the happiness which he enjoyed in the Stevenson household.

THE CRAVEN STREET GAZETTE

Saturday, September 22, 1770.
THIS morning Queen Margaret, accompanied by her first maid of honour, Miss Franklin, set out for Rochester. Immediately on their departure, the whole street was in tears—from a heavy shower of rain. It is whispered, that the new family administration, which took place on her Majesty's departure, promises, like all other new administrations, to govern much better than the old one.

We hear that the great person (so called from his enormous size), of a certain family in a certain street, is grievously affected at the late changes, and could hardly be comforted this morning, though the new ministry promised him a roasted shoulder of mutton and potatoes for his dinner.

It is said, that the same great person intended to pay his respects to another great personage this day, at St. James's, it being coronation day; hoping thereby a little to amuse his grief; but was prevented by an accident, Queen Margaret, or her maid of honour, having carried off the key of the drawers, so that the lady of the bed-chamber could not come at a laced shirt for his Highness. Great clamours were made on this occasion against her Majesty.

Other accounts say, that the shirts were afterwards found, though too late, in another place. And some suspect, that the wanting a shirt from those drawers was only a ministerial pretence to excuse picking the locks, that the new administration might have everything at command.

We hear that the lady chamberlain of the household went to market this morning by her own self, gave the butcher whatever he asked for the mutton, and had no dispute with the potato-woman, to their great amazement at the change of times.

It is confidently asserted, that this afternoon, the weather being wet, the great person a little chilly and nobody at home to find fault with the expense of fuel, he was indulged with a fire in his chamber. It seems the design is, to make him contented by degrees with the absence of the Queen.

A project has been under consideration of government, to take the opportunity of her Majesty's absence for doing a thing she was always averse to, namely, fixing a new lock on the street door, or getting a key made to the old one; it being found extremely inconvenient, that one or other of the great officers of state should, whenever the maid goes out for a ha'peny worth of sand, or a pint of porter, be obliged to tend the door to let her in again. But opinions being divided, which of the two expedients to adopt, the project is, for the present, laid aside.

We have good authority to assure our readers, that a Cabinet Council was held this afternoon at tea; the subject of which was a proposal for the reformation of manners, and a more strict observation of the Lord's day. The result was a unanimous resolution, that no meat should be dressed tomorrow; whereby the cook and the first minister will both be at liberty to go to church, the one having nothing to do, and the other no roast to rule. It seems the cold shoulder of mutton, and the apple pie, were thought insufficient for Sunday's dinner. All pious people applaud this measure, and it is thought the new ministry will soon become popular.

We hear that Mr. Wilkes was at a certain house in Craven Street this day, and inquired after the absent Queen. His good lady and the children are well.

The report, that Mr. Wilkes, the patriot, made the above visit, is without foundation, it being his brother, the courtier.

Sunday, September 23.

It is now found, by sad experience, that good resolutions are easier made than executed. Notwithstanding yesterday's solemn order of Council, nobody went to church today. I seems the great person's broad-built bulk lay so long abed, that the breakfast was not over till it was too late to dress. At least this is the excuse. In fine, it seems a vain thing to hope reformation from the example of our great folks.

The cook and the minister, however, both took advantage of the order so far, as to save themselves all trouble, and the clause of cold dinner was enforced, though the going to church was dispensed with; just as common working folks observe the commandment. *The seventh day thou shalt rest,* they think a sacred injunction; but the other *six days thou shalt labor* is deemed a mere piece of advice, which they may practise when they want bread and are out of credit at the ale house, and may neglect whenever they have money in their pockets.

It must, nevertheless, be said, in justice to our court, that, whatever inclination they had to gaming, no cards were brought out today. Lord and Lady Hewson walked after dinner to Kensington, to pay their duty to the Dowager, and Dr. Fatsides made four hundred and sixty-nine turns in his dining-room, as the exact distance of a visit to the lovely Lady Barwell, whom he did not find at home; so there was no struggle for and against a kiss, and he sat down to dream in the easy chair, that he had it without any trouble.

Monday, Sept. 24.

We are credibly informed, that the great person dined this day with the Club at the Cat and Bagpipes in the City, on cold round of boiled beef. This, it seems, he was under some necessity of doing (though he rather dislikes beef), because truly the ministers were to be all abroad somewhere to dine on hot roast venison. It is thought, that, if the Queen had been at home, he would not have been so slighted. And though he shows outwardly no marks of dissatisfaction, it is suspected, that he begins to wish for her Majesty's return.

It is currently repeated, that poor Nanny had nothing for dinner in the kitchen, for herself and puss, but the scrapings of the bones of Saturday's mutton.

This evening there was high play at Craven Street House. The great person lost money. It is supposed the ministers, as is usually supposed of all ministers, shared the emoluments among them.

Tuesday, Sept. 25.

This morning the good Lord Hutton call'd at Craven Street House, and inquir'd very respectfully & affectionately concerning the Welfare of the Queen. He then imparted to the big Man a Piece of Intelligence important to them both, and but just communicated by Lady Hawkesworth, viz. that the amiable and delectable Companion, Miss D[orothea] B[lount] had made a Vow to marry absolutely him of the two whose Wife should first depart this life. It is impossible to express with words the various Agitations of mind appearing in both their Faces on this Occasion. *Vanity* at the Preference given them over the rest of Mankind; *Affection* to their present Wives, *Fear* of losing them, *Hope,* if they must lose them, to obtain the proposed Comfort; *Jealousy* of each other in case both Wives should die together: all working at the same time jumbled their Features into inexplicable confusion. They parted at length with Professions & outward Appearances indeed of ever-during Friendship; but it was shrewdly suspected that each of them sincerely wished

Health & long Life to the other's Wife; & that however long either of these Friends might like to live himself, the other would be very well pleas'd to survive him.

It is remark'd, that the Skies have wept every Day in Craven Street, the Absence of the Queen.

The Publick may be assured that this Morning a certain *great* Personage was asked very complaisantly by the Mistress of the Household, if he would chuse to have the Blade-Bone of Saturday's Mutton that had been kept for his Dinner today, *broil'd* or *cold*. He answer'd gravely, *If there is any Flesh on it, it may be broil'd; if not, it may as well be cold*. Orders were accordingly given for Broiling it. But when it came to Table, there was indeed so very little Flesh, or rather none, (Puss having din'd on it yesterday after Nanny) that if our new Administration had been as good œconomists as they would be thought, the Expence of Broiling might well have been saved to the Publick, and carried to the Sinking Fund. It is assured the *great* Person bears all with infinite Patience. But the Nation is astonish'd at the insolent Presumption, that dares treat so much Mildness in so cruel a manner!

A terrible Accident *had like to have* happened this Afternoon at Tea. The Boiler was set too near the End of the little square Table. The first Ministress was sitting at one End of the Table to administer the Tea; the *great* Person was about to sit down at the other End, where the Boiler stood. By a sudden Motion the Lady gave the Table a Tilt. Had it gone over, the G.P. must have been scalded, perhaps to Death. Various are the Surmises and Observations on this Occasion. The Godly say it woud have been a just Judgment on him, for preventing, by his Laziness, the Family's going to Church last Sunday. The Opposition do not stick to insinuate that there was a Design to scald him, prevented only by his quick Catching the Table. The Friends of the Ministry give out, that he carelessly jogg'd the Table himself, & would have been inevitably scalded, had not the Ministress sav'd him. It is hard for the Publick to come at the Truth in these Cases.

At six o'clock this Afternoon, News came by the Post, that her Majesty arrived safely at Rochester on Saturday night. The Bells immediately rang—for Candles to illuminate the Parlour, the Court went into Cribbidge, and the Evening concluded with every other Demonstration of Joy.

It is reported that all the principal Officers of the State have received an Invitation from the Duchess Dowager of Rochester to go down thither on Saturday next. But it is not yet known whether the great Affairs they have on their Hands will permit them to make this Excursion.

We hear that from the Time of her Majesty's leaving Craven-Street House to this Day, no Care is taken to file the Newspapers; but they lie about in every Room in every Window, and on every chair, just where the Great Person lays them when he has read them. It is impossible Government can long go on in such Hands.

"To the Publisher of the Craven Street Gazette
"Sir, I make no doubt of the Truth of what the Papers tell us, that a certain great Person is half-starved on the Blade-Bone of a *Sheep* (I cannot call it *Mutton,* there being none on it) by a Set of the most careless, worthless, thoughtless, inconsiderate, corrupt, ignorant, blundering, foolish, crafty & knavish Ministers, that every got into a House and pretended to govern a Family and provide a Dinner. Alas for the poor old England of Craven Street! If they continue in Power another Week, the Nation will be ruined. Undone, totally undone, if I and my Friends are not appointed to succeed them. I am a great Admirer of your useful and impartial Paper; and therefore request you will insert this without fail, from
"Your humble servant,
"Indignation."

"To the Publisher of the Craven Street Gazette
"Sir, Your Correspondent, *Indignation,* has made a fine Story in your Paper against our Craven Street Ministry, as if they meant to starve his Highness, giving him only a bare Blade-Bone for his Dinner, while they riot upon roast Venison. The wickedness of Writers in this Age is truly amazing. I believe that if even the Angel Gabriel would condescend to be our Minister, and provide our Dinners, he could scarcely escape Newspaper

Defamation from a Gang of hungry, ever-restless, discontented, and malicious Scribblers.

"It is, Sir, a Piece of Justice you owe our righteous Administration to undeceive the Publick on this Occasion, by assuring them of the Fact, which is, that there was provided, and actually smoaking on the Table under his Royal Nose at the same Instant, as fine a Piece of Ribs of Beef roasted as ever Knife was put into, with Potatoes, Horse-radish, Pickled Walnuts, &c. which his Highness might have eaten of if so he had pleased to do; and which he forbore to do merely from a whimsical Opinion (with Respect be it spoken) that Beef doth not with him perspire well, but makes his Back itch, to his no small Vexation, now that he has lost the little Chinese ivory Hand at the End of a Stick, commonly called a Scratch back, presented to him by her Majesty. This is the Truth, and if your boasted Impartiality is real, you will not hesitate a Moment to insert this Letter in your next Paper.

"I am, tho' a little angry at present,
                    "Yours as you behave,
                              "A Hater of Scandal."

Junius and *Cinna* came to hand too late for this Paper, but shall be inserted in our next.

MARRIAGES, none since our last;—but Puss begins to go a-Courting.

DEATHS. In the back Closet and elsewhere, many poor Mice.

STOCKS. Biscuit—very low. Buckwheat & Indian meal—both sour. Tea, lowering daily—in the Canister. Wine, shut.

Wednesday, September 26. Postscript.—Those in the Secret of Affairs do not scruple to assert roundly, that the present First Ministress is very notable, having this Day been at Market, bought Mutton Chops, and Apples 4 a Penny, made an excelled Applepy with her own Hands, and mended two Pair of Breeches.

[4]

Polly Stevenson

If Margaret Stevenson was not Benjamin Franklin's wife, he was at least as close to her daughter as he was to his own. His relationship with Mary, or Polly as she was called, lacked the overt emotionalism revealed in his earlier correspondence with Catherine Ray. It is clear, however, that Polly was as pleased to be his daughter as he was to be her father.

TO MISS MARY STEVENSON

Craven Street, June 11, 1760

Dear Polly:

'Tis a very sensible Question you ask, how the Air can affect the Barometer, when its Opening appears covered with Wood? If indeed it was so closely covered as to admit of no Communication of the outward Air to the Surface of the Mercury, the Change of Weight in the Air could not possibly affect it. But the least Crevice is sufficient for the Purpose; a Pinhole will do the Business. And if you could look behind the Frame to which your Barometer is fixed, you would certainly find some small Opening.

There are indeed some Barometers in which the Body of Mercury at the lower End is contain'd in a close Leather Bag, and so the Air cannot come into immediate Contact with the Mercury; yet the same Effect is produc'd. For, the Leather being flexible, when the Bag is press'd by any additional Weight of Air, it contracts, and the Mercury is forced up into the Tube; when the Air becomes lighter, and its Pressure less, the Weight of the Mercury prevails, and it descends again into the Bag.

Your Observation on what you have lately read concerning Insects is very just and solid. Superficial Minds are apt to despise those who make that Part of the Creation their Study, as mere Triflers; but certainly the World has been much oblig'd to them. Under the Care and Management of Man, the Labours of the little Silkworm afford Employment and Subsistence to Thousands of Families, and become an immense Article of Commerce. The Bee, too, yields us its delicious Honey, and its Wax useful to a Multitude of Purposes. Another Insect, it is said, produces the Cochineal, from whence we have our rich Scarlet Dye. The Usefulness of the Cantharides, or Spanish Flies, in Medicine, is known to all, and Thousands owe their Lives to that Knowledge. By human Industry and Observation, other Properties of other Insects may possibly be hereafter discovered, and of equal Utility. A thorough Acquaintance with the nature of these little Creatures may also enable Mankind to prevent the Increase of such as are noxious, or secure us against the Mischiefs they occasion. These Things doubtless your Books make mention of: I can only add a particular late Instance which I had from a Swedish Gentleman of good Credit. In the green Timber, intended for Ship-building at the King's Yards in that Country, a kind of Worms were found, which every year became more numerous and more pernicious, so that the Ships were greatly damag'd before they came into Use. The King sent Linnæus, the great Naturalist, from Stockholm, to enquire into the Affair, and see if the Mischief was capable of any Remedy. He found, on Examination, that the Worm was produced from a small Egg, deposited in the little Roughnesses on the Surface of the Wood, by a particular kind of Fly or Beetle; from whence the Worm, as soon as it was hatched, began to eat into the Substance of the Wood, and after some time came out again a Fly of the Parent kind, and so the Species increased. The season in which this Fly laid its Eggs, Linnæus knew to be about a Fortnight (I think) in the Month of May, and at no other time of the Year. He therefore advis'd, that, some Days before that Season, all the green Timber should be thrown into the Water, and kept under Water till the Season was over. Which being done by the King's Order, the Flies missing their usual Nest, could not increase; and the Species was either destroy'd or went elsewhere; and the Wood was effectually preserved; for, after the first Year, it became too dry and hard for their purpose.

There is, however, a prudent Moderation to be used in Studies of this kind. The Knowledge of Nature may be ornamental, and it may be useful; but if, to attain an Eminence in that, we neglect the Knowledge and Practice of essential Duties, we deserve Reprehension. For there is no Rank in Natural Knowledge of equal Dignity and Importance with that of being a good Parent, a good Child, a good Husband or Wife, a good Neighbour or Friend, a good Subject or Citizen, that is, in short, a good Christian. Nicholas Gimcrack, therefore, who neglected the Care of his Family, to pursue Butterflies, was a just Object of Ridicule, and we must give him up as fair Game to the satyrist.

Adieu, my dear Friend, and believe me ever

Your affectionately,

B. FRANKLIN.

[5]

The Shipley Girls

Franklin was his most charming self with the daughters of his friend Jonathan Shipley, Bishop of St. Asaph, as shown by his account of a coach ride to London with eleven-year-old Kitty and his epitaph for Georgiana's pet squirrel.

TO MRS. JONATHAN SHIPLEY

August 12, 1771

Dear Madam,

This is just to let you know that we arriv'd safe and well in Marlborough Street about six, where I deliver'd up my Charge:

The above seems too short for a Letter; so I will lengthen it by a little Account of our Journey. The first Stage we were rather pensive. I tried several Topics of Conversation, but none of them would hold. But after Breakfast we began to recover spirits, and had a good deal of Chat. Will you hear some of it? We talk'd of her Brother, and she wish'd he was married. "And don't you wish your Sisters married too?" "Yes. All but Emily; I would not have her married." "Why?" "Because I can't spare her, I can't part with her. The rest may marry as soon as they please, so they do but get good Husbands." We then took upon us to consider for 'em what sort of Husbands would be fittest for every one of them. We began with Georgiana. She thought a Country Gentleman, that lov'd Travelling and would take her with him, that lov'd Books and would hear her read to him; I added "that had a good Estate and was a Member of Parliament and lov'd to see an Experiment now and then." This she agreed to; so we set him down for Georgiana, and went on to Betsy. "Betsy," says I, "seems of a sweet mild Temper, and if we should give her a Country Squire, and he should happen to be of a rough, passionate Turn, and be angry now and then, it might break her Heart." "O, none of 'em must be so, for then they would not be good Husbands." "To make sure of this Point, however, for Betsy, shall we give her a Bishop?" "O, no, that won't do. They all declare against the Church, and against the Army; not one of them will marry either a Clergyman or an Officer; that they are resolved upon." "What can be their reason for that?" "Why you know, that when a Clergyman or an Officer dies, the Income goes with 'em; and then what is there to maintain the Family? There's the Point." "Then suppose we give her a good, honest, sensible City Merchant, who will love her dearly and is very rich?" "I don't know but that may do." We proceeded to Emily, her dear Emily, I was afraid we should hardly find any thing good enough for Emily; but at last, after first settling that, if she did marry, Kitty was to live a good deal with her; we agreed that as Emily was very handsome we might expect an Earl for her. So having fix'd her, as I thought, a Countess, we went on to Anna-Maria. "She," says Kitty, "should have a rich Man that has a large Family and a great many things to take care of; for she is very good at managing, helps my Mama very much, can look over Bills, and order all sorts of Family Business." "Very well; and as there is a Grace and Dignity in her Manner that would become the Station, what do you think of giving her a Duke?" "O no! I'll have the Duke for Emily. You may give the Earl to Anna-Maria if you please: But Emily shall have the Duke." I contested this Matter some time; but at length was forc'd to give up the point, leave Emily in Possession of the Duke, and content myself with the Earl for Anna-Maria. "And now what shall we do for Kitty? We have forgot her, all this Time." "Well, and what will you do for her?" "I suppose that tho' the rest have resolv'd against the Army, she may not yet have made so rash a Resolution." "Yes, but she has: Unless, now, an old one, an old General that has done fighting, and is rich, such a one as General Rufane; I like him a good deal; You must know I like an old Man, indeed I do: And some how or other all the old Men take to me, all that come to our House like me better than my other Sisters: I go to 'em and ask 'em how they do, and they like it mightily; and the Maids take notice of it, and say when they see an old Man come, 'There's a Friend of yours, Miss Kitty.' " "But then as you like an old General, hadn't you better take him while he's a young Officer, and let him grow old upon your Hands, because then, you'll like him better and better every Year as he grows older and older." "No, that won't do. He must be an old Man of 70 or 80, and take me when I am about 30: And then you know I may be a rich young Widow." We din'd at Staines, she was Mrs. Shipley, cut up the Chicken pretty handily (with a little Direction) and help'd me in a very womanly Manner. "Now," says she, when I commended her, "my Father never likes to see me or Georgiana carve, because we do it, he says, badly: But how should we learn if we never try?" We drank good Papa and Mama's Health, and the Healths of the Dutchess, the Countess, and Merchant's Lady, the Country Gentlewoman, and our Welsh Brother. This brought their Affairs again under Consideration. "I doubt," says she, "we have not done right for Betsy. I don't think a Merchant will do for her. She is much inclin'd to be a fine Gentlewoman; and is indeed already more of the fine Gentlewoman, I think, than any of my other Sisters; and therefore she shall be a Vice Countess."

Thus we chatted on, and she was very entertaining quite to Town.

I have now made my Letter as much too long as it was at first too short. The Bishop would think it too trifling, therefore don't show it him. I am afraid too that you will think it so, and have a good mind not to send it. Only it tells you Kitty is well at School, and for that I let it go. My Love to the whole amiable Family, best Respects to the Bishop, and 1000 Thanks for all your Kindnesses, and for the happy Days I enjoy'd at Twyford. With the greatest Esteem and Respect, I am, Madam, Your most obedient and humble Servant. . . .

[6]

TO MISS GEORGIANA SHIPLEY

September 26, 1772.

Dear Miss,

I lament with you most sincerely the unfortunate end of poor MUNGO. Few squirrels were better accomplished; for he had had a good education, had travelled far, and seen much of the world. As he had the honour of being, for his virtues, your favourite, he should not go, like common skuggs, without an elegy or an epitaph. Let us give him one in the monumental style and measure, which, being neither prose nor verse, is perhaps the properest for grief; since to use common language would look as if we were not affected, and to make rhymes would seem trifling in sorrow.

EPITAPH.

Alas! poor MUNGO!
Happy wert thouh, hadst thou known
Thy own felicity.
Remote from the fierce bald eagle,
Tyrant of thy native woods,
Thou hadst nought to fear from his piercing talons,
Nor from the murdering gun
Of the thoughtless sportsman.
Safe in thy wired castle,

GRIMALKIN never could annoy thee.
Daily wert thou fed with the choicest viands,
By the fair hand of an indulgent mistress;
But, discontented,
Thou wouldst have more freedom.

Too soon, alas! didst thou obtain it;
And wandering,
Thou art fallen by the fangs of wanton, cruel RANGER!

Learn hence,
Ye who blindly seek more liberty,
Whether subjects, sons, squirrels or daughters,
That apparent restraint may be real protection;
Yielding peace and plenty
With security.

You see, my dear Miss, how much more decent and
proper this broken style is, than if we were to say, by
way of epitaph,

Here SKUGG
Lies snug,
As a bug
In a rug.

and yet, perhaps, there are people in the world of so little
feeling as to think that this would be a good-enough epitaph for poor Mungo.

If you wish it, I shall procure another to succeed him;
but perhaps you will now choose some other amusement.

Remember me affectionately to all the good family,
and believe me ever, Your affectionate friend. . . .

[7]

Deborah's Last, Lonely Years

In Philadelphia Deborah was unhappy and lonely, her health worsening. "I am very low speretted . . . so very lonely," she wrote her husband. Their correspondence during her declining years reveals Franklin at his worst. He sent her gifts and some affection, but neither in quantities sufficient to allay her increasing unhappiness. His generally brief letters lack the chatty quality which she would have appreciated; instead, he made her into the American secretary of his expanding affairs and criticized her freely when she blundered. Thoroughly at home in England, he constantly wrote her of his imminent return while assuring his English friends that he was preparing to transplant his family to English soil. He even allowed jealousy to aggravate her loneliness: when he took a trip to France in 1767 he did not write, but let Mrs. Stevenson describe in detail to Deborah the letters she got from him. As if it were not enough to have to be told of her husband's whereabouts by a woman who had, in many ways, usurped her place, Mrs. Stevenson added salt to the wounds by telling her that she was close enough to Franklin to know that he had had "Blind Boils so call'd" on his back when he left for France. And then Franklin wrote his wife that Margaret Stevenson was "the best Woman in England. . . ." The philosopher had trained himself to be an agreeable companion—he was more skillful than most men at the art of pleasing—but when it came to his wife this otherwise most charming of men was willing only to nod civilly when he should at least have forced a smile.

BENJAMIN TO DEBORAH

December 21, 1768

My Dear Child,

I have now before me your Favours of Oct. 1, 18. 23. 30. and Nov. 5, which I shall answer in order.

I wonder to hear that my Friends were backward in bringing you my Letters when they arrived, and think it must be a mere Imagination of yours, the Effect of some melancholy Humor you happen'd then to be in. I condole with you sincerely on poor Debby's Account, and hope she got well to her Husband with her two Children.

You say in yours of Oct. 18, "For me to give you any Uneasiness about your Affairs here, would be of no Service, and I shall not at this time enter on it." I am made by this to apprehend that something is amiss, and perhaps have more Uneasiness from the uncertainty, than I should have had if you had told me what it was. I wish therefore you would be explicit in your next. I rejoice that my good old Friend, Mr. Coleman, is got safe home, and continues well. Upon what you write me now about the Watches, I shall, if I find I can afford it; for I understand the Ballance of the Post Office Account which I must pay here, is greatly against me, owing to the large Sums you have received. I do not doubt your having applied them properly, and I only mention it, that if I do not send you a Watch, it will not be thro' Neglect or for want of Regard, but because I cannot spare the Cash, for I shall not like to leave Debts behind me here. Mrs. Stevens's Bills since her Marriage have been accepted as before, I should have mention'd it if they had not. Sally Franklin whom you inquire after is here at present under Mrs. Stevenson's care, but I expect her Father to fetch her soon. She presents her Duty.

Remember me respectfully to Mr. Rhodes, Mr. Wharton, Mr. Roberts, Mr. and Mrs. Duffield, Neighbour Thomson, Dr. and Mrs. Redman, Mrs. Hopkinson, Mr. Duché, Dr. Morgan, Mr. Hopkinson, and all the other Friends you have from time to time mention'd as enquiring after me. As you ask me, I can assure you, that I do really intend, God willing, to return in the Summer, and that as soon as possible after seeing and settling Matters with Mr. Foxcroft, whom I expect in April or May. I am glad that you find so much reason to be satisfy'd with Mr. Bache. I hope all will prove for the best. Capt. Falkener has been arrived at Plymouth some time, but the Winds being contrary could get no farther, so I have not yet received the Apples, Meal, &c., and fear they will be spoilt. I send with this, some of the new kind of Oats much admir'd here to make Oatmeal of, and for other Uses, as being free from Huskes; and some Swiss Barley 6 Rows to an Ear: perhaps our Friends may like to try them, and you may distribute the Seed among them. Give some to Mr. Roberts, Mr. Rhodes, Mr. Thomson, Mr. Bartram, our Son, and others.

I cannot comprehend how so very sluggish a Creature as Ben. Mecom is grown, can maintain in Philadelphia so large a Family. I hope they do not hang upon you: for really as we grow old and must grow more helpless, we shall find we have nothing to spare.

I hope the Cold you complain of in two of your Letters went off without any ill Consequences. We are, as you observe, blest with a great Share of Health considering our Years now 63. For my own part, I think of late that my Constitution rather mends: I have had but one Touch of the Gout, and that a light one, since I left you; It was just after my Arrival here, so that this is the 4th Winter I have been free. Walking a great deal tires me less than it used to do. I feel stronger and more active. Yet I would not have you think that I fancy I shall grow young again. I know that men of my Bulk often fail suddenly: I know that according to the Course of Nature I cannot at most continue much longer, and that the living even of another Day is uncertain. I therefore now form no Schemes, but such as are of immediate Execution; indulging myself in no future Prospect except one, that of returning to Philadelphia, there to spend the Evening of Life with my Friends and Family.

Mr. and Mrs. Strahan, & Mr. and Mrs. West, when I last saw them, desired to be kindly remembered to you. Mrs. Stevenson and our Polly send their Love. Mr. Coombe, who seems a very agreeable young Man, lodges with us for the present. Adieu, my dear Debby. I am, as ever, your affectionate Husband. . . .   [8]

DEBORAH TO BENJAMIN

November 20, 1769

. . . yister day I reseved yours dated September the 9 whare in you was so kind as to sende me Sir John Pringels advice to me . . . I am much obliged to you and to so worthey a good man as Sir John . . . my disorder was for this reson my distres for my dear Debbey misforten and her being removed so far from her friend and such a helpless famely and before I had got the better of that our Cusin Betsey macum was taken ill and so much distresst so soon that added to my one [own] dis satisfied distresed att your staying so much longer . . . bouth Salley and my self live so very lonley that I had got into verey low state and got into so unhapey a way that I cold not sleep a long time good old Mr. Whorton did come sometimes to aske how we did and asked us to cume to spend a day att his house . . . and while thair I lost all my memery I cold not tell aney thing but stayed all day but verey sleepey. and as soon as I got to bed I sleep all night and semd [seemed?] quite hapey and esey and I shold a got better but Salley was surprised att my sleepinge as I did . . . [I] supmited to be bleeded and took somthing agonste my one [own] Judgment to oblige Salley as shee was in such a Condison as shee was, I had no head ake or fever the Dr sed my blood was verey good but sed he wold sende to you I beg[g]ed him not but it gave me much onesey nes a boute it or wold not a lett you to a knowe a boute it I still sleep verey well and sleep as soon as night but did loos my apeytite and loos my memery . . . and then wold be better agen for some time after but this time I was verey ill . . . and thanke god while I semed to recover my memerey and thanke god I have my memery . . . I have had one fitt of the head ake. . . .

[9]

BENJAMIN TO DEBORAH

May 1, 1771

My dear Child

I wrote to you per Capt. Osborne, and have since received yours of Jan. 14 per Cousin Benezet, and of March 7, per the Packet.

The Bill on Sir Alexander Grant for £30 which you so kindly sent me inclos'd, came safe to hand. I am obliged too to Mr. Hall for enabling you on a Pinch to buy it. But I am sorry you had so much Trouble about it; and the more so, as it seems to have occasioned some Disgust in you against Messrs. Foxcrofts for not supplying you with money to pay for it. That you may not be offended with your Neighbours without Cause; I must acquaint you with what it seems you did not know, that I had limited them in their Payments to you, to the Sum of Thirty Pounds per Month, for the sake of our more easily settling, and to prevent Mistakes. This making 360 Pounds a year, I thought, as you have no House Rent to pay yourself, and receive the Rents of 7 or 8 Houses besides, might be sufficient for the Maintenance of your Family. I judged such a Limitation the more necessary, because you never have sent me any Account of your expences, and think yourself ill-used if I desire it; and because I know you were not very attentive to Money-matters in your best Days, and I apprehend that your Memory is too much impair'd for the Management of unlimited Sums, without Danger of injuring the future Fortune of your Daughter and Grandson. If out of more than £500 a Year, you could have sav'd enough to buy those Bills it might have been well to continue purchasing them. But I do not like your going about among my Friends to borrow Money for that purpose, especially as it is not at all necessary. And therefore I once more request that you would decline buying them for the future. And I hope you will no longer take it amiss of Messrs. Foxcrofts that they did not supply you. If what you receive is really insufficient for your support, satisfy me by Accounts that it is so, and I shall order more.

I am much pleased with the little Histories you give me of your fine Boy, which are confirmed by all that have seen him. I hope he will be spared and continue the same Pleasure and Comfort to you, and that I shall ere long partake with you in it. My Love to him, and to his Papa and Mama. Mrs. Stevenson too is just made very happy by her Daughter's being safely delivered of a Son; the Mother and Child both well. Present my affectionate re-

spects to Mrs. Montgomery with Thanks for her most obliging Present. It makes a nice Bag for my Ivory Chessmen, I am, as ever, Your Affectionate Husband
B. Franklin

[10]

DEBORAH TO BENJAMIN

[1772?]

My Dear Child

I reseved yours by the packet it gives me much plestuer to hear that you air well and happey I was in hopes that a packet or a vesill wold arived before this wente . . . as I was in hopes that [it] wold in forme when you intend to returne agen to your one home I conte write to you as I am so very unfitt to expres my self and not a bell to due as I yousd for that illness I hed was a polsey . . . my memery failes me I conte expres my self as I yousd to due I did tell your friend Dr Small when he was heare that I had thoute it was a polsey . . . my write hand is verey weak some times I am not abel to try on my close I am verey low sperreted that it is verey trubl sume to tell what I wold say of . . . I have bin verey un well for 5 or 6 days I donte make aney complaint to you. I saw yisterday that several vesils from N York and frome this place get to Ingland I belive Dr Small was in one of them I hope he is safe arived at home and well Mr. Beache ses that he is a good mon I hope Capt Falkner is safe arive and well . . . I must aske in faver for sume muslim for Salley to worke for her self I have one my self but have not wore it . . . let me know if you shold returned home this fall I heard that Mrs. Write has seen you but when shee wente I did not know when shee wente or I shold a given her a letter. . . .

[11]

BENJAMIN TO DEBORAH

Sept. 10, 1774

It is now nine long Months since I received a Line from my dear Debby. I have supposed it owing to your continual Expectation of my Return; I have feared that some Indisposition has rendered you unable to write; I have imagined any Thing rather than admit a Supposition that your kind Attention towards me was abated. And yet when so many other Old Friends have dropt a Line to me now & then at a Venture, taking the Chance of finding me here or not as it might happen, why might I not have expected the same Comfort from you, who used to be so diligent and faithful a Correspondent, as to omit scarce any Opportunity?

This will serve to acquaint you that I continue well, Thanks to God.—It would be a great pleasure to me to hear that you are so. My Love to our Children, and believe me ever

Your affectionate Husband

B Franklin

I recommend the Bearer Mr. Westley to your Civilities

[12]

WILLIAM TO BENJAMIN

Deborah died on December 19, and probably never received the preceding letter. Five days later William Franklin wrote his father a letter which must have left a life-long impression.

December 24, 1774

Hon'd Father:

I came here on Thursday last to attend the funeral of my poor old mother, who died the Monday noon preceding. Mr. Bache sent his clerk express to me on the occasion, who reached Amboy on Tuesday evening, and I set out early the next morning, but the weather being very severe and snowing hard, I was not able to reach here till about 4 o'clock on Thursday afternoon, about half an hour before the corpse was to be moved for interment. Mr. Bache and I followed as chief mourners; your old friend H. Roberts and several other of your friends were carriers, and a very respectable number of the inhabitants were at the funeral. I don't mention the particulars of her illness, as you will have a much fuller account from Mr. Bache than I am able to give. Her death was no more than might be reasonably expected after the paralytick stroke she received some time ago, which greatly affected her memory and understanding. She told me when I took leave of her on my removal to Amboy, that she never expected to see you unless you returned this winter, for that she was sure she should not live till next Summer. I heartily wish you had happened to have come over in the fall, as I think her disappointment in that respect prayed a good deal on her spirits. . . . Your dutiful son,

Wm. Franklin
[13]

"A Thorough Courtier"

With his wife dead, Franklin soon broke with his surviving son, William, over political issues. The two men disagreed over Parliament's harsh retribution for the Boston Tea Party, the father giving up in exasperation, "But you who are a thorough Courtier, see every thing with Government Eyes."

When war began, William chose the Loyalist side, and no correspondence passed between him and his father until 1784, when a brief reconciliation was effected. However, Franklin's will left his son little: "the part he acted against me in the late War, which is of public Notoriety, will account for my leaving him no more of an Estate he endeavoured to deprive me of." After this William severed all connections with the country of his birth: "The Revolution in America, and the shameful Injustice of my Father's Will, have in a manner dissolved all my Connexions in that Part of the World of a private as well as publick Nature."

The following letter was written by Franklin in response to an overture William made in 1784.

TO WILLIAM FRANKLIN

August 16, 1784.

Dear Son,

I received your letter of the 22nd past, and am glad to find that you desire to revive the affectionate Intercourse, that formerly existed between us. It will be very agreeable to me; indeed nothing has ever hurt me so much and affected me with such keen Sensations, as to find myself deserted in my old Age by my only Son; and not only deserted, but to find him taking up Arms against me, in a Cause, wherein my good Fame, Fortune and Life were all at Stake. You conceived, you say, that your Duty to your King and Regard for your Country requir'd this. I ought not to blame you for differing in Sentiment with me in Public Affairs. We are Men, all subject to Errors. Our Opinions are not in your own Power; they are form'd and govern'd much by Circumstances, that are often as inexplicable as they are irresistible. Your Situation was such that few would have censured your remaining Neuter, *tho' there are Natural Duties which precede political ones, and cannot be extinguish'd by them.*

This is a disagreeable Subject. I drop it. And we will endeavor, as you propose mutually to forget what has happened relating to it, as well as we can. I send your Son over to pay his Duty to you. You will find him much improv'd. He is greatly esteem'd and belov'd in this Country, and will make his Way anywhere. It is my Desire, that he should study the Law, as the necessary Part of Knowledge for a public Man, and profitable if he should have occasion to practise it. I would have you therefore put into his hands those Law-books you have, viz. Blackstone, Coke, Bacon, Viner, &c. He will inform you, that he received the Letter sent him my Mr. Galloway, and the Paper it inclosed, safe. . . .

I did intend returning this year; but the Congress, instead of giving me Leave to do so, have sent me another Commission, which will keep me here at least a Year longer; and perhaps I may then be too old and feeble to bear the Voyage. I am here among a People that love and respect me, a most amiable Nation to live with; and perhaps I may conclude to die among them; for my Friends in America are dying off, one after another, and I have been so long abroad, that I should now be almost a stranger in my own Country.

I shall be glad to see you when convenient, but would not have you come here at present. You may confide to your son the Family Affairs you wished to confer upon with me, for he is discreet. And I trust, that you will prudently avoid introducing him to Company, that it may be improper for him to be seen with. I shall hear from you by him and any letters to me afterwards, will come safe under Cover directed to Mr. Ferdinand Grand, Banker at Paris. Wishing you Health, and more Happiness than it seems you have lately experienced, I remain your affectionate father,

B. Franklin

[14]

The Ladies of France

"... as jolly as formerly, and as strong and hearty," was the way Franklin described himself in his seventy-second year. He was in France, and he delighted in being "very plainly dress'd, wearing my thin grey strait hair, that peeps out under my only Coiffure, a fine Fur Cap, which comes down my Forehead almost to my spectacles. Think how this must appear among the Powder'd Heads of Paris!"   [15]

Franklin's charm and his immense popularity made him a valued member of any salon, and so he was avidly pursued by the Frenchwomen of the day. (In a contemporary French satire, there was a louse who had resided on many of the great heads of France and had moved to Franklin's gray hair. The louse described a dinner party at which Franklin was introduced to a young lady. She reads him a rather poor poem of her own composition, and as she finishes he embraces her with ardor [but with-

out removing his glasses] and whispers, "Until this evening, my divine one.")

Franklin explained the ladies' attention to him in a letter to his stepniece in Boston.

TO MRS. ELIZABETH PARTRIDGE

October 11, 1779

Your kind Letter, my dear Friend, was long in coming; but it gave me the Pleasure of knowing that you had been well in October and January last. The Difficulty, Delay and Interruption of Correspondence with those I love, is one of the great Inconveniences I find in living so far from home: but we must bear these & more, with Patience, if we can; if not, we must bear them as I do with Impatience.

You mention the Kindness of the French Ladies to me. I must explain that matter. This is the civilest nation upon Earth. Your first Acquaintances endeavour to find out what you like, and they tell others. If 'tis understood that you like Mutton, dine where you will you find Mutton. Somebody, it seems, gave it out that I lov'd Ladies; and then every body presented me their Ladies (or the Ladies presented themselves) to be *embrac'd,* that is to have their Necks kiss'd. For as to kissing of Lips or Cheeks it is not the Mode here, the first, is reckon'd rude, & the other may rub off the Paint. The French Ladies have however 1000 other ways of rendering themselves agreeable; by their various Attentions and Civilities, & their sensible Conversation. 'Tis a delightful People to live with . . .

Adieu, my dear Child, & believe me ever. Your affectionate Papah. . . .

[16]

A Treaty of the Heart

In France Franklin fell in love. When he met Madame Brillon in 1777 she was in her thirties, married to a rich and uninterested financier twenty-four years her senior. In their correspondence she addressed Franklin as "mon chér papa," and he replied to "ma trés chére enfante." It was Katy Ray all over again; he reminded her of the commandment to increase and multiply, told her he loved her "like a Father, with all my Heart," and admitted that "I sometimes suspect the Heart of wishing to go further, but I try to conceal that." In July of 1782 Franklin took a few moments away from his work on a peace treaty to propose another treaty to Madame Brillon.

TO MADAME BRILLON

WHAT a difference, my dear Friend, between you and me!—You find my Faults so many as to be innumerable, while I can see but one in you; and perhaps that is the Fault of my Spectacles.—The Fault I mean is that kind of Covetousness, by which you would engross all my Affection, and permit me none for the other amiable Ladies of your Country. You seem to imagine that it cannot be divided without being diminish'd: In which you mistake the nature of the thing and forget the Situation in which you have plac'd and hold me. You renounce and exclude arbitrarily every thing corporal from our Amour, except such a merely civil Embrace now and then as you would permit to a country Cousin,—what is there then remaining that I may not afford to others without a Diminution of what belongs to you? The Operations of the Mind, Esteem, Admiration, Respect, & even Affection for one Object, may be multiply'd as more Objects that merit them present themselves, and yet remain the same to the first, which therefore has no room to complain of Injury. They are in their Nature as divisible as the sweet Sounds of the Forte Piano produc'd by your exquisite Skill: Twenty People may receive the same Pleasure from them, without lessening that which you kindly intend for me; and I might as reasonably require of your Friendship, that they should reach and delight no Ears but mine.

You see by this time how unjust you are in your Demands, and in the open War you declare against me if I do not comply with them. Indeed it is I that have the most Reason to complain. My poor little Boy, whom you ought methinks to have cherish'd, instead of being fat and Jolly like those in your elegant Drawings, is meagre and starv'd almost to death for want of the substantial Nourishment which you his Mother inhumanly deny him, and yet would now clip his little Wings to prevent his seeking it elsewhere!—

I fancy we shall neither of us get any thing by this War, and therefore as feeling my self the Weakest, I will do what indeed ought always to be done by the Wisest, be first in making the Propositions for Peace. That a Peace may be lasting, the Articles of the Treaty should be regulated upon the Principles of the most perfect Equity & Reciprocity. In this View I have drawn up & offer the following, viz.—

ARTICLE 1.

There shall be eternal Peace, Friendship & Love, between Madame B. and Mr F.

ARTICLE 2.

In order to maintain the same inviolably, Made B. on her Part stipulates and agrees, that Mr F. shall come to her whenever she sends for him.

Art. 3.

That he shall stay with her as long as she pleases.

Art. 4.

That when he is with her, he shall be oblig'd to drink Tea, play Chess, hear Musick; or do any other thing that she requires of him.

Art. 5.

And that he shall love no other Woman but herself.

Art. 6.

And the said Mr F. on his part stipulates and agrees, that he will go away from M. B.'s whenever he pleases.

Art. 7.

That he will stay away as long as he pleases.

ART. 8.

That when he is with her, he will do what he pleases.

ART. 9.

And that he will love any other Woman as far as he finds her amiable.

Let me know what you think of these Preliminaries. To me they seem to express the true Meaning and Intention of each Party more plainly than most Treaties.—I shall insist pretty strongly on the eighth Article, tho' without much Hope of your Consent to it; and on the ninth also, tho' I despair of ever finding any other Woman that I could love with equal Tenderness: being ever, my dear dear Friend,

Yours most sincerely
BF

[17]

Rejected Suitor

When Franklin sailed from France in 1785, he left behind two saddened women, Mesdames Brillon and Helvétius. The latter was a rich widow in her sixties who lived at Auteuil. A beautiful woman of great charm and intellect, she was called Notre Dame d'Auteuil, *and her daughters the* Etoiles. *Her active salon had included, at one time, Voltaire, and was joined by Franklin in the late 1770s. The man from Philadelphia was bewitched by Madame Helvétius and eventually proposed marriage. She rejected him, but their relationship continued amicably. Her attraction for him can best be understood from two letters, one from his own pen and the other written by John Adams's wife.*

TO MADAME HELVÉTIUS

[September 19, 1779]

I see that statesmen, philosophers, historians, poets, and men of learning of all sorts are drawn around you, and seem as willing to attach themselves to you as straws about a fine piece of amber. It is not that you make pretensions to any of their sciences; and if you did, similarity of studies does not always make people love one another. It is not that you take pains to engage them; artless simplicity is a striking part of your character. I would not attempt to explain it by the story of the ancient, who, being asked why philosophers sought the acquaintance of kings, and kings not that of philosophers, replied that philosophers knew what they wanted, which was not always the case with kings. Yet thus far the comparison may go, that we find in your sweet society that charming benevolence, that amiable attention to oblige, that disposition to please and be pleased, which we do not always find in the society of one another. It springs from you; it has influence on us all, and in your company we are not only pleased with you, but better pleased with one another and with ourselves.

[18]

ABIGAIL ADAMS TO LUCY CRANCH

September 5, 1784

My Dear Lucy . . .

This lady I dined with at Dr. Franklin's. She entered the room with a careless, jaunty air; upon seeing Ladies who were strangers to her, she cried out, "Ah! Mon Dieu, where is Franklin? Why did you not tell me there were ladies here?" You must suppose her speaking all this in French. "How I look!" said she, taking hold of a Chemise made of Tiffany, which she had on over a blue lute-string, and which looked as much upon the decay as her beauty, for she was once a handsome woman; her hair was frizzled; over it she had a small straw hat, with a dirty gauze half-handkerchief round it, and a bit of dirtier gauze, than ever my maids wore, was bowed on behind. She had a black gauze scarf thrown over her shoulders. She ran out of the room; when she returned, the Doctor entered at one door, she at the other, upon which she ran foreward to him, caught him by the hand,

"Hélas! Franklin;" then gave him a double kiss, one upon each cheek, and another upon his forehead. When we went into the room to dine, she was placed between the Doctor and Mr. Adams. She carried on the chief of the Conversation at dinner, frequently locking her hand into the Doctor's, and sometimes spreading her arms upon the backs of both the gentlemen's chairs, then throwing her arm carelessly upon the Doctor's neck. . . . I own I was highly disgusted, and never wish for an acquaintance with any ladies of this cast. After Dinner she threw herself upon a settee, where she showed more than her feet. She had a little lap-dog, who was next to the Doctor, her favorite. This she kissed, and when he wet the floor she wiped it up with her chemise. This is one of the Doctor's most intimate friends, with whom he dines once every week, and she with him. . . .

[19]

Home Again

Back in Philadelphia Franklin corresponded with his friends across the sea and induced Polly Stevenson Hewson to emigrate with her children; her mother and her husband had died. Content in the bosom of his family, he wrote, probably for the last time, to his old friend Bishop Shipley.

TO JONATHAN SHIPLEY

February 24, 1786

Dear Friend,

I received lately your kind letter of Nov. 27th. My Reception here was, as you have heard, very honourable indeed; but I was betray'd by it, and by some Remains of Ambition, from which I had imagined myself free, to accept of the Chair of Government for the State of Pennsylvania, when the proper thing for me was Repose and a private Life. I hope, however, to be able to bear the Fatigue for one Year, and then to retire. . . .

As to my Domestic Circumstances, of which you kindly desire to hear something, they are at present as happy as I could wish them. I am surrounded by my Offspring, a Dutiful and Affectionate Daughter in my House, with Six Grandchildren, the eldest of which you have seen, who is now at a College in the next Street, finishing the learned Part of his Education; the others promising, both for Parts and good Dispositions. What their Conduct may be, when they grow up and enter the important Scenes of Life, I shall not live to *see,* and I cannot *foresee.* I therefore enjoy among them the present Hour, and leave the future to Providence.

He that raises a large Family does, indeed, while he lives to observe them, *stand,* as Watts says, a *broader Mark for Sorrow;* but then he stands a broader Mark for Pleasure too. When we launch our little Fleet of Barques into the Ocean, bound to different Ports, we hope for each a prosperous Voyage; but contrary Winds, hidden Shoals, Storms, and Enemies come in for a Share in the Disposition of Events; and though these occasion a Mixture of Disappointment, yet, considering the Risque where we can make no Insurance, we should think ourselves happy if some return with Success. My Son's Son, Temple Franklin, whom you have also seen, having had a fine Farm of 600 Acres convey'd to him by his Father when we were at Southampton, has drop'd for the present his Views of acting in the political Line, and applies himself ardently to the Study and Practice of Agriculture. This is much more agreeable to me, who esteem it the most useful, the most independent, and therefore the noblest of Employments. His Lands are on navigable water, communicating with the Delaware, and but about 16 Miles from this City. He has associated to himself a very skillful English Farmer lately arrived here, who is to instruct him in the business, and partakes for a Term of the Profits; so that there is a great apparent Probability of their Success.

You will kindly expect a Word or two concerning myself. My Health and Spirits continue, Thanks to God, as when you saw me. The only complaint I then had, does not grow worse, and is tolerable. I still have Enjoyment in the Company of my Friends; and, being easy in my Circumstances, have many Reasons to like Living. But the Course of Nature must soon put a period to my present Mode of Existence. This I shall submit to with less Regret, as, having seen during a long Life a good deal of this World, I feel a growing Curiosity to be acquainted with some other; and can chearfully, with filial Confidence, resign my Spirit to the conduct of that great and good Parent of Mankind, who created it, and who has so graciously protected and prospered me from my Birth to the present Hour. Wherever I am, I hope always to retain the pleasing remembrance of your Friendship, being with sincere and great Esteem, my dear Friend, yours most affectionately, B. FRANKLIN.

P.S. We all join in Respects to Mrs. Shipley, and best wishes for the whole amiable Family.

[20]

VI

SOMETHING OF HIS RELIGION

"Sams Religion is like cheddar cheese," said Franklin in Poor Richard's Almanack, 1734, " 'Tis made of the milk of one & twenty Parishes." The author's own mind did not naturally run in theological channels. The precisionism of his Puritan heritage was alien to his own broad secular spirit, and he thought of New England's brand of Calvinism as "dry doctrine."

He had, however, no more enthusiam for disagreement with religion than for devotion to it. "There are some Things in your New England Doctrines and Worship which I do not agree with," he wrote his sister when she admonished him for his secularism, "but I do not therefore condemn them, or desire to shake your Belief or Practise of them."

Franklin's beliefs did to a large extent remain those of his Puritan predecessors, drained of mystical sanction and supported, rather, by social necessity.

A Practical Theology

A good illustration of the facility of Franklin's theology and the pragmatic criteria by which he judged religion is a letter he wrote, as an adult, to his father and mother.

TO JOSIAH AND ABIAH FRANKLIN

April 13, 1738

Honour'd Father and Mother

I have your Favour of the 21st of March in which you both seem concern'd lest I have imbib'd some erroneous Opinions. Doubtless I have my Share, and when the natural Weakness and Imperfection of Human Understanding is considered, with the unavoidable Influences of Education, Custom, Books and Company, upon our Ways of thinking, I imagine a Man must have a good deal of Vanity who believes, and a good deal of Boldness who affirms, that all the Doctrines he holds, are true; and all he rejects, are false. And perhaps the same may be justly said of every Sect, Church and Society of men when they assume to themselves the Infallibility which they deny to the Popes and Councils. I think Opinions should be judg'd of by their Influences and Effects; and if a Man holds none that tend to make him less Virtuous or more vicious, it may be concluded he holds none that are dangerous; which I hope is the Case with me. I am sorry you should have any Uneasiness on my Account, and if it were a thing possible for one to alter his Opinions in order to please others, I know none whom I ought more willingly to oblige in that respect than your selves: But since it is no more in a Man's Power *to think* than *to look* like another, methinks all that should be expected from me is to keep my Mind open to Conviction, to hear patiently and examine attentively whatever is offered me for that end; and if after all I continue in the same Errors, I believe your usual Charity will induce you rather to pity

and excuse than blame me. In the mean time your Care
and Concern for me is what I am very thankful for.

As to the Freemasons, unless she will believe me when
I assure her that they are in general a very harmless sort
of People; and have no principles or Practices that are
inconsistent with Religion or good Manners, I know no
Way of giving my Mother a better Opinion of them than
she seems to have at present (since it is not allow'd that
Women should be admitted into that secret Society). She
has, I must confess, on that Account, some reason to be
displeas'd with it; but for any thing else, I must entreat
her to suspend her Judgment till she is better inform'd,
and in the mean time exercise her Charity.

My Mother grieves that one of her Sons is an Arian,
another an Arminian. What an Arminian or an Arian is,
I cannot say that I very well know; the Truth is, I make
such Distinctions very little my Study; I think vital Religion has always suffer'd, when Orthodoxy is more regarded than Virtue. And the Scripture assures me, that
at the last Day, we shall not be examin'd what we *thought*,
but what we *did;* and our Recommendation will not be
that we said *Lord, Lord,* but that we did GOOD to our
Fellow Creatures. See Matth. 2[5].

We have had great Rains here lately, which with the
Thawing of Snow in the Mountains back of our Country
has made vast Floods in our Rivers and by carrying away
Bridges, Boats, &c. made travelling almost impracticable
for a Week past, so that our Post has entirely mist making
one Trip.

I know nothing of Dr. Crook, nor can I learn that any
such Person has ever been here.

I hope my Sister Janey's Child is by this time recovered. I am Your dutiful Son

BF

[1]

"A Dissertation on Liberty and Necessity, Pleasure and Pain"

Only once did Franklin mistake logic for reason and thus paint himself into an unreal dogmatic corner. In his only formal adventure in theology, addressed to his friend James Ralph, the young rebel allied himself with deism, the fashionable heresy of the day.

TO JAMES RALPH

1725

SIR,

I have here, according to your Request, given you my *present* Thoughts of the *general State of Things* in the Universe. Such as they are, you have them, and are welcome to 'em; and if they yield you any Pleasure or Satisfaction, I shall think my Trouble sufficiently compensated. I know my Scheme will be liable to many Objections from a less discerning Reader than your self; but it is not design'd for those who can't understand it. I need not give you any Caution to distinguish the hypothetical Parts of the Argument from the conclusive: You will easily perceive what I design for Demonstration, and what for Probability only. The whole I leave entirely to you, and shall value myself more or less on this account, in proportion to your Esteem and Approbation.

Sect. I *Of* Liberty *and* Necessity

I. *There is said to be a* First Mover, *who is called* GOD, *Maker of the Universe.*

II. *He is said to be all-wise, all-good, all powerful.*

These two Propositions being allow'd and asserted by People of almost every Sect and Opinion; I have here suppos'd them granted, and laid them down as the Foundation of my Argument; What follows then, being a chain of Consequences truly drawn from them, will stand or fall as they are true or false.

III. *If He is all-good, whatsoever He doth must be good.*
IV. *If He is all-wise, whatsoever He doth must be wise.*

The Truth of these Propositions, with relation to the two first, I think may be justly call'd evident; since, either that infinite Goodness will act what is ill, or infinite Wisdom what is not wise, is too glaring a Contradiction not to be perceiv'd by any Man of common Sense, and deny'd as soon as understood.

V. *If He is all-powerful, there can be nothing either existing or acting in the Universe against or without his Consent; and what He consents to must be good, because He is good; therefore* Evil *doth not exist.*

Unde Malum? has been long a Question, and many of the Learned have perplex'd themselves and Readers to little Purpose in Answer to it. That there are both Things and Actions to which we give the name of *Evil,* is not here deny'd, as *Pain, Sickness, Want, Theft, Murder,* &c. but that these and the like are not in reality *Evils, Ills,* or *Defects* in the Order of the Universe, is demonstrated in the next Section, as well as by this and the following Proposition. Indeed, to suppose any Thing to exist or be done, *contrary* to the Will of the Almighty, is to suppose him not almighty; or that Something (the Cause of *Evil*) is more mighty than the Almighty; an Inconsistence that I think no One will defend: and to deny any Thing or Action, which he consents to the existence of, to be good, is entirely to destroy his two Attributes of *Wisdom* and *Goodness.*

There is nothing done in the Universe, say the Philosophers, *but what God either does, or* permits *to be done.* This, as He is Almighty, is certainly true: But what need of this Distinction between *doing* and *permitting?* Why, first they take it for granted that many Things in the Universe exist in such a Manner as is not for the best, and that many Actions are done which ought not to be done, or would be better undone; these Things or Actions they cannot ascribe to God as His, because they have already attributed to Him infinite Wisdom and Goodness; Here then is the Use of the Word *Permit;* He *permits* them to be done, *say they.* But we will reason thus: If God permits an Action to be done, it is because he wants either *Power* or *Inclination* to hinder it; in saying he wants *Power,* we deny Him to be *almighty;* and if we say He wants *Inclination* or *Will,* it must be, either because He is not Good, or the Action is not *evil,* (for all Evil is contrary to the Essence of *Infinite Goodness.*) The former is inconsistent with his before-given Attribute of Goodness, therefore the latter must be true.

It will be said, perhaps, that *God permits evil Actions to be done, for* wise *Ends and Purposes.* But this Objection destroys itself; for whatever an infinitely good God hath wise Ends in suffering to *be,* must be good, is thereby made good, and cannot be otherwise.

VI. *If a Creature is made by God, it must depend upon God, and receive all its Power from Him; with which Power the Creature can do nothing contrary to the Will of God, because God is Almighty; what is not contrary to His Will, must be agreeable to it; what is agreeable to it, must be good, because He is Good; therefore a Creature can do nothing but what is good.*

This Proposition is much to the same Purpose with the former, but more particular; and its Conclusion is as just and evident. Tho' a Creature may do many Actions which by his Fellow Creatures will be nam'd *Evil,* and which will naturally and necessarily cause or bring upon the Doer, certain *Pains* (which will likewise be call'd *Punishments;*) yet this Proposition proves, that he cannot act what will be in itself really Ill, or displeasing to God. And that the painful Consequences of his evil Actions (*so call'd*) are not, as indeed they ought not to be, *Punishments* or Unhappiness, will be shewn hereafter.

Nevertheless, the late learned Author of *The Religion of Nature,* (which I send you herewith) has given us a Rule or Scheme, whereby to discover which of our Actions ought to be esteem'd and denominated *good,* and which *evil:* It is in short this, "Every Action which is done according to *Truth,* is good; and every Action contrary to Truth, is evil: To act according to Truth is to use and esteem every Thing as what it is, *&c.* Thus if *A* steals a Horse from *B,* and rides away upon him, he uses him not as what he is in Truth, *viz*. the property of another, but as his own, which is contrary to Truth, and therefore *evil*." But, as this Gentleman himself says, (sect. I. Prop. VI.) "In order to judge rightly what any Thing is, it must be consider'd, not only what it is in one Respect, but also what it may be in any other Respect; and the whole Description of the Thing ought to be taken in: So in this Case it ought to be consider'd, that *A* is naturally a *covetous* Being, feeling an Uneasiness in the want of *B's* Horse, which produces an Inclination for stealing him, stronger than his Fear of Punishment for so doing. This is *Truth* likewise, and *A* acts according to it when he steals the Horse. Besides, if it is prov'd to be a *Truth*, that *A* has not Power over his own Actions, it will be indisputable that he acts according to Truth, and impossible he should do otherwise.

I would not be understood by this to encourage or defend Theft; 'tis only for the sake of the Argument, and will certainly have no *ill Effect*. The Order and Course of Things will not be affected by Reasoning of this Kind; and 'tis as just and necessary, and as much according to Truth, for *B* to dislike and punish the Theft of his Horse, as it is for *A* to steal him.

VII. *If the Creature is thus limited in his Actions, being able to do only such Things as God would have him to do, and not being able to refuse doing what God would have done; then he can have no such Thing as Liberty, Free-will or Power to do or refrain an Action.*

By *Liberty* is sometimes understood the Absence of Opposition; and in this Sense, indeed, all our Actions may be said to be the Effects of our Liberty: But it is a Liberty of the same nature with the Fall of a heavy Body to the Ground; it has Liberty to fall, that is, it meets with nothing to hinder its Fall, but at the same Time it is necessitated to fall, and has no Power or Liberty to remain suspended.

But let us take the Argument in another View, and suppose ourselves to be, in the common sense of the Word, *Free Agents*. As Man is a Part of this great machine, the Universe, his regular Acting is requisite to the regular moving of the whole. Among the many Things which lie before him to be done, he may, as he is at Liberty and his Choice influenc'd by nothing, (for so it must be, or he is not at Liberty) chuse any one, and refuse the rest. Now there is every Moment something *best* to be done, which is alone then *good*, and with respect to which, every Thing else is at that Time *evil*. In order to know which is best to be done, and which not, it is requisite that we should have at one View all the intricate Consequences of every Action with respect to the general Order and Scheme of the Universe, both present and future; but they are innumerable and incomprehensible by any Thing but Omniscience. As we cannot know these, we have but as one Chance to ten thousand, to hit on the right Action; we should then be perpetually blundering about in the Dark, and putting the Scheme in Disorder; for every wrong Action of a Part, is a Defect or Blemish in the Order of the Whole. Is it not necessary then, that our Actions should be over-rul'd and govern'd by an all-wise Providence?—How exact and regular is every Thing in the *natural* World! How wisely in every Part contriv'd! We cannot here find the least Defect! Those who have study'd the mere animal and vegetable Creation, demonstrate that nothing can be more harmonious and beautiful! All the heavenly Bodies, the Stars and Planets, are regulated with the utmost Wisdom! And can we suppose less Care to be taken in the Order of the *moral* than in the *natural* System? It is as if an ingenious Artificer, having fram'd a curious Machine or Clock, and put its many intricate Wheels and Powers in such a Dependance on one another, that the whole might move in the most exact Order and Regularity, had nevertheless plac'd in it several other Wheels endu'd with an independent *Self-Motion*, but ignorant of the general Interest of the Clock; and these would every now and then be moving wrong, disordering the true Movement, and making continual Work for the Mender: which might better be prevented, by depriving them of that Power of Self-Motion, and placing them in a Dependance on the regular Part of the Clock.

VIII. *If there is not such Thing as Free-Will in Creatures, there can be neither merit nor demerit in Creatures.*

IX. *And therefore every Creature must be equally esteem'd by the Creator.*

These Propositions appear to be the necessary Consequences of the former. And certainly no Reason can be given, why the Creator should prefer in his Esteem one Part of His Works to another, if with equal Wisdom and Goodness he design'd and created them all, since all Ill or Defect, as contrary to his Nature, is excluded by his Power. We will sum up the Argument thus, When the Creator first design'd the Universe, either it was His Will and Intention that all Things should exist and be in the Manner they are at this Time; or it was his Will they should *be* otherwise, *i.e.* in a different Manner: To say it was His Will Things should be otherwise than they are, is to say Somewhat hath contradicted His Will, and broken His Measures, which is impossible because inconsistent with his Power; therefore we must allow that all Things exist now in a Manner agreeable to His Will, and in consequence of that are all equally Good, and therefore equally esteem'd by Him.

I proceed now to shew, that as all the Worlds of the Creator are equally esteem'd by Him, so they are, as in Justice they ought to be, equally us'd.

Sect. II.

. . . I shall here subjoin a short Recapitulation of the Whole, that it may with all its Parts be comprehended at one View.

1. *It is suppos'd that God the Maker and Governour of the Universe, is infinitely wise, good, and powerful.*

2. *In consequence of His infinite Wisdom and Goodness, it is asserted, that whatever He doth must be infinitely wise and good;*

3. *Unless He be interrupted, and His Measures broken by some other Being, which is impossible because He is Almighty.*

4. *In consequence of His infinite Power, it is asserted, that nothing can exist or be done in the Universe which is not agreeable to His Will, and therefore good.*

5. *Evil is hereby excluded, with all Merit and Demerit;*

and likewise all preference in the Esteem of God, of one Part of the Creation to another. This is the Summary of the first Part.

Now our common Notions of Justice will tell us, that if all created Things are equally esteem'd by the Creator, they ought to be equally us'd by Him; and that they are therefore equally us'd, we might embrace for Truth upon the Credit, and as the true Consequence of the foregoing Argument. Nevertheless we proceed to confirm it, by shewing *how* they are equally us'd, and that in the following Manner.

1. *A Creature when endu'd with Life or Consciousness, is made capable of Uneasiness or Pain.*

2. *This Pain produces Desire to be freed from it, in exact proportion to itself.*

3. *The Accomplishment of this Desire produces an equal Pleasure.*

4. *Pleasure is consequently equal to Pain.*

From these Propositions it is observ'd,

1. *That every Creature hath as much Pleasure as Pain.*

2. *That Life is not preferable to Insensibility; for Pleasure and Pain destroy one another: That Being which has ten Degrees of Pain subtracted from ten of Pleasure, has nothing remaining, and is upon an equality with that Being which is insensible of both.*

3. *As the first Part proves that all Things must be equally us'd by the Creator because equally esteem'd; so this second part demonstrates that they are equally esteem'd because equally us'd.*

4. *Since every Action is the Effect of Self-Uneasiness, the Distinction of Virtue and Vice is excluded. . . .*

5. *No State of Life can be happier than the present, because Pleasure and Pain are inseparable. . . .*

I am sensible that the Doctrine here advanc'd, if it were to be publish'd, would meet with but an indifferent Reception. Mankind naturally and generally love to be flatter'd: Whatever sooths our Pride, and tends to exalt our Species above the rest of the Creation, we are pleas'd with and easily believe, when ungrateful Truths shall be with the utmost Indignation rejected. ''What! bring ourselves down to an Equality with the Beasts of the Field!

with the *meanest* part of the Creation! 'Tis insufferable!''
But, (to use a Piece of *common* Sense) our *Geese* are but
Geese tho' we may think 'em *Swans;* and Truth will be
Truth tho' it sometimes prove mortifying and distasteful.

[2]

A Reconsideration of Freethinking

*The young Franklin soon became dissatisfied with free-
thinking. The most succinct articulation of his changed
feeling on the subject came much later, however, when
he was 73. Franklin described his feelings about his earlier theological writings in a letter to an Englishman who
was putting together an edition of his papers.*

TO BENJAMIN VAUGHN

November 9, 1779

. . . It was addressed to Mr. J. R., that, is, James
Ralph, then a youth of about my age, and my intimate
friend; afterwards a political writer and historian. The
purport of it was to prove the doctrine of fate, from the
supposed attributes of God; in some such manner as this:
that in erecting and governing the world, as he was infinitely wise, he knew what would be best; infinitely good,
he must be disposed, and infinitely powerful, he must be
able to execute it: consequently all is right. There were
only an hundred copies printed, of which I gave a few to
friends, and afterwards disliking the piece, as conceiving
it might have an ill tendency, I burnt the rest, except one
copy, the margin of which was filled with manuscript
notes by Lyons, author of the Infallibility of Human
Judgment, who was at that time another of my acquaintance in London. I was not nineteen years of age when
it was written. In 1730, I wrote a piece on the other side
of the question, which began with laying for its foundation this fact: ''That almost all men in all ages and countries, have at times made use of prayer.'' Thence I

reasoned, that if all things are ordained, prayer must among the rest be ordained. But as prayer can produce no change in things that are ordained, praying must then be useless and an absurdity. God would therefore not ordain praying if everything else was ordained. But praying exists, therefore all things are not ordained, etc. This pamphlet was never printed, and the manuscript has been long lost. The great uncertainty I found in metaphysical reasonings disgusted me, and I quitted that kind of reading and study for others more satisfactory. . . .

[3]

Articles of Belief and Acts of Religion

Franklin escaped the theology of Puritanism but not its psychology. The introspective and instructive urge which produced the autobiography is a direct descendant of the impulse which moved seventeenth-century English Puritans to write their autobiographies. Also in this line is Franklin's penchant for drawing up lists clarifying his beliefs for himself.

1728

FIRST PRINCIPLES

I believe there is one supreme, most perfect Being, Author and Father of the Gods themselves. For I believe that Man is not the most perfect Being but one, rather that as there are many Degrees of Beings his Inferiors, so there are many Degrees of Beings superior to him.

Also, when I stretch my Imagination thro' and beyond our System of Planets, beyond the visible fix'd Stars themselves, into that Space that is every Way infinite, and conceive it fill'd with Suns like ours, each with a Chorus of Worlds forever moving round him, then this little Ball on which we move, seems, even in my narrow Imagination, to be almost Nothing, and myself less than nothing, and of no sort of Consequence.

When I think thus, I imagine it great Vanity in me to

suppose, that the *Supremely Perfect* does in the least regard such an inconsiderable Nothing as Man. More especially, since it is impossible for me to have any positive clear idea of that which is infinite and incomprehensible, I cannot conceive otherwise than that he *the Infinite Father* expects or requires no Worship or Praise from us, but that he is even infinitely above it.

But, since there is in all men something like a natural principle, which inclines them to DEVOTION, or the Worship of some unseen Power;

And since Men are endued with Reason superior to all other Animals, that we are in our World acquainted with;

Therefore I think it seems required of me, and my Duty as a Man, to pay Divine Regards to SOMETHING.

I conceive then, that the INFINITE has created many beings or Gods, vastly superior to Man, who can better conceive his Perfections than we, and return him a more rational and glorious Praise.

As, among men, the Praise of the Ignorant or of Children is not regarded by the ingenious Painter or Architect, who is rather honour'd and pleas'd with the approbation of Wise Men & Artists.

It may be that these created Gods are immortal; or it may be that after many Ages, they are changed, and others Supply their Places.

Howbeit, I conceive that each of these is exceeding wise and good, and very powerful; and that Each has made for himself one glorious sun, attended with a beautiful and admirable System of Planets.

It is that particular Wise and good God, who is the author and owner of our System, that I propose for the object of my praise and adoration.

For I conceive that he has in himself some of those Passions he has planted in us, and that, since he has given us Reason whereby we are capable of observing his Wisdom in the Creation, he is not above caring for us, being pleas'd with our Praise, and offended when we slight Him, or neglect his Glory.

I conceive for many Reasons, that he is a *good Being;* and as I should be happy to have so wise, good, and powerful a Being my Friend, let me consider in what manner I shall make myself most acceptable to him.

Next to the Praise resulting from and due to his Wisdom, I believe he is pleas'd and delights in the Happiness of those he has created; and since without Virtue Man can have no Happiness in this World, I firmly believe he delights to see me Virtuous, because he is pleased when he sees Me Happy.

And since he has created many Things, which seem purely design'd for the Delight of Man, I believe he is not offended, when he sees his Children solace themselves in any manner of pleasant exercises and Innocent Delights; and I think no Pleasure innocent, that is to Man hurtful.

I *love* him therefore for his Goodness, and I *adore* him for his Wisdom.

Let me then not fail to praise my God continually, for it is his Due, and it is all I can return for his many Favours and great Goodness to me; and let me resolve to be virtuous, that I may be happy, that I may please Him, who is delighted to see me happy. Amen!

ADORATION

Prel. Being mindful that before I address the Deity, my soul ought to be calm and serene, free from Passion and Perturbation, or otherwise elevated with Rational Joy and Pleasure, I ought to use a Countenance that expresses a filial Respect, mixed with a kind of Smiling, that Signifies inward Joy, and Satisfaction, and Admiration.

O wise God, my good Father!

Thou beholdest the sincerity of my Heart and of my Devotion; Grant me a Continuance of thy Favour!

1. O Creator, O Father! I believe that thou art Good, and that thou art *pleas'd with the pleasure* of thy children.—Praised be thy name for Ever!

2. By thy Power hast thou made the glorious Sun, with his attending Worlds; from the energy of thy mighty Will, they first received [their prodigious] motion, and by thy Wisdom hast thou prescribed the wondrous Laws, by which they move.—Praised be thy name for Ever!

3. By thy Wisdom hast thou formed all Things. Thou hast created Man, bestowing Life and Reason, and placed

him in Dignity superior to thy other earthly Creatures.—
Praised be thy name for Ever!

4. Thy Wisdom, thy Power, and thy Goodness are everywhere clearly seen; in the air and in the water, in the Heaven and on the Earth; Thou providest for the various winged Fowl, and the innumerable Inhabitants of the Water; thou givest Cold and Heat, Rain and Sunshine, in their Season, & to the Fruits of the Earth Increase.—
Praised be thy name for Ever!

5. Thou abhorrest in thy Creatures Treachery and Deceit, Malice, Revenge, [*Intemperance*,] and every other hurtful Vice; but Thou art a Lover of Justice and Sincerity, of Friendship and Benevolence, and every Virtue. Thou art my Friend, my Father, and my Benefactor.—
Praised be thy name, O God, for Ever! Amen!

[After this, it will not be improper to read part of some such Book as Ray's *Wisdom of God in the Creation,* or *Blackmore on the Creation,* or the Archbishop of Cambray's *Demonstration of the Being of a God,* &c., or else spend some Minutes in a serious Silence, contemplating on those Subjects.]

Then sing

MILTON'S HYMN TO THE CREATOR

"These are thy Glorious Works, Parent of Good!
Almighty, Thine this Universal Frame,
Thus wondrous fair! Thyself how wondrous then!
Speak ye who best can tell, Ye Sons of Light,
Angels, for ye behold him, and with Songs
And Choral Symphonies, Day without Night,
Circle his Throne rejoicing you in Heav'n,
On Earth join all ye creatures to extol
Him first, him last, him midst, and without End.
"Fairest of Stars, last in the Train of night,
If rather Thou belongst not to the Dawn,
Sure Pledge of Day! thou crown'st the smiling Morn
With thy bright Circlet, Praise him in thy Sphere
While Day arises, that sweet Hour of Prime.
Thou Sun, of this great World, both Eye and Soul,
Acknowledge him thy greater; Sound his Praise

In thy eternal Course; both when thou climb'st,
And when high Noon hast gain'd, and when thou fall'st.
Moon! that now meet'st the orient sun, now fly'st,
With the fixed Stars, fixed in their orb that flies,
And ye five other wandering Fires, that move
In mystic Dance not without Song; resound
His Praise, that out of Darkness called up Light.
Air! and ye Elements! the eldest Birth
Of Nature's womb, that in Quaternion run
Perpetual Circle, multiform, and mix
And nourish all things, let your ceaseless Change
Vary to our great Maker still new Praise.
Ye mists and Exhalations, that now rise
From Hill or steaming lake, dusky or grey,
Till the Sun paint your fleecy skirts with Gold,
In honour to the World's Great Author rise;
Whether to deck with Clouds the uncolor'd sky,
Or we the thirsty Earth wth falling show'rs,
Rising or falling still advance his Praise.
His Praise, ye Winds! that from 4 quarters blow,
Breathe soft or Loud; and wave your Tops, ye Pines!
With every Plant, in sign of worship wave.
Fountains! and ye that warble, as ye flow
Melodious Murmurs, warbling tune his Praise.
Join voices all ye living souls, ye Birds!
That singing, up to Heaven's high gate ascend,
Bear on your wings, & in your Note his Praise;
Ye that in Waters glide! and ye that walk
The Earth! and stately tread or lowly creep;
Witness *if I be silent*, Ev'n or Morn,
To Hill, or Valley, Fountain, or Fresh Shade,
Made Vocal by my Song, and taught his Praise.''

[Here follows the Reading of some Book, or part of a
Book, Discoursing on and exciting to Moral Virtue.]

PETITION

Inasmuch as by Reason of our Ignorance We cannot be
certain that many Things, which we often hear mentioned
in the Petitions of Men to the Deity, would prove real
Goods, if they were in our Possession, and as I have

reason to hope and believe that the Goodness of my Heavenly Father will not withold from me a suitable share of Temporal Blessings, if by a Virtuous and holy Life I conciliate his Favour and Kindness, Therefore I presume not to ask such things, but rather humbly and with a Sincere Heart, express my earnest desires that he would graciously assist my Continual Endeavours and Resolutions of eschewing Vice and embracing Virtue; which Kind of Supplications will *at least be thus far beneficial, as they remind me* in a solemn manner of my Extensive duty.

That I may be preserved from Atheism & Infidelity, Impiety, and Profaneness, and, in my Addresses to Thee, carefully avoid Irreverence and ostentation, Formality and odious Hypocrisy,—Help me, O Father!

That I may be loyal to my Prince, and faithful to my country, careful for its good, valiant in its defence, and obedient to its Laws, abhorring Treason as much as Tyranny,—Help me, O Father!

That I may to those above me be dutiful, humble and submissive; avoiding Pride, Disrespect, and Contumacy,—Help me, O Father!

That I may to those below me be gracious, Condescending, and Forgiving, using Clemency, protecting *innocent Distress*, avoiding Cruelty, Harshness, and oppression, Insolence, and unreasonable Severity,—Help me, O Father!

That I may refrain from Censure, Calumny and Detraction; that I may avoid and abhor Deceit and Envy, Fraud, Flattery, and Hatred, Malice, Lying, and Ingratitude,—Help me, O Father!

That I may be sincere in Friendship, faithful in trust, and Impartial in Judgment, watchful against Pride, and against Anger (that momentary Madness),—Help me, O Father!

That I may be just in all my Dealings, temperate in my Pleasures, full of Candour and Ingenuity, Humanity and Benevolence,—Help me, O Father!

That I may be grateful to my Benefactors, and generous to my Friends, exercising Charity and Liberality to the Poor, and Pity to the Miserable,—Help me, O Father!

That I may avoid Avarice and Ambition, Jealousie, and Intemperance, Falsehood, Luxury, and Lasciviousness,—Help me, O Father!

That I may possess Integrity and Evenness of Mind, Resolution in Difficulties, and Fortitude under Affliction; that I may be punctual in performing my promises, Peaceable and prudent in my Behaviour,—Help me, O Father!

That I may have Tenderness for the Weak, and reverent Respect for the Ancient; that I may be Kind to my Neighbours, good-natured to my Companions, and hospitable to Strangers,—Help me, O Father!

That I may be averse to Talebearing, Backbiting, Detraction, Slander, & Craft, and overreaching, abhor Extortion, Perjury, and every Kind of wickedness,—Help me, O Father!

That I may be honest and open-hearted, gentle, merciful, and good, cheerful in spirit, rejoicing in the Good of others,—Help me, O Father!

That I may have a constant Regard to Honour and Probity, that I may possess a perfect innocence and a good Conscience, and at length become truly Virtuous and Magnanimous,—Help me, good God; help me, O Father!

And, forasmuch as ingratitude is one of the most odious of vices, let me not be unmindful gratefully to acknowledge the favours I receive from Heaven.

THANKS

For peace and liberty, for food and raiment, for corn, and wine, and milk, and every kind of healthful nourishment,—Good God, I thank thee!

For the common benefits of air and light; for useful fire and delicious water,—Good God, I thank thee!

For knowledge, and literature, and every useful art, for my friends and their prosperity, and for the fewness of my enemies,—Good God, I thank thee!

For all thy innumerable benefits; for life, and reason, and the use of speech; for health, and joy, and every pleasant hour,—My good God, I thank thee! **[4]**

A Summary of Belief

Three years later Franklin again stated the essentials of his belief, this time more briefly.

DOCT. TO BE PREA[CHE]D

[1731]

That there is one God Father of the Universe.

That he [is] infinitely good, Powerful and wise.

That he is omnipresent.

That he ought to be worshipped, by Adoration Prayer and Thanksgiving both in publick and private.

That he loves such of his Creatures as love and do good to others: and will reward them either in this World or hereafter.

That Men's Minds do not die with their bodies, but are made more happy or miserable after this life according to their Actions.

That Virtuous Men ought to league together to strengthen the Interest of Virtue, in the World: and so strengthen themselves in Virtue.

That Knowledge and Learning is to be cultivated, and Ignorance dissipated.

That none but the Virtuous are wise.

That Man's Perfection is in Virtue. . . .   [5]

"Here is My Creed"

More than fifty years after Franklin's sister had first questioned his religion, she still had qualms. He reassured her in a short letter; then, a month before his death, he summarized his final credo in a letter to the President of Yale College.

October 19, 1789

Dear Sister:—

I received your kind Letter of September the 10th, by Cousin John Williams. I have also received and paid your Bill, and am pleased that you added to it on Account of your Wood. As to my Health, it continues as usual,—sometimes better, sometimes worse,—and with respect of the Happiness hereafter which you mention, I have no Doubts about it, confiding as I do in the Goodness of that Being who, thro' so long a Life, has conducted me with so many Instances of it. This Family joins in best wishes of Happiness to you and your's with your affectionate Brother. . . .

[6]

TO EZRA STILES

March 9, 1790

Reverend and Dear Sir,

. . . You desire to know something of my Religion. It is the first time I have been questioned upon it. But I cannot take your Curiosity amiss, and shall endeavour in a few Words to gratify it. Here is my Creed. I believe in one God, Creator of the Universe. That he governs it by his Providence. That he ought to be worshipped. That the most acceptable Service we render to him is doing good to his other Children. That the soul of Man is immortal, and will be treated with Justice in another life respecting its Conduct in this. These I take to be the fundamental Principles of all sound Religion, and I regard them as you do in whatever Sect I meet with them.

As to Jesus of Nazareth, my Opinion of whom you particularly desire, I think the System of Morals and his Religion, as he left them to us, the best the world ever saw or is likely to see; but I apprehend it has received various corrupting Changes, and I have, with most of the present Dissenters in England, some doubts as to his Divinity; tho' it is a question I do not dogmatize upon, having never studied it, and think it needless to busy myself with it now, when I expect soon an Opportunity of knowing the Truth with less Trouble. I see no harm, however, in its being believed, if that Belief has the good Consequence, as probably it has, of making his Doctrines more respected and better observed; especially as I do not perceive, that the Supreme takes it amiss, by distinguishing the Unbelievers in his Government of the World with any peculiar Marks of his Displeasure.

I shall only add, respecting myself, that, having experienced the Goodness of that Being in conducting me prosperously thro' a long life, I have no doubt of its Continuance in the next, though without the smallest Conceit of meriting such Goodness. . . .

P.S. . . . I confide, that you will not expose me to Criticism and censure by publishing any part of this Communication to you. I have ever let others enjoy their religious Sentiments, without reflecting on them for those that appeared to me unsupportable and even absurd. All Sects here, and we have a great Variety, have experienced my good will in assisting them with Subscriptions for building their new Places of Worship; and, as I have never opposed any of their Doctrines, I hope to go out of the World in Peace with them all. . . .   [7]

NOTES ON THE SOURCES

At the end of each of Franklin's papers in this book, there is a bracketed number. These refer to the sources from which each paper is taken. The following is a listing of these numbers together with the sources to which they refer. The complete titles of the sources follow this listing.

I. The Way to Wealth
1. Labaree, I, 99–100
2. Labaree, I, 100–101
3. Labaree, I, 270
4. Labaree, III, 306–8
5. *Poor Richard's Almanack,* 1758

II. Essays to Do Good
1. Labaree, I, 256–59
2. *A Catalogue of Books Belonging to the Library Company of Philadelphia* (Philadelphia, 1741), p. 56
3. *Pennsylvania Gazette,* February 4, 1735
4. Smyth, II, 228–32
5. Smyth, II, 386–96

III. The New Prometheus, I: Franklin the Scientist
1. Smyth, II, 362–64
2. Smyth, IV, 221
3. Labaree, I, 85, 87–88, 90, 93–95, 98–99
4. Bigelow, II, 161–65
5. Smyth, III, 273–75
6. Smyth, II, 302
7. Smyth, II, 302–10
8. Joseph Priestley, *History and Present State of Electricity* (1767), 171–72, quoted in Van Doren, *Autobiographical Writings,* 77
9. *Poor Richard's Almanack,* 1753

10. Smyth, VI, 44–47
11. Smyth, II, 246–49, 264–67
12. Smyth, III, 103–5
13. Smyth, IV, 163–69
14. Smyth, V, 543–45
15. Smyth, IX, 337–38
16. Smyth, IX, 483–85

IV. The New Prometheus, II: Franklin and the Revolution
1. Smyth, VI, 407
2. Smyth, IV, 413, 415, 418–19, 420, 421, 428–29, 445–46, 448
3. Smyth, V, 14–15
4. Smyth, VI, 118–24
5. Smyth, VI, 249–51
6. Labaree and Bell, *Mr. Franklin*, 30–34
7. Smyth, VII, 110–11
8. Van Doren, *Autobiographical Writings*, 460–61
9. Smyth, VII, 36
10. Smyth, IX, 22–23
11. Smyth, IX, 695–97

V. The Bosom of His Family
1. Manuscript, American Philosophical Society
2. *Pennsylvania Gazette*, December 30, 1736
3. Smyth, III, 288–89
4. Smyth, V, 272–80
5. Smyth, IV, 20–22
6. Labaree and Bell, *Mr. Franklin*, 22–25
7. Smyth, V, 438–39
8. Smyth, V, 182–85
9. Manuscript, American Philosophical Society
10. Smyth, X, 287–89
11. Manuscript, American Philosophical Society
12. Van Doren, *Autobiographical Writings*, 340
13. Duane, *Family Letters*, 59–60
14. Smyth, IX, 252–54
15. Smyth, VII, 26
16. Smyth, VII, 393–94

17. Van Doren, *Autobiographical Writings*, 584–86
18. Smyth, X, 442
19. *Letters of Mrs. Adams*, II, 53–57
20. Smyth, IX, 488, 490–91

VI. "Something of My Religion"
1. Labaree, II, 202–4
2. Franklin, *A Dissertation on Liberty and Necessity, Pleasure and Pain* (London, 1725), 3–14, 29–32
3. Smyth, VII, 411–12
4. Smyth, II, 92–100
5. Labaree, I, 213
6. Smyth, X, 43
7. Smyth, X, 84–85

THE SOURCES

Charles Francis Adams, ed., *Letters of Mrs. Adams, the Wife of John Adams*, 2 vols. (Boston: 1840).

American Philosophical Society, Philadelphia, Pa., manuscripts.

William Duane, ed., *Letters to Benjamin Franklin, from His Family and Friends, 1751–1790* (New York: 1859).

Leonard W. Labaree and Whitfield J. Bell, Jr., eds., *Mr. Franklin: A Selection from His Personal Letters* (New Haven: Yale University Press, 1956).

Leonard W. Labaree, *et al.*, eds., *The Papers of Benjamin Franklin*, 40 vols. (New Haven: Yale University Press, 1959–).

Albert Henry Smyth, ed., *The Writings of Benjamin Franklin: Collected and Edited with a Life and Introduction*, 10 vols. (New York: 1905–1907).

Carl Van Doren, ed., *Benjamin Franklin's Autobiographical Writings* (New York: The Viking Press, 1945).
——, ed., *The Letters of Benjamin Franklin and Jane Mecom* (Princeton: Princeton University Press, 1950).

John Bigelow, ed., *The Complete Works of Benjamin Franklin* (New York: 1887–1889).

ADDITIONAL READING

The definitive edition of Franklin's papers is that edited by Leonard W. Labaree, *et al.*, *The Papers of Benjamin Franklin*, 40 vols. (New Haven: Yale University Press: 1959–). The completeness and accuracy of Labaree's edition, which is still in process, is unmatched by any of the other collections of Franklin's writings; indeed, few editions of any American's works can equal it. Informative headnotes introduce most items, and both sides of the correspondence are included. While the remaining volumes of this new edition are in preparation, the reader will have to make do with *The Writings of Benjamin Franklin, Collected and Edited with a Life and Introduction* by Albert Henry Smyth, in 10 vols. (New York: 1905-1907).

The text of the original manuscript of the autobiography is that edited by Max Farrand (Berkeley: University of California Press, 1949). The editor's Introduction tells the fascinating story of the original manuscript's travels, and how he pieced together his edition from Franklin's manuscript, two French translations, and the version edited by Franklin's grandson, William Temple Franklin.

There are many Franklin biographies: the two best are a short piece by Carl Becker in Vol. VI of the *Dictionary of American Biography* (New York: Charles Scribner's Sons, 1931), and a full-length book by Carl Van Doren, *Benjamin Franklin* (New York: The Viking Press, 1939). Van Doren also wrote *Jane Mecom: The Favorite Sister of Benjamin Franklin* (New York: The Viking Press, 1950) and edited *The Letters of Benjamin Franklin and Jane Mecom* (Princeton: Princeton University Press, 1950). Another volume of Franklin correspondence is that edited by William Greene Roelker, *Benjamin Franklin and Catherine Ray Greene: Their Correspondence, 1755-1790* (Philadelphia: American Philosophical Society, 1949).

The reader interested in what scholars have said about Franklin should see *Benjamin Franklin and the American Character*, edited by Charles L. Sanford (Amherst Problems in American Civilization Series. Boston: D. C. Heath & Co., 1955). Especially notable in this collection is D. H. Lawrence's attack on Franklin and Gladys Meyer's examination of his techniques of social advancement, a subject which she covers in detail in *Free Trade in Ideas: Aspects of American Lib-*

eralism Illustrated in Franklin's Philadelphia Career (New York: Columbia University Press, 1941). An influential literary attack on Franklin was made by William Carlos Williams in "Poor Richard," in his *In the American Grain* (New York: New Directions, 1956).

There are two fine, one-volume collections of Franklin's writings: Frank Luther Mott and Chester E. Jorgenson, eds., *Benjamin Franklin: Representative Selections* (New York: American Book Co., 1936), and Carl Van Doren, ed., *Benjamin Franklin's Autobiographical Writings* (New York: The Viking Press, 1945).

AFTERWORD: IMAGINING BENJAMIN FRANKLIN

Imagine being Benjamin Franklin. Imagine that after a lifetime of private enterprise and public service, first as a printer, then as an internationally famous scientist, and finally as a statesman negotiating a reconciliation between the newly established United States and Great Britain, immediately following the biggest rift the First British Empire would suffer—imagine that your friends ask you to craft a narrative of your life. They desire you not only to tell the story of your life but also to undertake this task for the edification of others, especially the young. Your aims only partly overlap with theirs, because you know that there are parts of your life—the early loss of a favorite little boy to smallpox; the long separation from a daughter and a wife, whom you never really got to know; the late loss of your first son to British loyalism—that you are still attempting to understand yourself. How to write a story that has some coherence, though fracture is evident albeit well hidden from the world? But you comply with their wishes, because you have a sense that they are justified in their request, and so you try to conform the narration to the aim of edification.

What does the discoverer of the positive and negative charges in electricity, or the investigator who determined the pattern of the Gulf Stream, or the inventor who devised the flexible catheter and lightning rod, say to youth about himself? What does the creator of a glass musical instrument, the glass armonica, reveal to others? What does the civic leader who developed a philosophical society, library, hospital, fireplace, fire company, and college tell about his intellectual life? What does the prime negotiator of peace treaties between thirteen different colonies, on the one hand, and other countries, on the other, offer to a waiting world? What does the friend of philosophers, scientists, laborers, statesmen, and kings *say* to people about his life and belief in social obligations connecting people? How can such a person determine what would be most interesting to tell? How might he relate the vicissitudes of fortune, the acceptance of personal failures along with the triumphs, the dimensions of an interior life that recognized the importance of spiritual as well as secular activities, even though secular activities were for him those most compelling?

"Dear Son," Franklin began, in the midsummer of 1771. "I have ever had a pleasure in obtaining any little anecdotes of my ancestors. . . . Now imagining it may be equally agreeable to you to know the circumstances of *my* life—many of which you are yet unacquainted with—and expecting a week's uninterrupted leisure in my present country retirement, I sit down to write them for you." Imagining it might be agreeable and even useful to others, Franklin took on the task of self-writing. He had a complex conception of his task, for self-discovery and self-effacement are part of the process of writing, as living, an exemplary life. Evoking his ancestors, Franklin offered a model for his son and for future generations. The story of a man coming to maturity and that of a nation coming into existence became intertwined, the achievements of the individual foretelling the promise of a people.

Franklin's friend Abel James was given the first part of Franklin's autobiography to read. Fascinated with the idea of imagining Franklin's life for future generations, James entreated the autobiographer to continue. Franklin was in the middle of demanding, delicate negotiations with England. Despite the pressures, Franklin composed what L. Jesse Lemisch has called the most famous part of the autobiography, the one devoted to the "bold and arduous task of moral perfection." The vision of this task was Franklin's own, yet its inclusion in his autobiography was a specific response to Abel James's request. "Life is uncertain, as the preacher tells us," James had written to Franklin, continuing, "and what will the world say if kind, humane, and benevolent Ben Franklin should leave his friends and the world deprived of so pleasing and profitable a work, a work which would be useful and entertaining not only to a few but to millions?" He forced home his point by insisting: "I know of no character living, nor many of them put together, who has so much in his power as thyself to promote a greater spirit of industry and early attention to business, frugality, and temperance with the American youth." The goal of the autobiography would thus become, in large measure, the visible presence of Franklin as a model of industry, honesty, thrift, and success. The model carried the burden of a larger-than-life person, one who might be, as Abel James announced, "many" men "put together."

Thus it seems that Franklin's life story was, in the very process of its composition, governed by a self-consciously fallible espousal of a severely challenging ideal, that of "moral perfection." Humans are obviously fallible: they are liable to make mistakes. But only fallible beings can grow toward perfection. Their errors (as printers would say, their "errata") are not only signs of imperfection but also instruments to assist the potential for perfectibility. Picking up the burden of writing his life, Franklin took on the task of suggesting perfectibility possible, if mistakes could be recognized, acknowledged, and learned from. The writing itself, like the living of the life of moral perfection, would be one of self-government.

Like a few others whose lives intersected with the era of the American Revolution against Great Britain, Franklin comprehended that political self-government is impossible apart from personal self-sovereignty. He considered that if individuals have a right to govern themselves, the right resides in their ability to perfect themselves. Only the demands of self-rule call forth the maturity of self-governance. Unlike most others of his generation, Franklin was in the process of creating a storied life that would in effect become the foundational text for succeeding generations' growing filiopiety for the Revolutionary generation. That is to say that future generations learned from the life of Benjamin Franklin, in all its varied drafts as they circulated, that self-governing institutions at bottom rest upon the virtues and abilities of self-sovereign individuals, political autonomy being inseparable from personal autonomy. Hence Franklin's personal narrative has been understood to carry profound political implications.

The transformation of Franklin-the-man into Franklin-the-American-hero began before his death. Thomas Jefferson called Franklin "the greatest man and ornament of the age and country in which he lived." After Franklin died, the stories about him reached new mythic and heroic heights. His memory would serve as one of the foundational memories of the nation. From the early days of the nineteenth century onward, the view of Franklin as an exemplary American appears in poems, songs, newspaper and magazine articles, and books. Ordinary people, landed people, and revolutionary veterans read these portraits. The anecdotes of Franklin's life became known throughout the country. Robert Thomas, a bookseller in rural Massachusetts, announced in 1794 (just four years after Franklin's death) that his readers should settle in for the winter and get themselves into order for the new year. He advised his readers to "Call upon your debtors for settlement, see that your books are balanced before the new year opens." He recommended the reading of "The life of Dr. Franklin . . . for the amusement of winter evenings."

Franklin's life was taken as exemplary of industry, frugality, moderation, and toleration, and his accomplishments were directly linked in story and legend with a love of the nation he helped found. Mason Locke Weems, an itinerant bookseller who wrote mostly fictional vignettes based on passages of Franklin's life then entering circulation, walked country roads and sold his books during the first half of the nineteenth century. To "Parson" Weems, Franklin was the enemy of tyranny. Weems's *Life of Benjamin Franklin* (1845) evoked a Franklin whose moral perfection constituted an end to monarchical domination: "And to the galling sense of this villainous oppression, which never ceased to rankle on the mind of Franklin, the American people owe much of that spirited resistance to British injustice, which eventuated in their liberties." Such a reading of Franklin's life was central to the ideology of the glorious republic of Abraham Lincoln's day. In 1856 a story in the *New York Times* announced that Franklin "was the incarnation of the true American character. . . . Franklin was the true type of the pure, noble, republican feeling of

America." His life was not solely his own, for he belonged to the nation; indeed, he became the nation.

A century after Weems's imaginative appropriation of this cultural hero, at the conclusion of World War II, the figure of Franklin was still being pressed into national service. This was a time of triumphalism and even chauvinism, when the victory of the Allies was taken by many citizens of the United States as indisputable evidence of an invincible virtue. It is no surprise, then, that Franklin's career has been taken to epitomize all the virtues in which the material and moral progress of this vast and heterogeneous nation is rooted. Franklin became the icon of American democracy around the globe. In the middle of the twentieth century, a major project was initiated to collect, edit, and present Franklin's papers to the public as a full and reliable compendium, a magisterial collection called *The Papers of Benjamin Franklin*. Franklin would remain a cultural hero of the highest magnitude.

That Franklin became a national hero is finally not surprising. We often seek heroes to explain ourselves to ourselves. That is, in trying to figure out our way in the world as people and community members and citizens, we will seek out stories of others' lives to serve as counterpoints or models for our own lives. Such hero discovery can help individuals identify core sets of personal and social values that they wish to hold personally and within their communities. But if we emphasize Franklin as a model alone, seeking only the constellation of values in the person and his life that will reflect a vision of a potential life for ourselves, we can lose sight of this single man's lived experience. In so doing, we can undermine our ability to gain any important knowledge of his life's complexities because we are instead seeking our own or a nation's self-knowledge.

It is thus important to attempt to penetrate to Franklin's era and the influences both good and bad that conditioned his lifetime. In coming to terms with Franklin in light of his own era and life place, we can come to a richer, more exact understanding of the complexities of living, then and now, and we won't permit the model of the man, a sort of superhuman exemplar, to supercede the difficulties and complexities that a person encountered on his presumed way from rags to riches and fame. It is important to understand the fractures and fissures as well as the successes of cultural heroes.

Why did Franklin narrate his life in the way he did? What were the narrative models Franklin knew, and which ones did the autobiography reflect? How does his autobiography remodel those existing frames of narrative? Franklin was an insatiable reader throughout his life. While still a youth he read the best-known writers of his day, as L. Jesse Lemisch pointed out in the introduction: John Bunyan; Daniel Defoe; Cotton Mather; Anthony Ashley Cooper, the third Earl of Shaftesbury; John Locke; and Richard Steele. Given his Protestant and dissenting background, he also knew the Bible exceedingly well. The most commonly employed model for life writing in Franklin's day was that of spiritual autobiography, the journey of a soul toward light or the path taken by the good Christian to find paradise, or the heavenly city. John Bunyan's *Pilgrim's Progress,* a greatly admired narrative, was the best-read story of the spirit. Written for general readers, Bunyan's narrative traced the ups and downs in the life of Christian, the man seeking the best road to life—heavenly life, that is. Christian's path was not easy, and he made some errors along the way, but he eventually found himself traveling, if uncertainly, a road to spiritual well-being. *Pilgrim's Progress* is a narrative addressed to lost souls, offering advice for how to find oneself back in the arms of a loving father, the Christian God. By contrast, Franklin's *Autobiography* is a story addressed to humans on the path to self-discovery, whose experiences remain free of divine intervention, humans bent on imagining themselves becoming sovereign individuals and thus citizens worthy of being free to self-govern as citizens of a new republic.

While Franklin had developed during his lifetime his own articles of faith that broadly reflected what can be taken as Christian values—even if they do not indicate a concern about the divinity of Christ—the life journey he would relate for others would not be centered in Christian theology primarily or in any kind of spiritual mysticism. Yet as he wrote his life, Franklin employed a pattern strikingly like that of the ups and downs, the successes and failures, common to the mode of spiritual autobiography. Franklin's was the world of the enlightenment, the world that honored the material universe as offering the greatest opportunity for people to discover how best to live their lives, improve their conditions, and practice benevolence toward one another while creating a great civic community. Bunyan's pilgrim is a wayfarer who is traveling through this world in order to get to the next, life being a series of trials and temptations. Franklin's self is an actor caught up in an intensely engrossing worldly drama, full of opportunities for courageous action and inducements to experimental investigation into the natural world and the civic one.

Every life is in truth an experiment, a trial, in which the outcome hangs in the balance. Since progress is not guaranteed, nothing less than the self is on trial. How might we transform our inherited, constrained lives into unique, autonomous selves? This was Franklin's challenge. His became a story of moral regeneration, of how one finally can attempt to lead a moral life. It also became a story of the means to this-worldly success, revealing how Franklin developed and represented to others those values his friend Abel James identified as the "spirit of industry, and early attention to business, frugality, and temperance." Franklin included many of his successes in what he wrote, naming his youthful leadership roles, his inventions, his desire for moral perfection, his largely self-taught knowledge of arts and science. These were among characteristic successes that link Franklin's narrative with the mode of spiritual autobiography.

But as the road to moral perfection includes recognition of failure, Franklin also included his personal sorrows, his regrettable failures, his "errata." Franklin's adoption of the printers' term enabled him to elaborate a long opening metaphor about printing and authorship thus revealing a characteristically subtle humor evident throughout the narrative. In telling his story, he would "go over the same life from its beginning to the end only asking the advantage authors have of correcting in a second edition some faults of the first." "So would I also wish to change some incidents of it for others more favourable," he wrote. The approach makes the reader aware that life is a struggle, and the more moral the life, perhaps the greater the struggle. In suggesting that he might, if he could, change some of the "incidents," Franklin thus clarified that even Benjamin Franklin's life had faults, even his life included incidents of which the author was not proud. In imagining Benjamin Franklin's life, one would not escape its difficulties, in effect.

Franklin tried to work on his life narrative during his later years, but various events interceded to excuse his attention from the labor of writing about himself. He completed the first part at age sixty-five, when he was in England; the second in France, thirteen years later; and the third in Philadelphia, four years after that. At age eighty-four, he began the last section to be completed, taking his life story up to the time of his first attempts to negotiate with England. The life would not reach even the beginning of the American Revolution, in other words. Franklin's increasing negotiating activities, his age, and his weakening health all contributed to his inability to complete anything like his full life's story. But perhaps it would be useful to consider other reasons why he might have turned from writing and taken up other tasks instead.

Imagine being Benjamin Franklin! Self-narration is often a means of attaining self-possession, of owning up to our actions and of admitting our failures to act well. We come into possession of ourselves only when we in imagination, tethered to memory, recall the events of our lives and the sequences of these events. Like his life itself, the autobiographical world Franklin inhabited was not linear or progressive. Franklin's was a fractured life story, speaking a fractured life of effort and achievement, but both effort and achievement largely apart from his own family, amid a whirl of friends and associates. His was a life and life story wherein enemies could turn out to be friends, friends enemies. He lived in an often topsy-turvy world, where peace always seemed just too far off, war too imminent, and life too unpredictable for a humanist to accept. Were the pressures to create a uniform, neat narrative, at once useful and entertaining, too great, even for Benjamin Franklin? Was the possibility of writing a cohesive narrative too elusive because the life and the life's events were too fracturing?

Life writing carves out a space of movement between memory and hope, between the apparent recollection of the writer's actual experiences and the imagined possibility of a human world that the writer could have inhabited in an idealized version of him- or herself. The memory of the past creates a tension with the evocation of that possible world, where hope creates order, decorum, and civic piety as attainable goals. In such hopeful worlds, the memory of arbitrary events and infelicitous occasions of one's life is held in abeyance, with the possibility of perfection highlighted as the element potentially attained. Autobiography in this sense is a continuous redefining of self, a vacillation between remembered efforts and hoped for gains. Thus it can be said that autobiography gives witness to the individual's struggle for power to participate in the process of self-creation at the very same time that the individual recognizes the fissures and fractures that undermine authority over the life text being created.

Any actual self, like a life story of that self, is a host of possibilities and, in a certain sense, a contest between infelicity and perfection, between memory and hope. Benjamin Franklin was no exception. His integrity as a person stemmed not from an allegedly seamless unity, but from his resolute, defining insistence upon being the author of his own life and even the circumstances of that life, however fracturing and incomplete they might have seemed. He became the author of his own singular though fissured life. His commitment to self-government is of a piece with his insistence upon self-authorization and self-narration, even if the pieces of his character do not neatly fit together. Somewhat like the nation that itself took him up as its exemplar, Franklin is *e pluribus unum*, one out of many, just as his friend Abel James imagined centuries ago.

—Carla Mulford
Department of English
Pennsylvania State University